A DICTIONARY
OF
HORSE-DRAWN
VEHICLES

A DICTIONARY OF HORSE-DRAWN VEHICLES

Compiled by

D. J. M. SMITH

Foreword by H.R.H. The Prince Philip,
Duke of Edinburgh, K.G., K.T.

J. A. Allen & Co. Ltd.
1 Lower Grosvenor Place
Buckingham Palace Road
London SW1W 0EL

First published in Great Britain by
J. A. Allen & Co. Ltd.
1 Lower Grosvenor Place
Buckingham Palace Road
London SW1W 0EL

British Library Cataloguing in Publication Data
Smith, D.J. (Donald John), 1927–
A dictionary of horse-drawn vehicles.
1. Horse-drawn vehicles
I. Title
688.6
ISBN 0–85131–468–6

Printed in Great Britain at the University Printing House, Oxford

BUCKINGHAM PALACE.

I am delighted that a well informed author and an experienced publisher of equestrian books have collaborated to produce this comprehensive and concise dictionary. Horse-drawn vehicle builders were no more precise in naming their products than motor vehicle builders are today, although they did stick to standard descriptions for certain basic types. The great value of this dictionary is that it includes an exceptionally wide range of styles and types of vehicles under the names that might otherwise so easily be lost and forgotten.

1988

AUTHOR'S PREFACE

Specialising as I have for over forty years, I have long thought there was a need for a Dictionary that gave good coverage of commercial, utility, farm, and military vehicles, besides carriages and coaches. This work covers the whole range of horse drawn vehicles as no other appears to have done. It includes ancient, historical, British, and International types as used for pleasure, sport, ceremonial, public transport, trade, industry, military, and specialised purposes, such as fire engines, lifeboat carriages, and bathing machines. Whilst costs and dimensions tend to fluctuate over the years, these are mentioned wherever appropriate. There is a glossary of terms relating to carriage parts and accessories.

My efforts, hopefully, will interest not only amateurs or professionals of driving, but those by whom horse drawn vehicles are studied, collected, and admired.

D. J. M. SMITH

A

Abbot buggy. Australian buggy, although constructed to designs furnished by the Abbot, Downing Company of Concord, New Hampshire, U.S.A. Popular during the second half of the 19th century, in both town and country. Hung on semi-elliptical side springs and using pedal brakes. The wheelbase was fairly short while the half hood was usually kept in a raised position. Bodywork was similar to that of a Coal Box Buggy. *See* Coal Box Buggy.

Accommodation. Public service carriage of a type first constructed in North America about 1827. There was inside seating for twelve people, although an additional passenger might share the driving seat with the driver/conductor. First operated by a New York stagecoach proprietor named Brower. Driven between Bleeker Street and the outer suburbs, charging a shilling per head for any part of the journey. Passengers entered through side rather than end doors, in which the vehicle differed from the Coachee. Suspension was by means of thoroughbraces, in the style of the Concord Coach. Considered to be a short distance stagecoach rather than a forerunner of the Omnibus.

Acme sporting cart. Light, Australian gig of the late 19th century. Hung on a Dennett or three spring system. The driving seat was fully upholstered, including short armrests. There were half splashers or mudguards above both wheels.

Adopticon. Float or show wagon, drawn by six or more horses, first appearing in North America during the late 19th century. Able to convey a token payload it was mainly used for advertising purposes and in street parades. Introduced by a Colonel Haverly of Chicago, although the origin of its name is obscure.

Alderney milk float. English dairyman's float of the 1900's, with cranked axle and low-slung bodywork, hung on sideways semi-elliptical springs. Mounted through the front by means of a low step iron. Fitted with half-splashers above the wheels, also having a curved top or name board. There was a crosswise seat in the centre of the bodywork. Up to 15 cwts. capacity. Drawn by a large pony or cob.

Alexandra car. American version of the Dogcat phaeton, with dos-à-dos (back-to-back) seating, and cut under of the fore-wheels. *See* Dogcart and Dogcart Phaeton.

Alexandra dogcart.   English single or two-wheeled dogcart of the late 19th century. Constructed with straight rather than curved lines and a high dashboard. Slightly lower than the ordinary dogcart and thought to be more suitable for women drivers. High, broad splashers or mudguards protected the voluminous skirts of the period from mire and dust. Said to have been specially designed for Queen Alexandria, consort of Edward VIIth, when she was Princess of Wales.

Alley bodger.   Small, low-sided wagon, frequently running on iron wheels, used for general purposes, in the hop fields of Kent. Drawn by a single horse.

Alliance phaeton.   A lighter or sporting version of the Park Phaeton, popular during the 1850's and 1860's.

All-nighter.   American slang name for a night cab, operating in New York City during the hours of darkness. Usually a four-wheeler.

Ambulance.   This type of vehicle, eventually used as transport for invalids and casualties, derived from the French Hospital Ambulance, or mobile field hospital. It was originally a type of dressing station mounted on four wheels, containing medical supplies in the care of a commissioned surgeon and two or more orderlies. A slightly smaller version, designed by Baron Larrey, Chief Surgeon of the French Army, was introduced during the early 1790's, to convey sick and wounded from the front line to base hospitals. These were well-sprung, headed vehicles, on two or four wheels (according to size), drawn by either a pair or four-in-hand team. Patients lay in cots or on mattresses but later on stretchers. Two-wheeled types were mainly used in mountainous districts with narrow, uneven tracks.

A British military ambulance was introduced about ten years later, represented — throughout the 19th century — by several marks, until the appearance of motor vehicles. American military ambulances did not appear in large numbers until the Civil War of the 1860's. During earlier periods the wounded were transported in ordinary wagons or left to fend for themselves. In the American West a type of sleeping carriage, provided with hammocks for night travel, was known as an Ambulance.

The first civilian ambulance was a crude hand cart pushed from the rear. It assumed a modern, fully enclosed or panel-sided appearance by the 1880's, frequently having cranked axles and a clerestory roof (the latter for improved ventilation). Most ambulances were entered from the rear and provided with cut-under of the forewheels for turning in a confined space. They were among the first vehicles to be fitted with solid rubber tyres, wired or clinched in channels of the wheel rims. Usually drawn by a single horse in curved shafts.

In Britain, towards the end of the 19th century, a large number of four-wheeled cabs could be converted into ambulances, as the need arose. These would be large enough for a single stretcher case with attendant nurse or orderly.

Ambulance, horse.   Type of ambulance — on either two or four wheels — used to convey sick or injured horses, in both military and civil life. Low-slung, on cranked axles, entered over slatted ramps at either front or rear. Badly injured horses were winched into position by means of an off-side windlass. They could also be suspended in a body sling hung from an arched framework or hoop. Four-wheeled types were driven from a box seat while two-wheeled ambulances usually had a seat over the near-side wheel. Some military horse ambulances were drawn by a pair of horses, the near side horse attached by means of an outrigger or extension bar, ridden by a mounted driver.

Amepton.   Light, open carriage of the Landau-type, first appearing in London during the 1850's. Designed and patented by an Edwin Kesterton.

Americaine.   Name frequently used in Western Europe, especially France, to denote the American Buggy or Boguet. A number of these were fashionable in Paris, for a brief period, during the 1890's.

American break.   Passenger vehicle used in the Western States of America, for swift, long-distance travel. Seated six, with a slatted under-boot and ample luggage space. Very high for its short wheelbase. Drawn by four or more horses, changed at various staging posts. Hung on sideways elliptical springs, at front and rear.

American cab.   Two-wheeled cab, first used in the streets of New York about 1832. Mounted on cranked axles and having sideways elliptical or semi-elliptical springs. Entered from the rear, having seats for two passengers, on each side of the interior. The driver occupied a roofseat with angled footboard.

American cabriolet.   A four-wheeled, low-slung carriage popular in North America during the second half of the 19th century. Similar to the Victoria. Protected, at the rear, by a falling or half-hood. Drawn by a pair of horses in pole gear. Hung on full sideways elliptical springs, front and rear.

American coal wagon. Usually a high-sided, four-wheeled wagon, its loading platform lined with sheet iron. There were also low-sided types, some able to turn in full lock. Drawn by one or two horses, according to size. The driving seat was sprung although the body was unsprung or dead axle.

American dump wagon. American wagon, low-slung and designed on the hopper principle. Noted for a long wheelbase. Dead axle but having a fully sprung driving seat. There were cranked axles at the rear, while the fore-carriage had craned or gooseneck structure for underlock. Chain gears for opening and closing the bottom doors, when unloading, were operated either from a side windlass or lever on the fore-carriage. Usually drawn by a pair of horses in pole gear. *See* Dump Wagon.

American florist's van. Four-wheeled van used in the delivery of cut flowers and potted plants, especially in the streets of large American cities, up to the 1950's. Hung on several combinations of sideways and crosswise elliptical springs. Drawn by a single horse in straight or curved shafts. Either open or fully enclosed, the latter type having an effect of greenhouse windows. The driving position was frequently enclosed with an aperture for the reins above the dashboard.

American furniture van. American spring wagon, usually low-sided, having a long wheelbase and elevated driving seat. Hung on two sets of cross and side springs, front and rear. There were lashing rails above the single side planks, to which waterproof covers might be attached. Used for delivering furniture to houses and offices rather than removals. Drawn by either one or two horses.

American game cart. Light sporting vehicle on the lines of a phaeton, with two rows of forward facing seats. There was usually cut-under of the forecarriage for better turning angles. Hung on sideways elliptical springs, front and rear.

American garbage truck. A framework of parallel steel girders, running on four wheels, used for the door-to-door collection of refuse. Three large, demountable bins were slung between the girders, each bin having spring-controlled top-fillers. Matter could be tipped into the interiors by garbage men, with smaller bins or baskets, perched on single-plank running boards at the sides and rear of the vehicle. Drawn by a pair of medium-heavy horses in pole gear. The single driving seat would be mounted on two crosswise elliptical springs, although the main bodywork was unsprung or dead axle. Frequently painted bright yellow.

American gooseneck truck. Four-wheeled, low-loading truck or wagon, drawn by a single horse in shafts. Unsprung or dead axle, although the single driving seat would be mounted on fully elliptical springs. The platform, protected by stakes or stanchions, sometimes with crosswise boarding, would be much lower than the driving position. Rear wheels were usually cranked. Cut under of the fore-wheels was achieved by the use of curved irons or cranes, known in North America as goosenecks. A lever brake acted on both rear wheels. Near equirotal.

American gypsy van. This appeared mainly in the Atlantic Coast States from the 1860's to the 1920's. Very different from the gypsy vans of either Britain or Continental Europe, especially concerning their longer wheelbase. Sides were planked or panelled to the waistline, having decorative panels in the upper parts with painted landscapes or floral decorations. Windows, on each side, were square-topped, rounded or lancet shapes. The front entrance was reached via fixed steps on either side of a platform-like porch, beneath an extension of the roof canopy. Hung on crosswise elliptical springs at the front and sideways semi-elliptical springs at the rear. Drawn by a single horse.

American light delivery van. Light delivery van or wagon, used for retail trading. Featured a large goods compartment, with double doors at the rear. There would be a semi-enclosed driving seat and full cut-under of the forecarriage. Hung on reinforced but shallow platform springs. Drawn by a single horse or cob.

American light spring dray. Light delivery dray with both sprung seat and bodywork. Springs were sideways semi-ellipticals, front and rear.

American light trade cart. Two-wheeled delivery cart or van, fully enclosed and driven from an elevated rearward seat (off-entre to the right or off side), in the style of a Hansom Cab. The axle was cranked and the shafts well-curved. Access to the inner compartment was through single or double doors at the side of the driving seat. There was also a small rearward platform, useful for loading and unloading, while some had a forward roof rack. Drawn by a single horse or large pony. Hung on sideways elliptical or semi-elliptical springs. Half splashers protected both wheels.

American mail cart. Fully enclosed, two-wheeled van, hung on sideways, semi-elliptical springs. Drawn by a single horse or large pony. The single driving seat had curved side irons and a narrow footrest or toeboard, but minus a dashboard. Shafts were well-curved of flexible lancewood. A railed-up area to the rear of the driving seat, covering the head, could be used for empty mail bags. The upper part of the bodywork would be painted vermillion, while the lower half was dark blue with a white centre band or stripe. On the latter was printed 'U.S. MAIL'. Shafts and wheels were yellow, lined our in red.

American phaeton. North American version of the driving phaeton, popular throughout the greater part of the 19th century. Accommodated four on two forward facing seats, the latter well-upholstered with side rails and high back rests. The rear seats, were open, in the style of a Victoria, but minus the protection of a half hood. Floor of the rear part was frequently dropped or in the form of a shallow well. Splashers protected both front and rear wheels, meeting in the centre to form a crude step iron. There was full cut-under of the fore-carriage and both foot and dashboard. Hung on full sideways elliptical springs, front and rear. Drawn either by a single horse in shafts or pair in pole gear.

American prospector's wagon. Type of one-horse road wagon or buggy, having an unsprung body but sprung driving seat and low (unsprung) rearward seat. A lever brake acted on the rear wheels. Near equirotal. A railed-up area, between the seats, forming part of the traylike body, could be used for tools and light equipment. Popular in the days of gold prospecting, especially in the far West.

American removal van. Also known as a Moving Van. American version of the British Pantechnicon or four-wheel furniture Van. Usually drawn by three horses abreast. The enclosed driving seat, at or near roof level, was cantilevered above the front board. Strong pedal brakes acted on both rear wheels. Headed but without rounding boards. Hung on sideways semi-elliptical springs, front and rear. Much higher and slightly longer than the British type but without a rearward well.

American spring wagon. Low-sided goods delivery wagon, popular with retailers in many American towns and cities from the 1860's to the mid-1920's. The forecarriage was hung on crosswise elliptical springs, while the rearcarriage had lengthwise elliptical springs. Limited to half lock.

American spring wagon with cut-under. Similar to the American Spring Wagon but having full underlock. Hung on either crosswise elliptical or inverted semi-elliptical springs, front and rear. Like many American wagons of the 19th century, it had a

solid lengthwise underperch, between fore and rear carriages.
American street flusher. Water tank wagon with a powerful
flushing apparatus, its use dating from the early 1900's. Drawn by
a pair of horses in pole gear but having its pump worked by an
automobile-type petrol engine. The largest tanks would be up to
700 gallons capacity. Hung or sideways semi-elliptical springs,
front and rear. The single driving seat was on a level with the tank-
top, supported by brackets and sometimes by leaf springs.
Many vehicles of this type were owned by the street-cleansing
departments of American cities, manufactured by the Tiffin
Wagon Company of Ohio, established during the 1870's.
American timber wagon. Timber carrying vehicle in which the
fore and rearcarriages were connected by an improvised coupling
or reach pole, cut from a forest tree. There were heavy brakeblocks
on the hind wheels, operated by means of a bow-shaped brake-
lever. Drawn by either horses or oxen, sometimes mixed teams.
Amesbury trap. American four-wheeled driving vehicle with
near-equirotal wheels and dos-à-dos seating, as in a dogcart
phaeton. Hung on crosswise elliptical springs, front and rear.
Drawn by a single horse.
Amish buggy. Type of American Buggy favoured by members of
the Amish religious sect and community. These people are settled
in the states of Pennsylvania, Ohio and Indiana, where they live by
farming in the style of their ancestors, not allowed to change their
habits, transport or modes of dress, according to articles of faith.
The majority still use buggies and road wagons, especially when
driving to church or making social calls.

The Amish Buggy, still manufactured in fair numbers, is of a
basic tray-shape. It has a high-backed driving seat, wide enough
for two, a leather-covered dashboard, folding hood and brass-
mounted candle lamps. A slightly later type is more of a
box-shape, enclosed on three sides by leather screens or roll-
down blinds, for all-weather protection. There is characteristic
crosswise-elliptical springing at both front and rear. Such vehicles
are easy to repair, light to handle and convenient to store. Wheels
are near-equirotal. Usuaully drawn by a single horse.
Angular landau. Landau with a square, angular profile. An
alternative name for the Square or Shelburne Landau. *See* Landau.
Animal transport cart. Two-wheeled military cart of a type
mainly used in India and the Far East. Drawn by a pair of horses,
ponies or mules, harnessed to a centre-pole by semi-circular bands
attached to the cart saddles, known as belly-bugles. Still used in

France, especially by units of the Indian Army attached to the British Expeditionary Force, as late as 1940.

Araba. Turkish wagon of the 18th and 19th centuries, having a canopy top and crosswise seating. Used by women of the harem. Drawn by a pair of oxen or horses, guided by dismounted servants.

Arcera. A four-wheeled carriage of Ancient Rome, usually headed. Drawn by either horses or oxen.

Arkansas log truck. Light weight logging or lumber truck, used in the south western states of the U.S.A. End gears were connected by a short reach pole. Bolsters were set low, held in place by diagonal iron stays. Drawn by a pair of horses in pole gear.

Army wagon. Four Mule, Four-wheeled army supply wagon, drawn by either mules or horses. Widely used in the United States Army from the period of the Civil War onwards. Also known as an Escort Wagon. Its canvas head or cover was supported on a row of hoops (tilts).

Army wagon. Six Mule, A larger and slightly later vrsion of the Four Mule Army Wagon.

Ascot Landau. English vehicle of the Landau-type, reserved for the traditional drive down the course at Royal Ascot, in which the Royal Family and their guests are taken to a special enclosure. Drawn by teams of four horses each, controlled by postillions. Lower and lighter than the ordinary State Landau, but with rearward seats for footmen or carriage servants.

Asylum van. Ambulance-type wagon or van, used in North America by mental homes and insane asylums. Fully enclosed with barred or netted windows on either side of the bodywork. The rearward door was entered via a wooden step on steel brackets. Drawn by one or two horses. Mounted, front and rear, on semi-elliptical side springs.

Australian bow wagon. Australian farm wagon, dating from the 1870's, of a type first used in the State of Victoria. Noted for its low, single plank, sides, short wheelbase and curved bows or sideboards protecting both front and rear wheels. Unsprung or dead axle. Drawn by a single heavy horse in shafts or tandem pair.

Australian road wagon. Australian driving wagon, akin to the phaeton, used on rougher roads of country districts and the outback. Most had a large umbrella basket and rearward boot. Drawn by a single horse, the shafts — curving under its dashboard — being attached to the fore-axletree. A narrow but substantial perch prevented full underlock. A pedal brake operated on the rear wheels. Like the American Buggy, it was hung on crosswise elliptical springs, front and rear.

Australian oil and colourman's wagon.   Light dray of a type used in Australian townships by painters, decorators and builders' merchants. Introduced during the early 1900's. Sometimes adapted for the delivery of plate glass, when the demountable driving seat might be lowered and sheets of glass, wrapped in blankets, fitted into special racks reserved for the purpose. Some vehicles of this type had slatted floors. Drawn by a single horse in shafts or a pair in pole gear. Hung on semi-elliptical side springs at the front and full elliptical side springs at the rear. Small fore wheels turned in full lock. A pedal brake acted on both rear wheels.

Australian passenger wagon.   An Australian version of the North American Concord Coach, with canopy top and side blinds. Mounted on thoroughbraces rather than steel springs. There was room for eight inside passengers with two on the box. Drawn by teams of four or six horses.

Australian spring dray.   Two-wheeled dray or heavy cart, used in Australian cities and townships, to recover dead or injured horses. Could be tipped in a rearward direction, having an ample, slatted ramp over which a carcass might be winched. Either plank or panel-sided. Hung on sideways semi-elliptical springs. Driven from a low cross bench in the fore-part, reached by means of shaft steps.

Austrian Landau.   A vehicle of Central Europe, more in the style of a Victoria than the conventional Landau. Protected by a fixed head of the canopy type. Usually drawn by a pair of horses in pole gear.

Auto-top buggy.   Tray-bodied American Buggy, making use of a folding top or hood, similar to that of the 'T' Model Ford. Popular during the 1900's.

Avondale.   Alternative name, frequently used in North America, for the Governess Car or Tub Cart.

Aylesbury wagon.   Box-type English farm or road wagon, with high spindle sides and a fairly short wheelbase. Used both on the land and for market work. Turned in limited lock. Drawn by a single horse.

Ayrshire harvest cart.   Low-sided harvest cart found in the Western Lowlands of Scotland. Frequently unsprung or dead axle. As with some other Scottish and Irish vehicles of this type, linchpins were fitted on the outer surface of the nave, frequently working loose through vibration. Some types were fitted with semi-permanent end ladders.

Azaline. Tub-bodied American Buggy with high, panelled sides. A type used in Pennsylvania and other Atlantic Coast States of the U.S.A.

B

Back action. American term for a small trailer hitched to the rear of a larger vehicle.

Back door cab. Type of Wagonette-Brougham of the late 19th century, entered from the rear. Many were privately owned although even larger numbers plied for hire. Hung on sideways elliptical springs, front and rear.

Baggage cart. Two-wheeled vehicle, used in transporting military stores, especially from the late Middle Ages to the mid-17th century. Usually hooded or headed with low, wickerwork sides. Wheels were often solid or disc-types. Sometimes drawn by a pair of horses in double shafts or pole gear, but more frequently by a single horse.

Baggage wagon. Larger, four-wheeled version of the Baggage Cart used, from the late Middle Ages, in transporting military stores. A protective canvas cover was supported by tilts. Drawn by two or more horses in pole gear. A larger version, for civilian use, would be the Carrier's Wagon, later developing into the Stage Wagon. *See* Carrier's wagon and Stage wagon.

Baker's van. Either a two or four-wheeled delivery van, known in America as a Bakery Wagon. It appeared in several different types and styles, mainly between the 1860's and the late 1950's. A familiar example, in Britain, was the two-wheeled or Coburg Cart, but on many delivery rounds there were larger, four-wheeled types. Most appear to have been hung on sideways elliptical springs at the front and sideways semi-elliptical springs at the rear. By the mid-1930's large numbers had acquired pneumatic tyres, in common with the majority of commercial vans of those days.

The more traditional type could be loaded from the rear by means of double doors. Modern vans frequently had sliding doors or panels at the sides. The driver's seat was a cross-bench under a hood or forward extension of the roof, sometimes curving downwards towards the dashboard. A few had small lights or windows on either side of the driving seat. Shafts were either straight or curved. The average van cost about £45, although a Coburgh or two-wheeler would cost less than half this price.

Bakery wagon. American four-wheeled equivalent of the Baker's

Van. Square-shaped and usually headed, hung on semi-elliptical springs, front and rear. The sides were of straight, panelled wood, while the driving seat was semi-enclosed. Drawn by a single horse.

Ballesden cart/car.   Version of the English Dogcart with slatted sides.

Banbury miller.   An Oxfordshire version of the Miller's Wagon. Usually appeared with a bowed canvas top, supported by hoops, and having single shafts.

Band wagon.   Large four-wheeled vehicle, used in circus and carnival parades as a mobile bandstand. Drawn by four/six horses or even larger teams. Noted for ornate side panels and encrustations of gilded wood or plasterwork. There were two main versions, one in which the musicians sat on parallel seats inside the body of the wagon, while the other was a carrying box with crosswise seating at a higher level. The interior of the latter type was also used as storage space for instruments and general equipment. Both were driven from a high box seat, by a liveried coachman. Wheels often had decorative in-filling between the spokes, known as a 'sunburst' effect. Usually hung on sideways semi-elliptical springs, front and rear.

Bandy.   Native cart of India, normally a small platform between two wheels, sometimes headed or hooded by a canopy of rough matting. Drawn either by a yoke of small oxen or a pair of large ponies. An unsprung or dead axle type, often with disc wheels.

Barco de tierra.   Spanish Earth-Boat. Roughly made cart or wagon, with wickerwork sides, used by Spanish settlers on the Pampas of South America. A characteristic feature was its high wheels with numerous spokes. Drawn by pairs or larger teams of horses or oxen.

Barge.   Term used in New England and the Atlantic Coast States of North America for a crudely-built excursion wagon. This had lengthwise seating in the style of a wagonette and could be drawn by either one or two horses, the latter in pole gear. Driven from an elevated box seat and hung on elliptical or semi-elliptical side springs, front and rear. Entrance for passengers was from the rear by means of folding steps. Seated four to six, plus the driver. Open rather than headed, used mainly for sight-seeing and short distance travel.

Barge wagon.   A late type of English farm wagon, with straight-plank sides and prominent outraves, dating from the 1890's. The small front wheels were able to turn in full underlock, frequently having iron naves. Factory-made rather than constructed by village craftsmen. Drawn by a single horse in shafts but sometimes assisted by a chain horse in tandem.

Barker quarter landau.   Landau of the mid-19th century with a dropped centre or well, but having curved rather than square corners. *See* Landau.

Barouche.   The name derives from the Latin 'birotus' — meaning two-wheeled. In ancient times it was a small pleasure cart or car but developed into a larger or four-wheeled type. The later German equivalent was the 'barutsche', akin to the lighter and more elegant Caleche. The German type was introduced to Britain during the 1760's and widely known as a 'German Wagon'. A member of the coach family it had full undergear and lower quarters or panels but minus upper panels and only partly covered by a rearward or half-hood. Passengers normally faced in the direction of travel, although some vehicles had folding seats, on which others might be seated vis-à-vis. Essentially a town vehicle for summer driving, although some eventually had a protective screen able to close against the raised hood. The box seat, as with the landau and certain types of chariot, was well raised above the bodywork. Usually drawn by two horses in pole gear.

Barouche-Landau.   Sporting barouche with a higher than average box seat. Popular in England from the late 18th century and frequently driven by amateurs. There was usually a rearward or rumble seat for grooms. Driven to a four-in-hand team.

Barouche-sociable.   Barouche with a double hood or two half-hoods, protecting both front and rear of the vehicle.

Barouchet.   Small or cut-down type of barouche, driven to a single horse. Popular during the early 19th century. Sometimes minus the box seat, to be driven from the interior. Also known as a Demi-barouche or Couplet.

Barrel top.   Round-topped Gypsy or tinker's caravan. An alternative name for the Bow Top. A type claimed to have originated in South Yorkshire or Humberside.

Basket phaeton.   Also known as a 'Ladies' Basket Phaeton'. Designed during the 1860's and used for park driving in fashionable districts. Constructed either with or without a rumble seat. Basketwork sides were of curved or rounded profile. While British versions had sideways elliptical springs, an American type had crosswise ellipticals, similar to a buggy or road wagon.

Bathing machine.   Boxlike mobile dressing room mounted on large wheels, the latter either straight or dished. Drawn by a single horse, attached by chain traces and ridden rather than driven.

When sea water was level with the axletrees the horse was unhitched and steps let down at the front. For a return journey to the promenade the horse was harnessed to the rear of the machine and steps retracted. Sides of the bodywork, originally oval or octagonal but later square, were often striped in primary colours. Wheels tended to be equirotal or the same size, front and rear. The prototype is claimed to have been used at Weymouth by George III, at a period when sea bathing first became popular for reasons of both fashion and health.

Bath wagon. Type of small, dead axle wagon, drawn by a pony or donkey. Mainly used, during the 18th century, to convey portable bathtubs to and from summer houses.

Battery wagon. 1. Military vehicle, sometimes articulated, with a detachable rearward section, connected to the forepart by a coupling pole. Used in the American Army of the mid-19th century, to accompany field or siege batteries of the artillery, containing stores and spares. Drawn by two or more horses harnessed in pole gear.

2. A type of headed or enclosed military wagon, used by the Signal Corps of the American Army, as a mobile telegraphic office. Replaced by motor vehicles during the 1930's.

Battlesden cart/car. Small, handy pleasure vehicle, popular in England during the second half of the 19th century. Driven to a large pony or small cob. Similar to a single or two-wheeled dogcart but with a much lower body, in which it resembled the Malvern Cart.

Beach phaeton. American four-wheeled phaeton, frequently used for summer excursions at seaside resorts. Fairly low and open-sided, easy to enter. The forecarriage had full cut-under. Hung on sideways elliptical springs, front and rear. Drawn by a pair of cobs or large ponies, in pole gear.

Beach wagon. American pleasure wagon used for holiday excursions, especially at the coastal resorts of New England. Introduced during the 1860's, remaining popular until the 1900's. Of simple, traylike construction, but having a double row of seats facing forward. There was a canopy top, mounted on standards, and open sides. Hung on sideways elliptical springs. Drawn by a single horse.

Beaufort cart. Country driving cart related to the Norfolk Cart. A type frequently driven by Edward VII while staying at Sandringham. The shafts were well-curved and the sides of the body slatted, especially above the wheeltops. Hung on a Dennett or three-spring arrangement. A rearward footrest or tailboard could be let down for dos-à-dos passengers. Usually drawn by a small horse, about 15 hands high.

Beaufort phaeton. An enlarged version of the slightly smaller Mail Phaeton, with crosswise seats for two extra passengers or grooms. Designed by the then Duke of Beaufort, a founder-member of the Coaching Club. Mainly used for private driving and to exercise coach or carriage horses.

Bedford cart. English farm cart with fixed raves or sideboards above high wheels. Made in various sizes and capacities between 25 and 35 cwts. An unsprung or dead axle cart, drawn by a single horse.

Beer patrol wagon. An American two-wheeled cart (despite its name). Used in urban areas for the street delivery of beer in keg and barrel. A type introduced by the Ohlsen Company of Cincinnati, Ohio, had a revolving frame. Mainly popular during the late 19th and early 20th centuries. Drawn either by a single horse or pair of horses in pole gear.

Beer wagon. The standard brewer's dray of North America. Any type of four-wheeled wagon or dray used in the delivery of beer barrels. Frequently drawn by matching teams of heavy horses, chosen for good conformation and smart action, serving as an advertisement for the firm they represented.

Beet sugar gear. American carrying frame, often mounted with high-sided bodywork, used in carrying the sugar beet crop. Some had side-tipping facilities. Noted for small but strongly made wheels with broad treads, able to handle considerable loads. Drawn by teams of horses or mules, although in later years, by traction engines or farm tractors.

Belgian road cart. Light, two-wheeled driving and exercise cart, popular in Belgium during the 1900's. Hung on a three-spring system with pivoting shackles. Noted for its low bodywork and wide gauge or track, which made it safe for road work with inexperienced horses.

Benna. Crude farm cart of Ancient Rome, drawn by either a pair of oxen or horses. While the floor was of wooden planks the sides were of thick ropes, woven from grass or straw.

Bent panel cart. Light, two-wheeled dogcart, the sides tending to curve outwards. A shallow well protected the feet. Favoured by lady drivers on account of its greater protection from mud and splashes. The side slats or louvres were usually false. Drawn by a small horse or large pony in curved shafts.

Berkshire wagon. Large, bow-type wagon with a deeply waisted recess at the sides for improved underlock. Noted for its shafts, set between hounds or projections of the under-forecarriage, and closed-in outraves.

Berlin or Berline. Type of coach or chariot and the undergear on which it was supported. Said to have been invented during the mid-17th century by Colonel Philip de Chiese, a Piedmontese engineer employed by the Elector of Brandenburgh. Also attributed to the French designer and clock-maker, Roubo. So-named as its first public appearance was in the streets of Berlin. It made use of two parallel under supports or braces — in longitudinal plan — outside the main bodywork. On some types the braces could be tightened, raised or lowered by means of an attached windlass. Not widely popular in Britain or the American colonies until the mid-18th century. The main novelty lay in its suspension, features of which were adopted by the Concord stage coach and several similar vehicles. Usually drawn by a pair of horses in pole gear.

Berlin coach. Vehicle with the body of an ordinary coach carried on the suspension system of a Berlin.

Berlinet or Berlinette. Diminutive of Berlin. A smaller version of the Berlin with coupé or cut-down bodywork.

Berlingot. A narrow vis-à-vis coach or semi-open carriage, in which two persons sat facing each other. Also known as a 'Vis-à-vis'. *See* Vis-à-vis.

Berlin rockaway. Light passenger vehicle of North America with full-sized panels and glazed upper quarters. Not a true Berlin as it was hung on leaf springs rather than braces.

Beverley car. Square-sided version of the Governess Car. Finished with varnish over natural wood rather than in solid colours.

Bian. Large, four-wheeled version of the Irish Jaunting Car. Mainly used for long distance journeys in Southern Ireland, in districts not served by stage coaches. As with the smaller car, passengers sat back-to-back down the sides to the vehicle, facing outwards. Protection for the lower limbs was provided in the form of knee flaps. Introduced by Charles Biancononi of Dublin, a naturalised Irishman of Italian descent, concerned with the improvement of social conditions and public transport in his adopted country, during the early 19th century.

Bier. An open truck or carriage on which a coffin may be taken to the place of burial. Usually manhandled but sometimes adapted for pony draught.

Bike wagon. Light exercise wagon or runabout favoured in the United States of America from the 1880's to the 1900's. Similar to an American Buggy, with or without cut-under, also having wire-spoked wheels, rubber tyres, tubular framework and other features in common with a bicycle. A few early types had firm but narrow wooden spokes with small hubs. Drawn by a single horse or pony, according to size. It eventually developed into the show wagon, especially when making use of cut-under for full underlock.

Birotum. A small gig or chariot of Ancient Rome, drawn by a single horse. Used both for public hire and private use, especially during the reign of Constantine the Great (313–337 A.D.). Frequently provided with a rearward luggage rack. There was an extensive range of street ranks, inns and posting houses where the Birotum could be hired.

Bishop. An elderly vehicle refurbished to appear new and up-to-date. The term originally referred to a dishonest practice, dating from the late 16th century, in which the teeth of old horses were filed-down to make them seem younger.

Black and tan. Four-wheeled cab of the 'growler' type, appearing in the streets of New York from the 1880's. Coloured tan below and black above the waistline. They often ran a cheap service, considered disreputable in more fashionable quarters.

Black Maria. Four-wheeled police or prison van, the name originating in London during the early Victorian era. Most early types were emblazoned with the letters 'V.R.' and the royal crest. 'Maria' or 'Ria' was a nickname for Victoria, especially among the East-enders. This vehicle was an oblong, boxlike van, in a jet black livery, frequently without windows, although some had a glazed and slatted clerestory for improved ventilation. Driven from a high seat at roof level. Entered through a rearward door via two steps. Hung on sideways elliptical springs, front and rear. Draw by a pair of horses in pole gear. Used in Britain and North America until replaced by motor vehicles during the 1920's.

Boat carriage. Large break with both crosswise and sideways-on passenger seats. There was an elevated box seat for the driver and a rearward or low rumble seat for a groom. Mounted on both an underperch and cee-springs. Bodywork was in the form of a large rowing boat, complete to the last details of keel and gunwales. Headed with an awning or canopy, supported on eight standards. Introduced during the second half of the 19th century and mainly used in India or other dominion/colonial countries east of Suez.

The forecarriage turned in full lock. Drawn by teams of four or six horses.

Boat wagon. A shallower and slightly smaller vrsion of the Barge Wagon. *See* Barge Wagon. Introduced during the early 1900's. Usually factory built. Drawn by a single horse.

Body break. Large type of passenger break or wagonette, with an elevated driving seat. Drawn by a pair of horses in pole gear. Seated six or eight passengers on either transverse or longitudinal seating.

Boer treck wagon. Long wheel-based wagon used by the South African Boers in their landward trecks or migrations of the 19th century. The plank sides and flooring were easy to dismantle for crossing broad rivers and rock-strewn terrain. Sides were much higher at the rear than the front, a feature of the Dutch tradition from which it derived. A covered wagon with felt and canvas top supported on ten semi-circular hoops that resembled those of the North American Prairie Schooner. Drawn by varied numbers of horses or oxen, harnessed in pole gear. Minus a tailboard although a rearward inclined cratch or shelf was supported, between the rear wheels, on letting-down chains.

Boguet. 1. French version of the American four-wheeled buggy.
2. French version of the English or two-wheeled buggy.

Boiler trolley. Heavy delivery vehicle on iron disc-wheels, many of which were owned by the main line railway companies from the 1880's. Used in transporting boilers, castings and large machine parts. They had low clearance above road level and were little more than a longitudinal framework with bolsters at each end. Tare weight would be in the region of 6 tons, with a capacity of over 40 tons. Usually drawn by a large team of shire-type horses or 'waggoners', reserved for this work, the wheelers in double shafts rather than pole gear.

Boiler wagon. A lighter version of the Boiler Trolley, much higher above road level and mounted on iron-shod wooden wheels, with metal or wooden hubs. Drawn by large teams but more likely to have the wheelers in pole gear rather than shafts.

Bolster wagon. 1. A primitive type of four-wheeled buggy, without rearward springs. Suspension was by means of side bars/ braces and crosswise bolsters.

2. A commercial wagon on which an overhanging load was supported by crosswise bolsters.

Bonaventia. Name used in Pennsylvania (U.S.A.), for a type of American Buggy, also known as a Jenny Lind. *See* Jenny Lind.

Bone shaker.   Slang name for any type of cheap, hired carriage.
Boston chaise.   American single horse chaise, popular in New England during the first half of the 19th century. Noted for its folding or falling hood, curved shafts and suspension of leather side braces, the latter often combined with cee-springs. Essentially a two-wheeled vehicle for two occupants or a driver and passenger.
Bottle delivery van.   American, two-wheeled delivery van, hung on sideways elliptical springs, with high wheels and curved shafts. The semi-enclosed driving seat had a low footboard. Frequently in the form of a large imitation bottle with square sides. Drawn by a singe horse or pony, according to size. Used for both delivering and advertising any type of wet goods from brown sauce to patent medicine and wines or spirits.
Boule.   Berlin-type coach of the early 18th century, of Germanic origins. Mounted on a combination of side braces and cee-springs. Quarters of the bodywork tended to bulge outwards, although with limited headroom of the interior. Drawn by four horses, controlled by a single postillion on the nearside wheeler. Space in the forepart, normally occupied by a box seat, was used for luggage.
Boulnois cab.   Patent cab introduced on the streets of London during the early 1830's. Two passengers entered from the rear and sat facing each other in a sideways-on position. The driving seat was at roof level but, unlike that of a Hansom Cab, at the front rather than the rear of the bodywork. Due to its elongated dimensions and seating plan it was frequently known as a Minibus. Named after its inventor, William Boulnois.
Boulster wagon.   An enlarged type of Bolster Wagon (*See* Bolster Wagon 1), frequently used in public service. Noted for its two or three rows of crosswise seating and a hard or standing top. The bodywork was raised on bolsters or boulsters but all seats were sprung individually. Usually open-sided but with roller blinds, side curtains and a driving apron across the forward seating. Drawn by one or two horses, the pair harnessed in pole gear. First used and constructed in New Jersey, U.S.A. — invented by Amos Stiles of Moorestown, New Jersey, in 1814.
Bounder.   Oxford. Slang name for a fast, light dogcart on a pair of high wheels. Driven either to a single horse or tandem. Seated four, dos-à-dos. Hung on sideways semi-elliptical springs. Wheel spokes were painted bright red. Also known as the Oxford Cart, named after the city of its origins and frequently driven by sporting undergraduates.

Bow-fronted brougham.   Brougham in which the usually straight
front panel or window (windscreen) was curved or bow-fronted.
Bow-fronted hansom.   Version of the Hansom Cab, often
privately owned and popular with professional men. Fully
enclosed and entered through a side door, the forepart having a
characteristic curved or bow-shape.
Bow-topped caravan.   Also known as a Bow Top. Gypsy living
van with a bow-shaped roof or top, although some were more
square in outline than others. The roof covering was canvas or
tarpaulin, weather-proof and lined — on the inside — with
chenille matting, the whole supported by bowlike hoops. The ends
of the van were usually boarded-up or enclosed. Each vehicle
contained a cooking stove; both fixed and folding items of
furniture, with two bunks. Entered through a front door and
porch over steps that were let down between the shafts. Hung on
semi-elliptical side springs, front and rear. A screw-down brake
acted on the rear wheels, operated from the porch.
Bow wagon.   Dead axle farm wagon of traditional English
design, mainly associated with the Cotswolds and South West
Midlands. The sides and outraves were arched above the rear
wheels. Waisted at the fore-end to improve the turning circle.
Usually painted straw yellow with red wheels and under works.
Drawn by a single horse in shafts or larger team in Tandem/
trandem. Also known as the Farmer's Wagon.
Box.   The Box or Box Cart was a version of the European
Tumbril, as used in Scotland or the North of England. Open and
low-sided, there were both tipping and non-tipping versions.
Unsprung or dead axle.
Box body cart.   Strongly made, plank-sided cart, mainly con-
structed in Britain for export to her colonies and other tropical or
sub-tropical countries. Noted for its square or boxlike structure
and high-sided appearance. Fitted with iron naves and frequently
having iron spokes. Drawn by a single horse or mule.
Box wagon.   Dead axle farm wagon of traditional design.
Associated with the East Midlands and eastern countries of
England. Designed with higher, straighter sides than the Bow
Wagon but having a shorter wheelbase. Usually painted blue with
red wheels and underworks. The waisted sides allowed a limited
turning circle.
Bracket-fronted wagon.   American name for any type of vehicle
in which the footboard is supported by brackets, continuous with
the bodywork.

Bradford cart. Open, low-slung cart, hung on sideways semi-elliptical springs. Frequently had an elevated cross seat mounted in a central position. Sides and rear were guarded by low rails and spindles. Used by street traders and for local collection/delivery purposes. Drawn by a large pony or small cob.

Brake. Alternative spelling of Break, mainly favoured in England during the second half of the 19th century. *See* Break.

Break. Heavy four-wheeled passenger vehicle with an elevated driving seat, originally used for training and breaking young horses, also for exercise purposes. From the mid-19th century many were fitted with longitudinal seating which could be removed when luggage was carried. Drawn by a pair of horses in pole gear. Virtually an enlarged version of the wagonette. In many cases a hired, rather than a privately owned vehicle.

Breaking cart. Two-wheeled training or exercise vehicle, used for breaking single horses to draught. Noted for its skeletal structure and elevated driving seat, being a smaller version of the Skeleton Break or Brake. *See* Skeleton Break. Many were owned by large commercial firms and the cartage departments of railway companies.

Brett. Travelling carriage, widely used in the Atlantic Coast States of North America. A transatlantic version of the European Britzska. Drawn by two or more horses in pole gear.

Brewer's covered wagon. English light, four-wheeled delivery van or wagon, having a framed top or cover of waterproofed material, supported on tilts. Fitted with a shallow footboard but minus a dashboard. Driven from a crossbench under an awning, well back from the front of the vehicle. Hung on sideways semi-elliptical springs, front and rear. Made in three full-horse sizes, the largest able to carry up to ten barrels. Cost about £52 — late 19th century.

Brewer's crank-axle float. Long, low two-wheeled vehicle mounted on cranked-axles for greater ease of loading — lowering the height of the vehicle — especially the loading platform. Provided with extra raves or sideboards but seldom with splashers or mudguards. Sides were much higher at the front than the rear. Fitted with upward curving shafts. Made in four sizes, the largest — for one or two horses — up to a capacity of 2 tons. Could be headed with a tarpaulin or waterproof sheet drawn over tilts. Hung on sideways semi-elliptical springs. Introduced during the late 19th century. Cost between £20 and £30, according to size.

Brewer's straight axle delivery cart. Similar to the Brewer's

Crank-axle Float, but with a straight axle and much higher above ground level. Fitted with straight rather than curved shafts. Used for crates of bottled beer rather than barrels or casks. Frequently headed. Drawn by a single horse. Popular during the late 19th century.

Brewer's show dray/wagon.   Type of show vehicle similar to the Market Wagon, used by modern brewers for advertising and publicity purposes rather than deliveries. Driven from an elevated seat supported by iron standards or uprights. Plank, panel or spindle-sided. Frequently handled by large teams or pairs.

Brewer's show van.   While the Brewer's Show Dray or Wagon may have been adapted from an earlier service vehicle delivering crated bottles, the show van is purpose built for advertising, appearing in many harness classes at national and local horse shows. It is about 12 ft in length with an elevated driving seat, projecting and angled footboard, and pedal drum brakes. Some are now mounted on disc-wheels and pneumatic tyres, which are easier than spoked wheels to keep in good repair. Hung on semi-elliptical springs at the front and a three spring arrangement at the rear. Drawn by singles, pairs or larger teams, according to classes in which they are entered.

Brewer's two-wheeled dray.   Brewer's two-wheeled delivery dray of the mid-18th century. Three large barrels were mounted in a crosswise position, the driver sitting on the first barrel. Drawn by a pair of horses in tandem, the first horse guided by the assistant driver or trouncer.

Brewer's wagon.   Alternative name for the American Beer Wagon.

Brewster wagon.   Square-shaped American Buggy or road wagon. Hung on scroll springs. Manufactured in large numbers by the James B. Brewster Carriage Company of New York City, during the late 19th century. Noted for its superior workmanship and finish.

Bridal coach.   Ceremonial wedding coach of the late 19th century, similar to the Double Brougham. Coloured white, pink or silver with inlaid silverwork. Further noted for decorative heart and arrow motifs and heart-shaped candle lamps. Usually drawn by a pair of grey horses in pole gear. Popular in the United States of America and some Continental countries, rather than in Britain.

Brisker.   Slang name used by coachmen and grooms for the Britzska.

Brisker-phaeton.   Rearward hooded phaeton with well-upholstered passenger seats and a long wheelbase. Strong lever brakes acted on the rear wheels. Hung on sideways elliptical springs, front and rear.

Britton wagon. A lighter but slightly larger version of the Goddard Buggy. *See* Goddard Buggy. An American vehicle invented by John W. Britton of New York City in 1872.

Britzska. Also spelt Britzka, Britska, Britzschka and Britschka. Originally an open wagon of Poland and Eastern Europe. In Austria it developed as a passenger vehicle, for three or more people on crosswise seating, having an elevated boxseat at the fore-end. A version of the Austrian type appears to have reached Western Europe shortly after the Napoleonic Wars and to have become popular in England, as a travelling carriage, during the 1820's. The final version included a rearward platform with rumble seat, large enough for three carriage servants. With the adjustment of certain screens and panels the interior could be converted to a sleeping compartment, for one or two persons to lie at full length. Usually hung on cee-springs there was a sturdy underperch between the axles. In later years the box or driving seat was often removed and space acquired taken-up by a luggage boot. Until the coming of railways, ambassadors and high-ranking diplomats frequently travelled about Europe in the Britzska, accompanied by an armed escort. I. K. Brunel, engineer of the Great Western Railway, slept and travelled in such a vehicle for weeks on end, while surveying the main line between Bristol and London. Drawn by four or six horses at first coachman driven but later controlled by postillions.

Britzska chariot. Type of posting chariot modelled on the Britzska, known in Germany and Austria as the Eilwagen.

Britzska Landau. English version of the Britzska in which the hood was designed to lie flat in the style of a modern Landau. Patented by a London carriage builder named Hopkinson, about 1838.

Britzska phaeton. An elegant, lighter version of the Britzska, its suspension similar to that of the early phaeton. Elbow springs were used at the fore-end to increase luggage and passenger space.

Bronson wagon. American panel-sided passenger or driving wagon of the phaeton-type. It had two crosswise seats with high backrests, passengers facing in the direction of travel. Seldom headed. Hung on crosswise elliptical or semi-elliptical side springs, front and rear. Driven to a pair or horses in pole gear. Popular during the second half of the 19th century.

Brouette. Type of sedan chair on wheels, manually pushed or pulled by a single person between shafts. Invented by a Frenchman named Dupin in 1668, it was one of the first vehicles to use all-metal springs. A version introduced to England in 1715, could be drawn by a small pony, led on foot rather than driven.
Brougham. Small passenger vehicle of compromise, between a cab and a gentleman's private coach. Inspired if not actually designed by Lord Brougham — a statesman of the early 19th century, after whom it was named. It is now thought to have been based on an earlier Continental vehicle known as a Droiteschka Chariot. The first English version by Sharp and Bland, was too heavy and cumbersome, although a type built by Robinson and Cook in 1839, gave greater satisfaction.
Low-slung but fully panelled, the Brougham seated two passengers facing forward, screened from the driver by a square glass panel or windscreen. Apart from the much larger Double Brougham and a later bow-fronted version, there were two main types, both drawn by a single horse in shafts. The so-called Peters Brougham had angular lines, while the Barker Brougham was more elegant, with generous curves. Many old Broughams were eventually converted into cabs, remaining popular well into the 1920's and the age of the motor car. A few were even retained by private families, during the Second World War, as a petrol saving economy. Could be purchased from 100 gns. upwards.
Brougham Hansom. Type of Hansom Cab designed in 1887, driven from a seat on the fore-part of the roof. It held three or four passengers. Entered from the rear by means of a low step. Hung on sideways semi-elliptical springs.
Brougham van. Four-wheeled light delivery van. The same as an Omnibus Van. *See* Omnibus Van.
Brougham wagonnette. Small, enclosed wagonette, seating four passengers, or two per side. Fitted with a bow-fronted, frequently removable, top or head. Drawn by a single horse in curved shafts.
Brunswick. Type of light Surrey with a fixed head or top. Hung on crosswise elliptical springs, front and rear. Popular in the Middle West of North America during the 1890's and 1900's. Drawn by a single horse. Seated four people.
Brush van/wagon. Four-wheeled living van of the English Fens and East Anglia. Mainly used by sellers of brooms, brushes and baskets. Notable features included fixed steps forming a rearward entrance, panel sides and several roof and wall racks for the display of wares. A motorised version appeared during the early 1920's but

all types became very scarce shortly before the Second World War, as local trade diminished. Only one genuine example is known to have survived into the 1980's.

Buckboard/buck wagon. Four-wheeled, open passenger vehicle, popular in the Western States of North America from the 1830's to the 1900's. Constructed from strong but springy planks of ash wood, having one or two rows of crosswise seating. Drawn by a single horse or pair. Unsprung, apart from the resilience of its woodwork. Ideal for cross country driving where there were few roads or tracks.

Buckboard barouche. Large passenger vehicle constructed on the unsprung or buckboard principle. Used in the Western parts of North America as a stagecoach, before the introduction of the Concord Coach.

Buckboard mail. Large Buckboard, as built by the Studebaker Company, to convey luggage and mails in the far West of North America. An up-dated version of the Buckboard Barouche, popular during the 1890's, especially in regions beyond the reach of main line railways.

Buckboard wagon. Early type of American Buggy constructed on the unsprung or buckboard principle, but having a shorter wheelbase than most types.

Bucket-seat gig. Gig with two separate bucket-shaped seats for driver and passenger, respectively. Usually hung on a Dennett or three spring system.

Bucker. An all-night cab operating in the streets of New York and other American cities. Slightly more respectable than the Black and Tan. Also known as a Night Owl or Night Hawk.

Buckinghamshire cattle cart. Plank or panel-sided cattle cart, similar to the two-wheeled horse ambulance. Loaded from either end, when the horse was shut out, slatted ramps forming both head and tail-boards. Usually open topped. Drawn by a single horse.

Buckingham wagon. American open or semi-open phaeton, introduced in 1879. Designed to convey four passengers on crosswise seating. Drawn by a single horse.

Buckinghamshire wagons. These were either versions of the Box Wagon or the Bow-type. The so-called Chiltern Wagon of this county was a small box-type, frequently used for collecting stones turned-up by the plough.

Budwieser wagon. American/German beer wagon, similar to a stake-sided dray. Usually constructed with a sprung body, hung on sideways elliptical springs, driven from an elevated seat above the fore-axle. Drawn by eight horses or larger teams, frequently Clydesdales. Barrels were mounted in a sideways-on position, tilted outwards, a few hanging under the bodywork, beneath the loading platform.

Bugatti coach. Type of private road coach with a chariot-style body, able to seat two inside passengers only, but six more on roof seats. The inner compartment was seldom used. Only four of this type are known to have been completed, during the early 1900's. Designed by Ettore Bugatti of Paris, perhaps better known for his sports and racing cars of a later period.

Bugatti road cart. Elegant road or exercise cart with movable seats (covered by a Bugatti patent) and aluminium splashers. Designed for showing trotting horses during the early 1920's. Constructed in Paris under the supervision of Ettore Bugatti.

Buggy or buggie. 1. Light English-type gig, two-wheeled and with curved shafts. First popular during the early 19th century and revived about thirty years later. Drawn by a single horse or large pony, using a variety of steel suspension gear.

2. A whole family of medium-sized driving wagons. Popular in the United States of America from the 1830's to the 1920's. A simple type of phaeton with equirotal or near-equirotal wheels. Derived from a tray-bodied vehicle of Central European origins. The keynote of construction was combined cheapness and simplicity. Towards the end of the 19th century they underwent a form of mass-production, similar to the T-model Ford, which they outwardly resembled, especially in the cross-springing of their suspension (many of the early Fords were known as mechanical buggies). Still used — in limited numbers — by members of the Amish religious sect. American Buggies could be purchased at between 150 and 500 dollars.

Buggy, Amish. *See* Amish Buggy.

Buggy, boat. Boat-shaped American Buggy, mounted on four near-equirotal wheels but able to float. Invented by a Perry Davis of Rhode Island, U.S.A., in 1859. Slightly higher at the rear than the front, closely related to the earlier Yacht Buggy. On some versions the spoked wheels could be fitted with manually operated paddles, useful when crossing still waters or sluggish streams and rivers. Difficult to control where there was a strong current, through lack of steerage.

Buggy, coal box. Patent American Buggy, with a short wheel-base. Fairly high above road level but with a cut-back rear portion.

Said to resemble a grocer's coal box, once a feature in many country stores throughout North America. Designed by James Lawrence of the Brewster Carriage Company, New York, about 1861. Popular in some districts until the late 1920's.

Buggy, coal scuttle. Early variation of the Coal Box Buggy, made by a rival firm of carriage builders. Sides tended to be much lower than with the Coal Box type.

Buggy, Concord. American Buggy making use of sideways bracing rather than steel springs, as with the Concord Coach.

Buggy, Corning. Also known as the Corning Wagon. American Buggy with a fixed top or head and fairly high sides. First supplied to the specifications of an Erastus Corning of Albany, New York State, in 1875. Later manufactured under licence by the Brewster Carriage Company.

Buggy, Dexter. Low-slung, square-type of American Buggy, with patent platform suspension. Named after 'Dexter' a famous trotting horse and match winner of the late 19th century.

Buggy, doctor's. Dignified type of American Buggy or road wagon. Provided with rearward storage space for a medical bag and similar items. Widely used by doctors and other professional men from the 1880's to the 1920's. Also known as the Physician's Buggy or Phaeton. Frequently had a curved, fixed top, known as a Yandell — patented by a Doctor Yandell of Louisville, Kentucky. *See* Yandell Buggy.

Buggy, fantail. American buggy, with a rearward projection or fantail of the bodywork. Popular from the 1850's to the 1880's.

Buggy, ironage. All-metal American Buggy, constructed with side sheets of cast iron. Introduced about 1870. It had a short run of popularity as its various components soon began to work loose, making irritating clanking or squeaking noises.

Buggy, monitor. A type of American Coal Box Buggy with a deep or well-bottom and inward curving side panels. Designed by a J. W. Lawrence of New York City, in 1859.

Buggy, ogee. Early American Buggy, the design of its underside and rearward parts based on ogee or 'S' curves.

Buggy, piano box. A version of the square American Buggy of the 1850's, but sometimes having rounded corners. One of the most popular of the early types. Manufactured by R. M. Stivers and Company of New York City.

Buggy, show. An open American Buggy of the four-wheeled type, used for showing trotting horses or ponies at County Fairs and Agricultural Shows. It featured full cut-under of the forecarriage, wire-spoked wheels and solid or pneumatic rubber tyres. Popular from the late 1890's to the present day. Introduced to Britain as the Mill's Wagon.

Buggy, slide seat. American Buggy designed with movable or jump seats. Made with a double row of forward facing seats able to take four persons, including the driver.

Buggy, square box. An earlier version of the Piano Box Buggy, with square corners. *See* Buggy, Piano Box.

Buggy, Stanhope. Modification of the English (two-seater) Stanhope Gig. Designed with a falling hood and hung on sideways elliptical springs. The name was also borrowed for an American four-wheeled buggy, but this was inaccurate nomenclature.

Buggy, tub-body. Early American Buggy of the 1840's and 50's, with a tub-like, leather-covered body.

Buggy, yacht. A modification of the original or tray-bodied buggy, intended to imitate the lines of a pleasure yacht. First built in 1859, for the Brewster Carriage Company, by J. W. Lawrence. A stage of development towards the coalbox type.

Buggyette. Small, neat town Buggy of the English type, running on two wheels. Patented by the Indian carriage-building firm of Steuart and Company, Calcutta, during the late 19th century.

Builder's cart. Two-wheeled, tumbril-type cart, used — by British builders — in greater numbers than the four-wheeled wagon or van. Made to tip in a rearward direction. Raves or sideboards were used for the protection of overhanging loads, especially with the so-called London types. Advertised in such journals as 'The Clayworker' until the late 1940's. Frequently used on building sites and in brickworks or quarries until the post war period.

Builder's spring cart. Light builder's cart with panel sides, having a forward projection above the hind quarters of the single horse in shafts, to support pipes, poles and ladders, etc. Hung on both crosswise and sideways semi-elliptical springs. Up to 25 cwts. capacity. A large, two-horse type (the horses in tandem) carried upwards of 2 tons. Cost about £26 — during the 1890's.

Builder's van. Four-wheeled vehicle, with a short wheelbase, less frequently used on building sites than the Builder's Cart. Noted for high-planked or panelled sides and outward extension boards above the wheels. Drawn either by a single horse or pair of horses in pole gear. Up to three tons capacity. Usually dead axle, although some later types were hung on sideways semi-elliptical springs.

Builder's wagon. Also known as the Mill Wagon as similar types were frequently used by mill or factory owners. A commercial freight wagon drawn by a single horse. Made with low sides but frequently having high stakes or stanchions. used for conveying pipes, ladders or lengths of timber, especially to and from building sites.

Bull cart or float. Open but high-sided float, either two or four wheeled, used for transporting prize cattle.

Bulk gas van. A headed, panel-sided vehicle, running on four wheels. Usually drawn by two horses in pole gear. Mainly used in France and other European countries for the delivery of gas cylinders, especially during the 1900's. Usually hung on semi-elliptical springs, front and rear. Either led on foot or driven from a partly enclosed cross-bench, but seldom having foot or dash board.

Burmah buggy. Light gig or hooded buggy of the English type, running on two wheels. Hung on sideways semi-elliptical springs. Widely used, in Burma and India, during the second half of the 19th century. Drawn by a single pony.

Burton van. Type of living van seen on the English high roads from the 1890's to the 1930's. Used by showmen and hucksters rather than Gypsy folk. First made at Burton-on-Trent, Staffordshire, by the firm of Orton and Spooner, also noted for their fairground rides and sideshow equipment. The wheels of the Burton Van were near-equirotal, beneath rather than at the sides of the bodywork. Unlike Gypsy vans they kept more to surfaced roads than rutted lanes or uneven tracks, not requiring such large wheels or a broad gauge between them. Although there were windows at the rear and often on one side only, the third wall or side would be blank, as this was used for advertising purposes or as the backing for a sideshow. Most Burton Vans had a built-in safe for money and valuables.

Bus. 1. An abbreviation of Omnibus.

2. Slang name for any type of large passenger vehicle.

Business wagon. 1. Headed American Buggy, used by businessmen and commercial travellers. The sides were covered with canework, which was easier to keep clean than ordinary paintwork.

2. Light American delivery van, its lines similar to the Business Wagon (1). One of the smallest commercial vehicles in regular use.

Butcher's cart. In Britain this was usually a smart type of gig with well-ventilated bodywork. The high, single driving seat would be placed above a square carrying box or compartment, the fore-end of which frequently sloped forward with curved lines. Hung on sideways semi-elliptical springs, also with crosswise rearwards springing. Access to the inner compartment, lined with zinc, was via a rearward door or tailboard, the latter secured at 45 degrees by letting-down chains. There would be low handrails round the top and external parts of the compartment, where empty baskets might be lodged. Shafts were upward curved rather than straight, giving the body a slight rearward tilt when the horse was put to. Frequently driven to a quality hackney or hackney-type with smart action, drawing the admiration of passers-by as a publicity gimmick.

Butcher's van/mobile shop. A type of four-wheeled Butcher's Van as used in both Britain and North America, during the first half of the 20th century. These were not merely for delivery purposes, but sold meat products at the kerbside and from door-to-door, customers frequently sheltered by a sideways-on or rearward awning. The interior, lined with white cotton duck for better insulation, had cuts of meat hanging from overhead racks, a counter, chopping block and refrigeration compartment. British types, mainly seen in the expanding outer suburbs of large towns, were pioneered by the Co-Operative Society about 1922. They were smaller than the American vehicles of the same period, using a single horse between shafts rather than a pair in pole gear. American vans were usually much higher, both in the bodywork and above road level, mounted on a combination of cross and side springs. British vans had sideways elliptical springs only. Driving seats on both types, were crosswise benches, either partly or fully enclosed, mounted by means of a single step iron.

C

Cab. The name of this vehicle is derived from Cabriolet, meaning a two-wheeled coach, frequently used for public hire. Such vehicles, in their original form, came to London from Italy, via Paris, during the early 19th century. They were at first rivals of the already established hackney coaches and limited by Parliament to carry one passenger only, sharing a seat with the driver. There were also limitations concerning the amount of luggage carried. About 1823 the driver's portion of the seat was extended over the off-side wheel and later separated from the passenger seat.

Throughout the remainder of the century cabs developed in many varied guises, both as two and four-wheeled vehicles.

Restrictions were eventually relaxed, concerning the number of passengers and amount of luggage. The main types, by the 1860's, were the four-wheeled Growler, often adapted from the Brougham and Clarence, and the two-wheeled Hansom. The increased number of omnibuses, towards the end of the century, however, caused a considerable decline in the use of cabs — both two and four-wheelers — which were eventually replaced by motor cabs or taxis during the 1900's.

Growlers were driven from a box seat, while Hansoms were controlled from a rearward skeleton seat at roof level. Later types were fitted with taximeters, for recording distances and fares, from which the name Taxi derives.

Cab, crystal. American four-wheeled cab, widely used in New York City during the 1870's and 80's. Characterised by large glass windows or lights, in place of opaque side panels. Designed by A. S. Dodd of Dodd's Express Company, both cab owners and haulage contractors.

Cab-fronted gig. Also known as a Morgan Cart, after its designer and builder, during the 1890's. The low entrance and dashboard often curved to the rear end of the shafts, resembling the fore-end of a Hansom Cab. Some later types were hooded.

Cab. Hansom. Two-wheeled cab invented by a professional architect named Joseph Hansom, by whom the first design was patented in 1834. First known as the Hansom Safety Cab. Its main features were low-slung bodywork, high wheels and a rearward driving seat — the latter not at first evident. The purpose of its design was to combine speed with safety, having a low centre of gravity, essential for safe cornering and overtaking. Wheels were originally 7′6″ in diameter, later becoming much smaller although still large in proportion. The dashboard was curved at the rear of the shafts, bringing the hind-quarters of the horse fairly near the vehicle, for better control. There would be room for two passengers facing forward, on a single cross-seat, their legs protected by knee flaps.

About 1836 a carriage builder named Chapman redesigned the Hansom with cranked axles, also introducing side windows and improving the driver's seat. Forder of Wolverhampton made further innovations by lightening the vehicle, although returning to straight axles. It was in this final phase of development, during the 1880's and 90's, that it became the most typical cab of an era, noted for its swift approach on solid rubber tyres and the jingle of a warning bell. A version of the Hansom Cab was to be found in

many cities of the British Isles and throughout the world, but —
apart from a few in New York — it did not make a great
impression in the United States of America.

A later bow-fronted Hansom was fully enclosed and entered
through a side door, frequently hired or owned by doctors
and professional men. There were even a few Three-wheeled
Hansoms, with coil springs above the fore-wheel, rather than the
more usual semi-elliptical leaf springs. Some cabs were used
mainly in the summer and at seaside resorts, where more open
types with falling, half-hoods were popular.

From the 1890's nearly all Hansom Cabs had solid rubber tyres
and were hung on semi-elliptical side springs. Horses drawing
them were usually younger and better quality than those harnessed
to other cabs. The drivers were also younger, fitter men than the
drivers of Growlers, some even wealthy amateurs driving as a
hobby. Being smart and attractive, some fitted with interior
mirrors and solid silver accessories, these vehicles were often hired
by society bachelors and clubmen keeping late hours. They were
seldom used by unescorted women of good reputation, by whom
they were considered fast and not quite respectable.

Cabinet maker's furniture van. Medium-sized (four-wheeled)
furniture van, used by cabinet-makers and wholesalers in the
furniture trade. The lower parts of these vehicles, would have
mahogany panels but with outward extended raves or sideboards
of cheaper wood. There would be a straight or curved top (head),
boarded-up inside, of waterproofed canvas. Upper parts were
frequently ledged with an effect of overhang above the wheels.
Between 7 and 8 feet in length, up to a capacity of 2 tons. Drawn
by one or two horses, the pair harnessed in pole gear.

Cab, Kellner. A four-wheeled cab widely used in Paris from the
1880's. Designed by a French carriage-builder after whom it was
named. More spacious but substantial than the average four-
wheeler of this period.

Cab, Murch's. Also known as Murch's Chariot. A four-wheeled
cab, designed by a C. Murch of Cincinnati, Ohio, U.S.A., about
1880. It carried six passengers and had a large roofrack for
luggage, also an ample footboard. The framework was based on
'T'-shaped angle-irons, supported by patent low-slung suspension.
Entrance was through a rear door, via folding steps. Popular in
most American cities for between fifteen and twenty years. Large
and heavy but with a short wheelbase, able to turn in its own
length. Drawn by a medium-heavy horse.

.

Caboose. 1. An enclosed, box-shaped van of the American West, used by peddlars trading in remote areas. A combined caravan and shop-on-wheels, drawn by a pair of horses in pole gear. A notable feature was the tall 'bin' or stovepipe, often leaning at an odd angle.
2. The rearward brakevan on an American freight train.

Cabriole. Alternative name for a Cabriolet. *See* Cabiolet.

Cabriolet. A name derived from the French version of the Italian 'capriolo' for a kid or young goat. This relates to the skipping, capering movements of a kid and the swaying of a two-wheeled vehicle at speed. The original version, in Italy and France, was mounted very high above road level, with flexible shafts, its suspension being either whip or cee-springs. It came to England during the 1800's and was adopted as a fashionable mode of conveyance (over short distances) by members of the wealthier classes, tending to oust the slightly earlier curricle. It was much safer to drive than the curricle, although capable of high speed. English versions became much lower than their Continental counterparts and easier to mount, by means of a low shaftstep. Usually drawn by a powerful coach horse of the hunter type. Owner-driven, the groom was usually a short youth or mature male of stunted growth, standing on a rearward platform or dummy board.

Cage wagon. Vehicle used by travelling menageries and circuses in which to both exhibit and transport dangerous wild animals, such as tigers, wolves, etc. There were sturdy bars on both sides, while the ends were boarded-up and of solid construction. While in transit the bars would be covered by screens or shutters. Usually low-slung on platform springs but sometimes dead axle, with small equirotal wheels. Driven from a cross seat at roof level, with a forward projecting footboard. Corner pillars, end and rounding boards would be richly ornamented with carved and gilded work. Wheels frequently had a sunburst effect or infilling.

Caisson. French — caisse, a box or chest. Originally an ammunition cart or limber used by an artillery battery in the field. In later years it became an articulated vehicle, in which the fore and rear parts could be detached and used independently. In some cases the fore-part supported the trail of a field gun, furnished with seats on which the gun crew might ride. It could be further used in the military train, to contain tools and spare parts while supporting one or more spare wheels.

Calash. Czech — kolesa. A wheeled carriage or pair of large wheels. Sometimes spelt Calèche. In the French Canadian provinces, the calèche was a giglike vehicle driven from a narrow seat above the dashboard.

In most parts of Western Europe it was recognised as a development of the four-wheeled Barouche, often with extra seating and improved suspension. An even earlier but related vehicle, popular in London and Paris during the mid-18th century, was a light coach with five glasses or windows, that either resembled or inspired a female head-dress on a wire framework, also known as a 'calash'.

Calèche. 1. A development of the Barouche or German Wagon. Some later types were mounted on extra cross springs, for better suspension. An example would be the Eight-spring Caleche, popular in the Atlantic states of North America during the 19th century. *See* Calash.

2. Two-wheeled chaise or gig, drawn by a single horse. Usually hooded. Popular in Canada during the French colonial period. *See* Calash.

Caleche, Nantucket. Two-wheeled, unsprung or dead axle passenger cart, as used on Nantucket Island, Massachusetts, U.S.A., from the late 18th century. Fitted with cane-bottomed chairs lashed to the framework of the vehicle by stout cords.

Calesa. Two-wheeled passenger cart or heavy gig, used in the Phillipines from the mid-19th century to the 1940's. The driver frequently sat in the rear part of the vehicle, as with an English farm or dairy float. Hung on sideways semi-elliptical springs. Drawn by a single horse.

Calesin. Diminutive of Calesa. Small, two-wheeled passenger cart, usually hooded. Used in the Philippines throughout the greater part of the 19th century. Drawn by a single pony.

Calesso. Italian name for a two-wheeled, hooded gig, popular from the late 18th century until the 1900's.

Calf cart. Type of market cart, with a crosswise driving seat or bench, popular in English rural areas from the late 18th to the mid-19th centuries. Usually unsprung or dead axle. Calves, sheep and other small livestock were transported to market in the rearward part, secured under nets.

California passenger wagon. Type of semi-open Concord coach, mounted on thoroughbraces. Seated six inside passengers on cross benches, with two on the elevated box seat. Drawn by teams of four or more horses in pole gear.

California wagon. Strongly built American farm wagon, as used by settlers on the Western or Pacific seaboard. The driving seat might be sprung although the main bodywork was dead axle or unsprung. Sides were usually boarded-up but sometimes protected by side stakes. Most versions featured powerful lever brakes, acting on the rear wheels. There would be a large tool box at the fore-end.

California wood spring wagon. Type of American Buggy, similar to the Coal Box Buggy, but mounted on thoroughbraces. Extensive use was also made of flexible wooden springs, from which the name derives. Manufactured by the Kimball Carriage-building Company of San Francisco, from the mid-1860's. Mainly used in the Western states.

Calliope. Steam organ mounted on a horse-drawn wagon, frequently appearing in circus and carnival parades, especially in North America, from the mid-19th century. Most were fitted with a battery of up to 32 steam whistles operated from a central keyboard. Steam pressure would be in the region of 120 lbs p.s.i.

Camel top van. Type of 19th century delivery van, running on either two or four wheels, having an arched section of the roof (said to resemble the hump of a camel) at the fore-end, above the driving position. A feature, at one period, of many vans used for railway cartage and parcel delivery services.

Camp wagon. Alternative name for the American 'Chuck' or food wagon, also known as the Round-up Wagon. A four-wheeled vehicle, drawn by two or more horses in pole gear, used as a mobile canteen on farms and ranches in Western states of North America. Usually dead axle but having a fully sprung driving seat. A canvas top would be stretched over hoops or tilts. Similar vehicles were also used in the wagon trains of early settlers.

Canadian top buggy. Headed, tray-shaped American Buggy of a type once popular in the maritime provinces of Canada. Featured well-upholstered seating, high-sided bodywork and a high-straight dashboard. Hung on crosswise elliptical springs, front and rear.

Canoe cabriolet. Carbiolet with a curved or canoe-shaped body, popular during the second half of the 19th century. Some were hung on cee-springs, while others had a combination of both cee and sideways elliptical springs.

Canoe Landau. A graceful, rounded version of the landau, popular — in different sizes — throughout the greater part of the 19th century. Usually mounted on cee-springs although some larger versions also had a full underperch and elliptical springs of the forecarriage. Passengers sat two per side or vis-à-vis, protected in wet weather by half hoods — made to lie flat when not in use. Drawn either by a pair in pole gear or a single horse in shafts, according to size and weight, both driven from a skeleton box-seat. Larger types used for ceremonial purposes frequently had a rear seat for grooms or footmen, their fast trotting teams of four or six controlled by postillions.

Canoe. Open Quarter Victoria. Open Victoria of the panel boot type, having a curved, shallow underside, in the style of a Canoe Landau. Usually hung on sideways semi-elliptical springs or with rearward springs mounted on projections known as dumb-irons.

Canopy top phaeton. Light phaeton noted for its removable front or driving seat, frequently driven from the interior of the vehicle. Protected by a canopy top with deep fringes.

Canopy top Surrey. Tray-bodied (family) passenger vehicle of North America, noted for its long wheelbase. Headed by a fringed canopy supported on corner pillars. Hung on sideways elliptical springs at the rear and crosswise elliptical springs at the front.

Canopy top wagonette. American type wagonette, hung on sideways elliptical springs, front and rear, also having a short wheelbase and movable canopy top. There were large fenders of mudguards above the rear wheels only. Drawn by a single horse or large pony.

Canterbury phaeton. Light passenger vehicle hung on sideways elliptical springs, front and rear. Said to resemble the body of a wagonette on the underworks of a phaeton. Passengers sat inward-facing, on longitudinal benches, entering through a rear door.

Cape cart. Large, two-wheeled country cart of South Africa, seating three passengers and a driver. Hung on thoroughbraces and protected by a falling hood. Driven to a pair of swift horses in a type of curricle gear with centre pole. It originated among Dutch settlers in Cape Province during the early 19th century, but was later exported to both Australia and New Zealand. The rear part could be converted to a sleeping compartment. Frequently served as a form of military transport, for higher ranking officers, during the Boer War. now almost extinct, apart from a few preserved as museum pieces.

Car. Name derived from the Latin Carrus, denoting a four-wheeled vehicle, first used in the territory of Gaul. Carrus also means a chariot and a few early types may have run on two-wheels. The Old French 'Char' or 'Car' signifies any type of small pleasure vehicle, which now survives in poetic jargon.

In Britain, at least from the mid-19th century, a car meant a superior type of two-wheeled vehicle, as opposed to a mere cart — the latter often cheaply or roughly made. Popular types were the Governess Car, Ralli Car, Moray Car, etc. In Ireland the Jaunting or Side Car was known as a 'car' more as a contraction of speech than an indication of quality.

According to American and modern usage (in English-speaking countries), the name also refers to a railway or tramcar, such as a passenger car, box car, freight car, etc. In Britain it is also a contraction of motor car.

Caravan. 1. A house-on-wheels of many different types, used by Gypsies, tinkers, showmen, hucksters and other nomadic people, especially from the mid-19th century to the 1930's. Said to have developed from a tent rigged on a cart, used as a market stall by day and sleeping quarters at night.

2. A medieval long-cart or wagon of the 13th and 14th centuries. Usually an unsprung passenger vehicle, drawn by three horses in trandem, controlled by a postillion on the shaft horse.

Car, bobtail. Slang name for a small horse-drawn tram or street car, especially in cities of North America during the late 19th century. Usually operated without a conductor, fares paid to the driver on entering the vehicle.

Caretta. 1. A country cart of Sicily and Southern Italy, popular from the Middle Ages to the mid-20th century. Drawn by a single horse or pony in straight shafts. The body and framework was richly carved while side panels were painted with scenes from legends, biblical stories, etc. There are now motorised versions of this vehicle, many of which are still hand-decorated.

2. An early form of coach or carriage running on four wheels, used mainly in Italy for ceremonial purposes. Frequently lined with scented leather and costly textiles. There are records of such a vehicle used by Pope Gregory Xth in 1273. Now regarded as an ancestor of most modern passenger vehicles.

Carette. 1. Four-wheeled horse bus or short stage coach, appearing in the suburbs of many Australian towns and cities. Introduced by the firm of Duncan Frazer, about 1895, first appearing in the streets of Adelaide, South Australia. Popular until the early 1920's. Driven from a raised seat at the fore-end, protected by an extension of the roof canopy. Some later types had a separate smoking compartment. Seating was on longitudinal benches, facing inwards. Drawn by two horses in pole gear.

2. Low-slung omnibus, hung on sideways semi-elliptical springs and cranked axles. Drawn by two horses in pole gear. Mainly

appeared in the streets of Chicago during the 1890's and 1900's.
Car, funeral. 1. Name widely used in North America for a
horse-drawn hearse or funeral carriage. Not widely used until the
mid-19th century, as — before this period — the coffin would be
conveyed to the churchyard either on a hand-cart or farm wagon
adapted for the purpose.
  2. Specially constructed vehicle used at a state funeral, drawn
by men or large teams of horses. Usually draped with flags and
national emblems. Wheels were usually equirotal.
Car, horse. Also known as a street car. Name used in North
America for a horse-drawn vehicle, worked over a street tramway
or light railway, frequently on channel rails. Invented by an
American engineer known as John Stephenson, to run over steel
tracks between New York City and the then distant suburb of
Harlem, in 1831.
Cariole. Two-wheeled gig with narrow bodywork, frequently
unsprung or dead axle, used in country districts of Norway
throughout the 19th century. Driven from a low rearward
platform, also used as a luggage grid. Drawn by a single horse or
large pony harnessed between exceptionally long shafts, which
offered a certain amount of resilience. Only one passenger could be
conveyed at a given time. The graceful bodywork was not unlike
the Continental Chaise, from which it may have derived, during
the 1800's.
Carman's cart. Similar to the London Forage Cart, but used —
during the second half of the 19th century — for general delivery
purposes. Spindle or open-sided, having top raves to support an
overhanging load, and a forward projecting ladder (rack) above the
hindquarters of the shaft horse. Drawn by a single horse or tandem
pair. Hung on sideways elliptical springs. Up to loads of 35 cwts.
in the larger sizes and 15 cwts. in the smaller or cob sizes.
Caroche. An open carriage, drawn by six or more horses. Used
in France during the late 15th and early 16th centuries, mainly for
ceremonial purposes. A boxlike, dead axle type running on
equirotal wheels, but fitted with luxurious internal appointments.
Carosse. Dead axle coach or carriage of French origins, used
during the mid-17th century. Drawn by teams of four or more
horses. From the 1640's a few were hung on leather side or
thoroughbraces, while others may have developed a form of strap
suspension. Front and rear wheels were of contrasting sizes, the
forewheels sometimes very small. The box seat, above the fore
axle, would be draped with an elaborate fringed hammercloth and

other embroidery. There were neither doors nor windows in the conventional sense, side apertures (on either side) occupied by removable seats facing outwards. The occupants of side seats were exposed to mud and grit flung up by the wheels and usually wore masks of iron or leather, lined with velvet. Side curtains, in place of glass windows, were of tooled leather, rolled back in warm weather. Most vehicles carried at least six people, in addition to the driver and servants perched on a rearward platform or dummy board. Overall length was between six and eight feet.

The ownership of large private coaches or family carriages, in most European cities, rose rapidly within a few years. From a few dozen during the 1600's (in London), owned by courtiers and high-ranking officials, there were soon over 15,000, some in the possession of the lesser nobility, wealthy merchants and even prosperous tradesmen.

Carosse coupé. A cut-down version of the larger Carosse, frequently known in Britain as the Small Carriage. Popular from the mid-17th century to the late 1720's, especially in France. Drawn by a pair of horses driven from a low box seat. There would be either thoroughbraces or strap suspension. Seated four vis-à-vis, with two footmen standing on a rearwind dummy board. Hinged doors and glass lights or windows appeared towards the end of the 17th century and were commonplace by the 1700's.

Carozzella. Italian four-wheeled pleasure carriage drawn by a small horse or large pony, popular in many coastal and tourist resorts from the early 19th century to the present day. Seats four, including the driver, facing forward on crosswise seats, one passenger sharing the box seat. The rear seat is protected by a falling or half hood. Hung on sideways elliptical springs, front and rear. Shafts are straight.

Carpentum. 1. Either a two- or four-wheeled passenger vehicle used in Ancient Rome from the 1st century A.D. Said to have been named after Carmenta, a worthy matron and mother of Evander, one of the founders of Rome. A luxury vehicle, hung on side braces of toughened leather. Entered from the rear. Drawn by a pair of horses harnessed in curricle gear.

2. A patent carriage of the mid-19th century, designed in England by a David Davis, about 1840. Related to the Victoria, low-slung but elegant. Usually headed with a fixed or standing top.

Carriage. From the Latin — carrus for wagon or dray, and the Old French carier — for wagon or cart. It may mean, in modern terms, either the underworks of a vehicle (also known as carriage parts), or an open/semi-open passenger vehicle of superior quality. Most carriages run on four wheels but there are a few two-wheeled types, including the curricle and cabriolet. Some invalid carriages have two and (less frequently) three wheels.

Carriage break. Large break drawn by a pair of coach horses or a four-in-hand team. Usually headed and sometimes used as a private or station bus. Entered from the rear by means of four inclined steps. Some had a rearward seat, in a sideways-on position, for a conductor-guard. Hung on semi-elliptical springs at the rear and full elliptical side springs at the front.

Carriage builder's truck. A specially constructed open vehicle on four wheels, used by carriage builders and repairers for delivery purposes. Either low-slung on small wheels or having larger rear wheels and a rearward sloping platform. The driving seat was fairly high and of skeletal structure. There was a powerful lever brake acting on the rear wheels and a cranked windlass on the near side.

Carriagem. Name used in Portugal and Brazil for any type of passenger cart or carriage.

Carri-coche. A cart-coach running on two wheels, drawn by a single horse or pair of ponies. Controlled by a mounted driver or postillion. Popular in the towns and cities of Brazil, during the 18th and 19th centuries. A headed vehicle, entered from the rear by means of a single step. Either four or six passengers sat facing each other, seated on rough benches in a sideways-on or longitudinal position. Later types had glazed windows or side glasses, protected by Venetian blinds.

Carrier's cart. Cart usually drawn by a single horse, that plied between towns and villages of Britain from the late 17th to the early 20th centuries. Usually hooded or headed, with waterproofed canvas or tarpaulins, supported by bow-shaped hoops. Used for the collection and distribution of parcels, luggage and small items of commercial goods, although most were also fitted with a crosswise bench for paying passengers.

Carrier's wagon. Large, four-wheeled version of the Carrier's Cart, either sprung or dead axle. Drawn by two horses harnessed in pole gear. There is a distinct relationship between this vehicle and the longer distance Stage Wagon.

Carrinho. A small, neat cart, mainly used for agricultural purposes. The Portuguese equivalent of the Carretta. Usually dead axle. Drawn by a single horse.

Carro.   Name used in Portugal and her colonies for any type of large vehicle, on either two or four wheels.
Carrocim.   Small Portuguese passenger or pleasure cart, similar to a light gig. Popular in country districts, during the mid-19th century.
Carromata.   Two-wheeled pony cart, with a fixed or standing top. Popular in the Philippines during the mid-19th century.
Carruca.   From the Latin — carrus. Either a privately owned coach or a type of superior stage wagon, both used in the days of the Roman Empire. Frequently drawn by teams of mules rather than horses. Private versions, owned by the nobility, were decorated, both internally and externally, with precious stones, inlaid work and painted side-panels.
Carrus.   Name used in Ancient Rome for any type of large road vehicle, drawn by mules, horses or oxen. Many ideas of design and construction, concerning the better types, are now thought to have derived from Gallic sources.
Carryall.   1. Name used in New England for any type of large horse-drawn vehicle.

2. A two-wheeled travelling chariot, popular in Western Europe during the 17th and 18th centuries.

3. English name, used during the late 17th century, for any type of travelling chariot.
Cart.   1. Name thought to be of either Celtic or Gallic origins, as were many early designs for this type of vehicle. In the broadest sense a cart was always two-wheeled, known to many early civilisations before the wagon. It could be used as either a passenger carrier or for merchandise and agricultural purposes. Even hunting and war chariots were a development of this theme. Advantages to favour carts were the greater speeds at which they might travel and their flexibility in difficult terrain.

2. In modern times the passenger cart was frequently a country or informal sporting vehicle, not as costly or well-furnished as coaches or carriages. They were frequently an individual means of transport, owner-driven. Examples include the dogcart, market cart, tub cart, etc., drawn by a cob or pony rather than a full-sized horse. A number of such vehicles occupy an area of compromise, termed carts by some people and cars or carriages by others. This chiefly relates to their use and standards of finish, although a source of controversy even among experts.
Cart-car.   A version of the Trottle Car, claimed to be an ancestor

of the Irish Jaunting Car. First used in Northern Ireland during
the mid-18th century.

Cart, Newport Pagnell. Small English pleasure cart, with
dos-à-dos seating for four, in the style of a dogcart. Mounted on
sideways elliptical springs. Although first constructed in the
Buckinghamshire town of Newport Pagnell, large numbers were
eventually constructed in Canterbury and other centres.

Cart, pony. Any type of light vehicle, running on two wheels,
drawn by a pony rather than a cob or full-sized horse.

Casket cart/wagon. Four-wheeled vehicle, usually headed and
panel-sided, used to convey a coffin on any occasion not directly
concerned with the funeral ceremony. Drawn by a single horse.

Catafalque. An open-sided funeral car, also a structure on which
a corpse lies in state before the funeral service.

Catalonian cart. Primitive two-wheeled vehicle, mainly for
agricultural work, drawn by a single horse or mule. First used in
the Spanish province of Catalonia. Usually unsprung or dead axle.
A version of the Carretta and Carrinho.

Catterick. Type of large, open wagonette, popular during the
second half of the 19th century, especially in the north of England,
west of the Pennines. Drawn by a pair of horses in pole gear.

Cee-spring Brougham. Brougham of the 1860's, hung on cee-
springs, also having an underperch. Slightly larger and heavier
than most vehicles of this type.

Cee-spring gig. Sporting gig of the early 19th century, hung on
cee-springs. Considered to be more comfortable than earlier types.

Cee-spring Ralli car. Unusual type of Ralli Car, hung on cee-
springs.

Celerity. Swift, open-sided stage coach used in the Atlantic coast
states of North America, during the first half of the 19th century.
A forerunner of the Concord Coach and the Mud Wagon.
Suspended on thoroughbraces rather than side springs. Interior
seating, of which there may have been three rows, could be
converted into beds by letting down the backrests. Drawn by
teams of four or more horses.

Chair. 1. Two-wheeled driving vehicle, popular in both Western
Europe and colonial North America, during the late 18th and early
19th centuries. A single chair mounted on a small platform or
framework, akin to the Gig and Continental Chaise. In the earlier
types suspension depended on resilient shafts, as with the
buckboard. Later versions had side springs or thoroughbraces.

The so-called Windsor Chair was constructed with the familiar rod-back support, seen in farmhouse kitchens for over two centuries.

2. A type of low-slung, four-wheeled carriage, that resembled a square Victoria, appearing in the Channel Islands during the second half of the 19th century, both as a public and private passenger vehicle. A number are still used on the Island of Sark where motor cars are banned.

Chair-back gig. Type of early gig popular during the late 18th century, fitted with a chair or stick-back seat. Prototypes of the 1780's were hung on shallow whip springs, but later versions had semi-elliptical springs.

Chaise. The name of this vehicle is a corruption of the French — chaire or seat. It was widely used in Western Europe and the North American Colonies, during the late 18th and early 19th centuries. Drawn by a single horse or cob between curved shafts. Unlike the Chair (1.) there was frequently room for at least one passenger to share the driving seat, protected by a falling hood. Usually mounted on thoroughbraces but sometimes on cee-springs, a combination of both or balanced on resilient shafts without further suspension. The 'One Horse Chaise' of New England, incorporated several modes of springing, including a wooden cantilever system, unique to this design. The French or Continental Chaise had a shell-like body of great elegance, renowned for its richly carved and painted side panels in the baroque-style.

Chaise-à-porteurs. Later known in England as a Post Chaise, being — at first — two- but later four-wheeled, hired for long distance travel. It is thought to have originated in France during the early 18th century.

Chaise, Quaker. Alternative name for the Grasshopper Chaise, hung on so-called grasshopper springs of shallow steels. Usually plain and lacking ornament or bright colours. Popular during the early 19th century.

Chamulcus. A small, open vehicle of Ancient Rome, used mainly for short journeys. A type of town gig drawn by a single horse or large pony.

Charabanc. Four-wheeled passenger vehicle of French origins, with two or more rows of crosswise seating. Mainly driven to a four-in-hand team. Usually open but sometimes fitted with a canopy head or cover mounted on standards. Frequently seen at race meetings and other sporting events, where it served as a mobile grandstand. Much higher above ground level than the Wagonette or Break. Kept by wealthy families with large country mansions and extensive coach-houses. The seating plan tended to vary, passengers facing either in the direction of travel or — on centre seats — vis-à-vis. Introduced during the 1830's, one of the prototypes being presented to Queen Victoria by Louis Philippe, King of the French, still kept at the Royal Mews, Buckingham Palace. Some types had a slatted under boot for sporting dogs, at both front and rear.

In later years a version of the Charabanc could be used for sightseing parties, school or church outings, etc., from which the motor charabanc or motor coach derived. During the second half of the 19th century a heavy type was used by several railway companies, seating about twenty passengers and a driver.

Charabanc break.   American name for the Charabanc.

Chariot.   The original meaning of the word is obscure but may derive from char, chair or charette, relating both to four and two-wheeled passenger vehicles of antiquity in which persons might be seated. There are two separate lines of development.

1. A two-wheeled hunting or war chariot, which may have originated in China or the Middle East. This was drawn by either a single horse or several horses abreast. Remains of this type were unearthed in Mespotamia dating from 2,000 B.C. Such vehicles were eventually used for chariot racing, certain forms of military training and ceremonial purposes. Both the Ancient Greeks and Romans indulged in the thrilling sport of chariot racing, which took place in an arena known as a hippodrome. The chariot used was high at the front, with sturdy wheels and a low centre of gravity, entered from the rear. Many war chariots, especially those of the Gallic and Celtic nations, were entered through the semi-open front. Teams were the Biga or pair-horse entry, ranging through the Triga and Quadriga to the ten-horse team or Decemina. The centre horse would be between shafts, while the outer horses were connected by traces only.

2. A four-wheeled coupé or cut-down coach, usually seating two passengers facing forward, popular from the late 17th to the late 19th centuries. Eventually replaced, for many duties, by the even lighter and more compact Brougham. Reserved, in later years for ceremonial or dress occasions. Usually drawn by two horses harnessed in pole gear. First hung on cee-springs but later on sideways elliptical springs, also furnished with an underperch. The high box seat would have an elaborate hammercloth. Liveried

footmen rode on a rearward dummy board. Later versions cost 500 gns. each and upwards.

Chariot du parc. French military wagon used throughout the 19th century for baggage purposes and supply work. Similar to the British General Service Wagon but much heavier and usually drawn by three horses abreast.

Chariot, gala. Alternative name, especially in America, for the Dress Chariot.

Chariot, scythe. War chariot of different periods and races, the wheel hubs fitted with sharpened blades. Used by the Ancient Britons, Assyrians and Persians, among other tribes and nations, to mow down the ranks of retreating infantry.

Chariottee. Light phaeton, with either a falling hood or fixed top, frequently driven by ladies in the southern states of North America. Eventually manufactured in large numbers by the firm of Demarest and Company.

Chatelaine. Miniature of pony gig, frequently driven by ladies in the southern states of North America, during the mid-19th century. Manufactured by the firm of Demarest and Company.

Cheshire farm cart. Plank-sided cart with removable side, front and rear boards. Frequently fitted with supporting ladders for an overhanging load. Unsprung or dead axle having a capacity of 35 cwts.

Chihauhau wagon. Heavy type of travelling wagon, used in Northern Mexico, especially from the second half of the 18th century. Usually unsprung or dead axle, headed with a lightweight top supported on hoops. Drawn by teams of various numbers, both horses and oxen. The covered wagon of Latin America.

Chilese car. Two-wheeled passenger car or cart, usually headed and of compact, elegant design. Used mainly in northern provinces and the streets of Santiago, Chile.

Chiltern corn chandler's cart or van. A heavy version of the Corn Chandler's Van, more akin to the Miller's Wagon. usually fitted with straight, single shafts and mail hubs/axles. Noted for its spindle sides and decorative chamfering. Out raves were outwardly inclined above the wheel tops. A wagon-type turntable of the forecarriage allowed full lock. The bodywork was fairly short for overall size and of equal height, front and rear, with straight toplines rather than curved or dipped upper works. Drawn by a medium-heavy horse in square or van-type shafts.

Chiltern stone wagon. Short-wheelbased, high-sided farm wagon, related to the box type. Used in the Chilterns for collecting stones and flints turned up by the plough. Drawn by a single horse.

Chinese tilted cart.   Flat cart of Ancient China mounted on disc wheels but later developing short spokes. Dead axle, drawn by a single horse between curved shafts. The sides were protected by stakes. On the western borders of the empire were some headed with tilts for use as living wagons or a temporary shelter for nomadic herdsmen.

Circular hearse.   American horse-drawn hearse of the 1880's, with circular or curved side windows/panels and bowed ends. The coffin was slid into place over a steel track of 18" gauge. There were ornate side rails within the bodywork, each rail festooned with silver cord.

Chuck wagon.   Also known as the Camp Wagon or Round-up Wagon. *See* Camp Wagon and Round-up Wagon. Now widely used in western rodeos and stampedes for an updated version of chariot racing.

Church break.   Dutch family wagon used for church and chapel-going. Same as Kirkbrik. *See* Kirkbrik.

Circus wagons.   Several types of transport wagon used by travelling circuses, usually drawn (before mechanisation) by large teams of heavy horses. These were packing wagons or trucks containing props and equipment needed in the show, cage wagons, living vans and band wagons. Even the more prosaic were carved and decorated to take part in the grand parade. Some vehicles, kept for display and publicity purposes only, were Tableau Wagons or trucks, painted and gilded, the wheels having an infilled or sunburst effect. Usually driven from elevated seats at roof level.

Cirriculus.   Diminutive of Currus. A small or miniature carriage used in Ancient Rome as the plaything of rich children. Sometimes drawn by a pony, goat or other small animal.

Cisium.   Name derived from the Latin — cito, for quick or speedy. A type of Roman gig, driven by fashionable young men, often at dangerous speeds. Wheels were fairly high and light for a vehicle of this period. There were apertures or slats of the side panels serving to increase lightness and for decorative effect. Usually drawn by a single horse of good quality and conformation, but less frequently by two or three horses abreast (Biga and Triga). Some larger types eventually carried a limited number of passengers on cross seats, also mails and luggage, operating a posting service unequalled in Europe for over a thousand years. Entered through the front.

City teaming gear. Front and rear limbers or bolster carriages connected by a reach pole, having upright corner posts on crosswise bolsters. Used in American cities, throughout the 19th century, for transporting pipes, logs and girders.

Clarence. English family coach first appearing during the 1840's. Named after the then Duke of Clarence, by whom such a vehicle may have been owned. Hung on either cee or elliptical springs, without an underperch. An enlarged version of the Brougham although seating four persons vis-à-vis. Less ornate than a town or state coach and minus the decorative hammer cloth. Constructed in large numbers by the London firm of Laurie and Marner. Declined in use from the mid-1880's. Many were converted to cabs. Drawn by a single horse.

Clarence-Landau. Also known as Simpson's Clarence-Landau, named after its designer. A patent vehicle frequently used in India and certain other dominion or colonial countries, east of Suez, especially during the late 19th century. The upper quarters could be lowered and raised at will, supported on special 'U'-shaped brackets. Glasses or windows were protected by slats/blinds.

Clarence rockaway. American passenger vehicle with a combined driving and passenger seat built into the bodywork, under an extension of the fixed top/head. Usually hung on sideways elliptical springs but sometimes with half-elliptical springs at the rear. Drawn by a single horse.

Close or closed carriage. A passenger vehicle without side windows or glasses.

Clothes basket. 1. Carriage or cart with a basketwork body.

2. Slang name for a Ralli-car. This was first used in the *Daily Telegraph*, when reporting a court case concerning the patent rights of its designer.

3. Any type of roughly made or badly designed passenger vehicle, especially those on two wheels.

Coach. Pasenger vehicle, in either private or public service, running on four wheels and always headed or enclosed. The modern coach, at least from the second half of the 17th century, was suspended on either springs or leather thoroughbraces — although early coaches were unsprung or dead axle. Although such vehicles were known to the Ancient Romans and earlier civilisations, their development appears to have been neglected for many years, partly because the use of wheeled vehicles was

considered effeminate, by those able to ride or walk (invalids and
older people were carried in litters), also because the roads of
Europe were (often) unsuitable for anything more than lumbering
wagons with broad wheel-treads. The nearest approach to a
modern coach in Western Europe was the Long Cart of the 13th
century, uncomfortable and seldom used.

What is now regarded as the true coach was introduced during
the late Middle Ages at the town of Kocs in Hungary, from which
the corruption of its name survives. Spreading westwards to
Austria and Germany, they were also popular in Holland and
Flanders, but neglected in England, France and Spain until the
late Tudor era of the 16th century.

The first coaches in Britain were imported from Holland or
Germany, used more for show than comfort or convenience. They
were at first without springs, brakes, doors or windows, while the
highways over which they travelled were often impassible —
through deep mud, floods, snow drifts and heavy ruts — for half
the year. When public coaches and stage wagons were run on a
nation-wide basis, their operations were frequently limited by
adverse weather conditions. The British prototype was designed
and constructed by a master wainwright known as Walter Rippon,
employed by the Duke of Rutland, about 1555. The Earl of
Arundel imported a coach from Germany in 1580, that soon
became the envy of the court circle and nobility, while Elizabeth I
ordered several coaches from Dutch builders. These were mainly
boxlike vehicles, semi-open but having leather curtains to protect
the apertures. Prince Rupert drove to the battle of Marston Moor
in a coach and six, while Oliver Cromwell — after he became Lord
Protector — frequently drove his own vehicle in Hyde Park as a
pastime and means of relaxation. There are records of Louis XIV
of France driving through Paris in a gilded coach during the
1650's, while many of the German princes were renowned for their
collections of private coaches and studs of powerful horses bred to
draw them. During the second half of the 17th century most
coaches and passenger carriages were supported by a strong
underperch of wood or metal, but this became less important as
steel springs were introduced and improved. So-called 'Daleme'
springing or a combination of leather straps and metal springs was
used throughout the 18th century. Cee or 'C' springs were
invented during the 17th century, but little used until their
reintroduction about a hundred years later.

Elliptical and semi-elliptical leaf springs came during the early

1800's, which helped to make coaches much lighter in design and balance. The underperch eventually declined and appeared only on some of the larger vehicles, while more coaches acquired full underlock for an improved turning circle. This latter was only possible (when a perch was used), by means of cranes, which assisted in lifting the bodywork for cut-under. With the passage of time coaches and carriages tended to become swifter, yet safer and stronger but less ornate. Smaller teams were needed as roads and vehicles improved, and by the late 18th century six and even four horse teams — apart from those drawing stage or ceremonial coaches — were a rare sight. The lumbering state or family coach gave way to the elegant chariot or coupé, while Brougham, Clarence and Victoria were only slightly more elaborate than street cabs. Eventually even wealthy people, living in towns and cities for at least part of each year, tended to give up their personal coaches, relying more on vehicles hired from job-masters by the season, along with horses, coachmen and carriage servants.

Stage coaches were public travelling coaches for nearly two centuries, although challenged by the railways on their main line routes during the late 1830's and early 1840's. It was essential, however, for smaller horse-drawn vehicles to meet the trains up to the 1920's and the era of popular motoring. Amateur coach driving has always been an interest of the wealthier and more exclusive classes, but underwent an important revival — in both Europe and North America — during the second half of the 19th century. A second revival, extended to the use, display and preservation of a wide range of horse-drawn vehicles of all types, came during the 1970's.

Coach, cardinal's.   State coach used for ceremonial purposes, by cardinals of the Roman Catholic Church. Painted red, which was the traditional colour of a cardinal's hat and robes. Usually ornate, heavy vehicles drawn by six or more horses. Driven from a box seat with a richly embroidered hammer cloth.

Coach, flying.   Primitive stage coach of the early 18th century, travelling between five and nine miles per hour. This, however, was much faster than the stage wagon or carrier's wagon. Advertised as late as 1750 as 'safe and comfortable'. Hung on whip or elbow springs. Drawn by a four-in-hand team.

Coach, four-in-hand.   Type of large coach, driven to a four-in-hand team, either for business or pleasure. Amateur coaching or driving a four-in-hand, was first made popular by George IV during his sojourn in Brighton, first as Prince of Wales and later as

Prince Regent. The art was revived and became even more popular during the mid-19th century, with the formation of several coaching clubs. The Four-Horse Club functioned between 1808 and 1826. A still flourishing Coaching Club was founded in 1870 while an American Club came five years later, its headquarters in New York City, but with a nation-wide membership. Vehicles used at meets were privately owned versions of early road and mail coaches.

Coach, gala. State coach or carriage, richly ornamented and used for ceremonial or show purposes.

Coach, hammercloth. State or formal coach, richly ornamented and using an elaborate cover over the box seat known as a hammer cloth.

Coach, mail. A public coach, first used in England to carry both passengers and the Royal Mail. The first vehicle of this type was planned and introduced by a John Palmer of Bath, intended to replace a far from reliable system of mounted postboys. It originally ran between London, Bath and Bristol, but later extended — as a system — to most parts of the country. In 1829 there were 94 full-sized mail coaches, thirty four years after the founding of the enterprise. These were supplemented by many stage coaches and smaller or pair-horse coaches on shorter routes.

The first type of mail coach was hung on elbow springs or braces and carried inside passengers only. The guard shared a box seat with the driver, mails and valuables being in a locker under their feet. An improved mail coach of the early 1800's had crosswise roof seats of gammon boards, for four outside passengers, while the guard — fully armed with cutlass, pistols and blunderbuss — travelled on a single seat at the rear of the vehicle above a rearward boot. Suspension was eventually in the form of combined crosswise and sideways semi-elliptical springs, connected by 'D' links, known as 'Telegraph Springs', first used on a coach known as 'The Telegraph'. The four-horse teams worked stages of 7 to 10 miles, between inns and posting houses, at an average speed of 10¾ m.p.h. They functioned with such regularity that townsfolk and villagers along the main routes set their clocks by them. They were not usually named coaches, an exception being 'Quick Silver', which ran on the southern route between London, Devonport and Falmouth. Its timing between London and Devonport was 217 miles in 11½ hours. Mail coaches travelled free on all roads not having to pay tolls on either bridges or at toll gates. Gate Keepers not having their gate ready on hearing the blast on the guard's horn, could be fined for neglect of duty. All other traffic had to make way for the Mail.

A type of vehicle run by the Post Office for mails only, was reintroduced towards the end of the 19th century on certain country routes, especially in the south of England, radiating from London. These ran until the early 1900's and although little more than large, enclosed vans, were known as Mail Coaches. Like the earlier and true mail coaches they had patent mail hubs and axles, each hub secured by three long screws that were unlikely to part company with the wheel, at the same time, during accidents or breakdowns.

Coach omnibus. Short distance stage coach, combining the best features of coach and bus, popular in the southern states of North America during the mid-19th century.

Coach, public. Stage or mail coach used in public service to carry both passengers and parcels. Also known as a Road Coach. *See* Coach, road.

Coach, regulation. Private coach or drag owned by a member of the New York Coaching Club. This has to conform to approved standards of smartness, safety and traditional appearance, based on English models.

Coach, road. Alternative name for the stage or public coach, driven between stages on approved long distance routes. They ran from the early 17th century to the mid-19th century, in many ways similar to the later mail coaches, although carrying a larger number of outside passengers. During the early 18th century poorer people, not able to afford seats, were carried in a basketwork rumble, suspended between the rear wheels. Cheaper than mail coaches, stage coaches were more colourful, even gaudy, painted with names and destinations, also pictures of running foxes, coach horns and crossed whips.

Those driven in later years, often for pleasure or show, were distinct from specially built drags or park drags and more workmanlike, if less elegant. The horses were frequently of mixed colours rather than well-matched teams, while the guard wore a traditional uniform with beaver hat and scarlet coat, rather than a family livery. A spare neck collar was frequently hung on the side of the coach.

Coach, Salisbury boot. Vehicle with a curved boot and driving seat above a tool box, detached from the rest of the bodywork.

Coach, stage. *See* Stage coach.

Coach, state. Ornate coach used by royalty and persons of rank or wealth, especially from the mid-18th century to the late 19th century. Retained to the present day for Royal and State ceremonial. Often carved, gilded and painted with great attention to detail. The box would be covered with a deeply fringed hammer cloth, while footmen often rode on a rearward platform or dummy board, dismounting to clear the way in a busy street, also lowering steps and opening doors. Rarely comfortable vehicles, being overlarge and subject to lateral sway. They usually retained an underperch even when mounted on elliptical or semi-elliptical springs. Cost between £500 and £800 during the 1880's.

Coachee. A type of small stage coach or public carriage, used in and around the larger American cities from the late 18th to the mid-19th centuries. Sometimes known as a Jersey Wagon, as they were first developed in the State of New Jersey, U.S.A. Headed but frequently semi-open. Entered from the rear by means of one or two steps. The driver sat under an extension of the roof canopy, at the fore-end. Windows, without glass, were protected by leather curtains or roll-down blinds. Two seats or benches for passengers were in a crosswise position. Hung on thoroughbraces rather than springs. Drawn by a pair of light-medium draught horses in pole gear.

Coachee-rockaway. Type of public carriage modelled on the earlier coachee, introduced — in America — about 1860. Larger, clumsier and less compact than the coachee. It carried eight people facing forward, or two more than its predecessor. Drawn by a pair of medium draught horses in pole gear.

Coal carriage. Four-wheeled wagon or trolley of the late 18th century, with spindled sides, used for delivering bagged house-coal.

Coal carts, trollies or wagons. Most British coal carts, widely used for the sale and street delivery of household-coal, from the late 18th to the mid-20th centuries, were four-wheeled vehicles misnamed. Their altlernative and correct titles should have been carriages, trollies, lorries, wagons or drays, according to size, type and area. In certain parts of Britain and North America, however, there appears to have been a rearward tipping cart, used for coal deliveries, made to resemble a high-sided tumbril.

The earliest type in Britain was the London Carriage or Trolley based on Moore's patent Coal Carriage. This was mounted on large, red-painted wheels, with brass axlenuts, able to turn in quarter lock only. Like most vehicles for selling coal, it had a shelf under the rear carriage for scales and weights. Driven from either a standing or seated position. While early types were dead axle, use was eventually made of sideways semi-elliptical springs. In hilly districts chain horses were used in tandem, but some coal carriages travelled in pairs, the horses harnessed together for the steeper gradients, taking one load forward at a time.

A flat, open dray or trolley was later used, although versions of the traditional coal carriage survived, in some parts of London and the Home Countries, until the 1950's. Most open trollies — without sides or spindles, had a colourful crosswise headboard, enscribed with the name and business address of the owners, that would be of enamelled metal fixed to a wooden framework on a row of iron bars. The driver of this type either had to stand behind the headboard or lead his horse on foot. Latest prices would be chalked-up on a square or rounded board at the side of the loading platform. Some types had a partition rail or rails in horizontal form, supported by stanchions, down the centre of the vehicle. Unlike the original coal carriage, later vehicles had much smaller, near equirotal wheels, able to turn in full lock. Most were hung on sideways semi-elliptical springs and carried dragshoes. There were seldom brakes or side lamps and a few examples were unsprung or dead axle. In the provinces some trollies were without headboards, while a few trollies had tailboards only. The average price would be £30.

Coal sack trolley.   Panel-sided cart, the fore-end having a bowed top and iron outraves down both sides. Fairly high above road level, running on a pair of high wheels with either wooden or iron naves. Drawn by a single horse in shafts. Used for conveying either coal or loads of empty sacks to and from a merchant's wharf. Made in two or more sizes, the largest up to 35 cwt. capacity. Cost about £28 during the 1900's.

Cobb coach.   Version of the American Concord Coach, used in the Australian outback, especially before the coming of the railways. Cobb and Company were authorised to carry the Royal Mail in all parts of the sub-continent. The vehicle was suspended on thoroughbraces of toughened leather, as with prototype. Unlike the American Concord there were roof seats or Gammon boards for outside passengers, while the driving seat — under which the mails were stowed — appeared to be lower and wider than on the original Concord. *See* Concord Coach.

Cob cart.   Two-wheeled vehicle suitable for a cob or small horse. Either sprung or dead axle.

Cob cart or phaeton.   Small version of the Phaeton, drawn by a cob or large pony.

Coburg. General purpose delivery van mounted on two wheels, the arched roof or head protected by a waterproof cover. Used mainly in England, either by bakers, drapers or haberdashers. Known in the former trade as the 'Small Bread Van'. Low-slung and entered from the front, rather like a Hansom Cab, its dashboard curved to the hindquarters of the horse. Frequently fitted with cranked axles and hung on sideways elliptical springs, although a straight-axle type was also well-known. Shafts were upward curving. Cost between £23 and £30 each.

Cocking cart. English sporting vehicle of the late 18th century, mounted on high wheels and having a slatted underboot, in which fighting cocks were taken to a match or main. There was often a high rearward seat for the groom. A later version, used mainly for pleasure driving, could be drawn by three horses abreast, as with the Roman triga. This was mainly popular in the United States of America, during the 1890's and 1900's.

Colonial wagon. Light-weight delivery van made in Britain for export to dominion and colonial countries of the British Empire. Usually drawn by two horses in pole gear. Made with panel sides and a straight, boarded top or head. The driver's cross bench, large enough for two, was under a slightly raised awning or canopy. Hung on four sets of leaf springs or two lengthwise and two crossways, front and rear. A powerful hand-lever brake, external to the bodywork, acted on both rear wheels.

Combat wagon. Limbered or articulated military wagon of the 1900's, used in the American Army to replace the Escort Wagon. Drawn by pairs or larger teams of horses/mules harnessed in pole gear. Driven from a double seat on the fore-part. Unsprung but usually with a sprung seat. A hand lever brake operated on the rear section. The conical metal hubs were without dust excluders or loops for drag-ropes, evident on similar British vehicles.

Combination cart. American two-wheeled exercise cart, being slightly larger and heavier than the Harness Race Cart. *See* Harness Race Cart.

Combined hearse-coach. Mourning coach in which a rearward compartment for six passengers was attached to the hearse section. The driver's seat was attached to the fore-part of the hearse. Drawn by two horses in pole gear. Frequently used for cheap funerals.

Comfortable. Australian version of the London Growler or four-wheeled cab. Seated four passengers vis-à-vis. Hung on sideways elliptical and semi-elliptical springs.

Concord. The most popular stage or public coach of North America, versions of which were later used in Australia, New Zealand and South Africa. There were several types, the finest and most popular constructed by the firm of Abbot, Downing and Company of Concord, New Hampshire. This was based on the earlier Troy Coach of New York State. Abbot, formerly an employee of Downing, but later his partner, is said to have re-designed the Troy Coach as the Concord, this being of comfortable but sturdy construction, gaining immediate support in emerging states of the American West. When first sold the Concord was known as 'The American Mail Coach'. This was during the mid-1820's, its fortunes continuing to prosper until the 1890's and dominance of the inter-continental railroad companies. Throughout this period it was the main form of long distance travel for the average citizen.

Concords used in Western territories were usually larger than those serving in the older, colonial states with better roads. They carried up to twelve passengers, although a few later types — from the 1860's — were designed for sixteen people. Those working between the towns of New England and on the Atlantic seaboard, rarely carried more than six passengers, more akin to the English Mail Coach. Some Concords carried outside passengers, several clinging to the roof rack or large hind boot, but this was only allowed at the personal discretion of the guard or messenger, by whom order was kept with a loaded shotgun (riding shotgun). While Concords in the East were more conservative in planning and outward appearance, the Western types were smothered with bright colours and painted designs, like circus wagons. A few were designed as leisure or sight-seeing vehicles, even from the earliest days, based on holiday resorts.

The general plan of the vehicle was oval or egg-shaped, hung on thoroughbraces of toughened leather, ensuring a fairly comfortable and jolt-proof ride on the wildest mountain passes and desert tracks. Passengers sat facing each other on double benches or vis-à-vis. Mails and valuables were carried in a fore-boot while ordinary luggage was strapped to the roof or contained within a rear-boot, the latter having a sloping top but well-strapped down. All types had a strong wooden underperch, comprising three longitudinal members extending the full-length of the under-side. Fore-wheels had threequarter lock under the foreboot, while an off-side pedal brake acted on the much larger rear wheels. Underworks were usually painted light yellow or cream, in contrast with darker or brighter upperworks. Teams of from four to eight horses, according to terrain and the size of the vehicle, were controlled from the box-seat by skilful drivers using their voices rather than whips, knowing their team members as individuals. With large teams small stones or pebbles might be thrown at the heads of the leaders, landing with remarkable accuracy, more telling than the toughest whipcord. With teams of six or eight a detached or extra coachpole was used, known as a swinger.

While the guard usually sat next to the driver, on some sixteen seaters, especially those intended for sight-seeing excusions, there was a separate guard's seat at the rear, perched on a skeleton framework.

Concord top buggy. American Buggy with near-equirotal wheels, hung on inverted semi-elliptical springs. The wheelbase was fairly short and the folding hood of a semi-enclosed type. Bodywork was identical with the Coal Box Buggy.

Concord wagon. Light passenger wagon or buggy, also known as a Pleasure Wagon. A type first constructed by the Abbot, Downing Company, responsible for the Concord Coach. Hung on steel reaches or bars and side springs, in combination. A notable feature was the high, cantilevered driving seat. Drawn by a single horse between shafts.

Conestoga wagon. Large American farm and freight wagon combining the essential features of both English and German vehicles of this type. First made and used in the Conestoga Valley of Lancaster County, Pennsylvania, during the 1750's, this being the home of both British and German settlers, the latter frequently known as Pennsylvanian Dutch. Cruder types of wagon or wain, on similar lines, may be traced to an even earlier period. Some were eventually used to carry merchandise and passengers between distant towns and settlements. Drawn by large teams of either horses or oxen, according to load.

Frequently used by farming families or pioneers in their great land treks, but rarely further West than the Mississippi Valley. At night, on long journeys, the team would be detached from draught gear, to feed from a rearward box hung under the tailgate. They were then turned out to graze or secured to the side of the wagon by tethering rings. Horses used were usually heavy draught types in the region of 17 hands high. Oxen were seldom in-spanned after the 1790's.

The Conestoga was essentially a covered wagon, its canvas top or head supported by sloping rather than upright tilts, but should not be confused with smaller covered wagons used by settlers of a later era. The floor and bodywork of wooden planking curved slightly downwards to the fore-carriage, for mainly decorative reasons. The sides were made of near-horizontal planking with detachable top and side planks for a higher than average load. Front boards and end/tail gates were inclined outwards at both front and rear, with a fair amount of overhang beyond the axletrees. The sloping tilts, often known as 'bows', were between eight and twelve in number. Loading platforms were an average of 13 feet long. A form of driving seat or lazy board pulled out from the front of the wagon, on the near side, while there was a large tool box, also on the near side, fixed between front and rear wheels. Capacity would be between four and five tons. Originally a dead axle wagon with a strong underperch or coupling pole, based on a double-'A' frame. Brakes were added to some examples and a few eventually had semi-elliptical side springs. Most types carried heavy drag-shoes, hung from the undersides. Brakes were operated by means of a rearward side level. Running gear was painted red while the body was dark blue and the canvas top either grey or off-white.

Although tending towards a boat-shape the Conestoga was far from water-tight and there is no truth in the widespread belief that it could be floated across rivers, where there were neither bridges nor fords. A few may have reached the Far West, during the 1830's and 40's, but they were not — in general terms — western wagons, in purpose or style, the latter having more angular or square outlines.

Continental dogcart.   High, angular-type of dogcart of the four-wheeled type. Sometimes made with large wheels, the felloes being of iron or steel. Hung on elliptical or semi-elliptical side springs. Drawn by a single horse in shafts or a pair in pole gear.

Continental wagons.   Usually more basic than those made in Britain, up to the period of mechanisation. Frequently open or ladder-sided, with or without raves to protect the wheels. Some, especially in Holland, tended to be higher at the rear than the front. Mainly dead axle rather than sprung types, especially for farm work. Pole gear was used rather than shafts – most wagons drawn by a pair of horses. Corner poles were frequently used in place of end ladders. Wagons used for taking the family to church or market were fitted with cross benches and featured external carvings or painted decorations.

Contractor's cart.   American version of the European Builder's Cart. A two-wheeled dump or tip cart but with fairly low sides.

Contractor's gear. American carrying frame on four wheels, with end bolsters, that could be adapted for use with several types of upper works. Mainly used on work sites in the building trade. Drawn by a pair or larger team, harnessed to pole gear with swingle-trees and chain traces.

Contractor's van. English high-sided wagon or open-topped van, with hinged top and side boards, but minus a driving seat. Hung on semi-elliptical side springs, front and rear. Fitted with either shafts or pole gear. Up to a capacity of 3 tons. Usually drawn by a pair of heavy horses. Cost between £42 and £45.

Contractor's wagon. Larger and four-wheeled version of the American Contractor's Cart, widely used on building sites and in construction work. It could be adapted for sideways or rearward tipping, especially when certain sideboards were removed. Dead axle. Drawn by two horses in pole gear.

Conveniency. Slang name for a coach or carrige, especially among puritans and Quakers, during the 17th and 18th centuries.

Conveyance. Name for any type of vehicle, including coaches, carriages and wheel-less drags or litters, etc.

Copaicut. Four-wheeled passenger wagon or phaeton, widely used in the North American colonies of the late 18th century. There were two cross seats in parallel, although the rear seat was rarely used, its back rest closed as a lid, useful for luggage space. The rear of the vehicle tended to slant in an outward direction. Hung on thoroughbraces rather than springs. Drawn by a single horse in shafts.

Copicutt. Alternative spelling for Copaicut. *See* Copaicut.

Coracle. Basketwork phaeton of the late 19th century, said to resemble a Celtic coracle, which was a shallow, oval-shaped skinboat, mounted on a framework of woven twigs/slats.

Cobillard. French combined hearse and mourning coach, thought to have developed from a primitive road coach. Later types had a coupè body at the front, attached to a glass-sided, rearward compartment for the coffin. The driver's seat was at roof level. Both fore and hind wheels were hung on sideways elliptical springs. A strong hand-lever brake acted on the rear wheels. Drawn by either a pair or four-in-hand team.

Corn chandler's van. Either an open or headed vehicle, on four wheels, similar to a Miller's Wagon but slightly smaller and more compact. Drawn by a single horse.

Cornish haywain. Harvest cart used in East Cornwall and parts of West Devon. There were low side rails and fixed ladders at each end, the latter inclined at about 60 degrees. The platform was of medium length. A bowed top rail was fitted above each wheel but did not over-hang in the form of an out-rave.

Cornish Jack wains. Farm vehicles used in the flatter, inland parts of Cornwall. Not typical of the area, as this was mainly cart or wheel-less drag country. Four-wheeled and either without sides or having extremely low sides, especially a type in South Cornwall. A type from North Cornwall had low side rails or raves over the forewheels only. Usually able to turn in full lock with small wheels and a long wheelbase for height and size. Drawn by a single horse in shafts, sometimes aided by a chain horse in tandem.

Cotswold harvest cart. Used in Oxfordshire, Gloucestershire and parts of South Worcestershire. Noted for low sides and tall end ladders. Bowed above the wheels, similar to the original hay wain. During the closing years of the 19th century, large numbers were factory rather than craftsman made.

Costermonger's cart. Two-wheeled cart used in the East End of London by costermongers or street traders, selling fruit and vegetables at the kerbside or in street markets. The vehicle was usually drawn by a small pony or donkey, although sometimes converted into a hand barrow. Most doubled as a cart and market stall. There were bars or spindles at the sides, much higher at the rear than the front. Some had a mid-way driving seat, with or without backrest, mounted on curved irons. Hung on sideways semi-elliptical springs.

Cotton frame and seedbed wagon. Heavy wagon used in plantations of the Gulf-states of North America (the deep south). Drawn by large teams of mules or horses. The inner bodywork had iron struts that held the load steady, especially bales of cotton. Those used in semi-tropical conditions were soaked in linseed oil to prevent the woodwork cracking or the paint scaling. Types used during the early 19th century had quarter lock but were without a driving seat, the teams led on foot. Later versions, appearing after the Civil War, had full underlock and sideways semi-elliptical springs, also a sprung driving seat.

Coucou. Two-wheeled public cab or cart, related to the Carrier's Cart. Used in country districts of Northern France, throughout the 18th and 19th centuries. Able to carry six or seven passengers on crosswise seating under a fixed hood. There were two side apertures but neither proper doors nor windows. The driver sat above an iron dashboard, half covered by a leather apron.

Passengers entered through the front end by means of shaft-steps,
to be known as 'rabbits'.

Country cart. 1. Country made driving cart, finished in a
grained and varnished effect rather than solid paintwork.

2. Type of gig relating to a Dogcart, seating four persons, dos-à-
dos. Less formal than the Dogcart, with open side panels.
Sometimes fitted with a swingletree or draught bar rather than
trace hooks, which allowed greater comfort and flexibility for the
horse, especially when used with breast harness.

Coupé. The name derives from the French word for cut. This
usually relates to a small coach or chariot with truncated
bodywork, designed in this way for greater compactness or to
improve appearance. Known in France as the carosse-coupé.

Coupè, boule. Small or cut-down version of the Boule, fashionable during the first twenty years of the 19th century. Noted for its
exaggerated curves, especially those with a fixed head or standing
top, which gave it an ovoid appearance. Drawn by a pair of horses
in the care of a postillion. *See* Boule.

Coupé, Dorsay. French-style coupé, introduced to Britain by
the expatriate French nobleman Count Dorsay. Similar to the
Brougham but with additional folding seats, double suspension
and an octagonal front. Also known as a Dorsay.

Coupé, double suspension. The American name for a Double
Suspension Coach or Coupé Dorsay. *See* Coupé Dorsay.

Coupé, rockaway. Small or cut-down version of the American
vehicle known as a Rockaway. Frequently used as a station wagon.
See Rockaway.

Court hansom. Alternative name for a rare type of four-wheeled
Hansom Cab, mainly in private ownership.

Courting cart. Low-slung, well-bottomed driving and exercise
cart, seating two persons, side-by-side, squeezed together in fairly
close proximity. Hung on sideways semi-elliptical springs.

Covent garden market gardener's wagon. Large, open wagon,
used for conveying bulk quantities of vegetables to the London
markets, especially to Covent Garden, from the Home Counties.
Panel-sided, with deep headboards or raves over the wheels, above
which there would be a structure of iron bars or removable
sidegates. Made in two full-horse sizes, with double shafts. The
larger type would be up to a capacity of 6 tons.

Corvina. Type of Gallic war chariot, with scythe-hubbed wheels.
Entered from the rear rather than the front. Drawn by a pair of

swift horses, harnessed by means of side traces and neck yoke. First used in Britain and Gaul at the time of the Roman conquests.

Crank axle luggage cart. A low-slung vehicle with prominent splashers or mudguards. Mounted on cranked axles and sideways semi-elliptical springs. In many features it resembled the dairy float, although with a much higher tailboard on letting down chains. Made in either cob or full-horse sizes. Loading capacity was between 14 and 20 cwts. Cost between £23 and £25.

Crane-necked carriage. Vehicle mounted fairly high above ground level, its bodywork suspended on curved irons or crane-necks, which assisted the fore-wheels to lock beneath the under-body.

Crane-necked phaeton. Driving phaeton of the late 18th century, the fore-wheels of which were fitted with cranes or arched suspension for safer turning. Drawn by a single horse, pair or team. With teams of four or six, one of the fore-horses would be controlled by a postillion. A type of vehicle popular with the younger, fashionable set of both sexes.

Craven cart. Small version of the Ralli Car, with dos-à-dos seating. Usually driven to a pony or small cob.

Crios. A battering ram used by the Ancient Greeks in siege warfare. Mounted on four disc-wheels to form part of the military train. Drawn by horses, mules or oxen.

Crock wagon. American farm wagon, square-bodied and high-sided. Frequently unsprung or dead axle. Known in the far West as a Jolt Wagon. With or without a sprung driving seat.

Curate cart. Type of country cart or small gig, mainly used during the second half of the 19th century. Seated two persons only. Drawn by a pony.

Curre. Small, box-bodied passenger wagon of medieval France. Dead axle or unsprung, with large equirotal wheels. It normally seated two passengers at a given time, usually persons of rank or wealth. Drawn by a pair of medium-heavy horses in pole gear, either led on foot or guided by a positillion. Rarely travelled at more than a fast walking pace. Some of the larger types had quarter lock of the forewheels. Headed by means of a tapestrywork cover over tilts or hoops.

Curricle. Name derived from the Latin – curriculum, a light chariot. In modern terms a two-wheeled carriage of Italian origins, either open or headed, but usually with a falling hood. Popular in Britain during the early 19th century, until overshadowed by the rising popularity of the Cabriolet. It normally seated two, side-by-side, but often with a liveried groom on a rearward or rumble seat. Hung on cee-springs.

The Curricle was drawn by a pair of swift horses harnessed by means of traces and a centre pole. Attachment between pole and body harness was through a 'T'-shaped bar and rollers, at the fore-end of the pole, said to correct the effects of sway or uneven motion. Main hauling power or draught, however, was through the traces. A fashionable means of transport for younger men, greater favoured – at one period – by the Duke of Wellington.

Curriculum. Type of racing chariot popular in Ancient Rome. Said to have derived from an earlier Etruscan vehicle. Drawn by a pair of swift horses, harnessed by means of a centre pole and neck yoke, from which curricle gear was developed.

Curtain quarter rockaway. Elegant but sturdy version of the American Rockaway, mainly used in the New England and Atlantic Coast states during the 1880's and 90's. The rear body was a separate passenger compartment while the fore-part had semi-open crosswise seating, shared by the driver and a single passenger. Side apertures were protected by curtains or blinds rather than glasses. Mounted on crosswise elliptical springs. Usually drawn by two horses in pole gear.

Cutter. 1. Type of small sleigh drawn by a single horse or pony.

2. Light, four-wheeled passenger vehicle, drawn by a single horse.

Cut-under buggy. American Buggy of the mid-19th century, designed with a raised arch of the fore-body for cut-under. This made it safer for turning, in heavy traffic or a confined space, than the more conventional vehicle.

Cut-under coal wagon. Low-sided American Coal Wagon, without a driving seat but having cut-under of the forecarriage. Drawn by a pair of horses in pole gear, driven from a standing position. Underlock was of considerable effect when easing the vehicle out of ruts or potholes.

Cut-under gig. A small, modern gig of an award-winning type, made to contemporary designs from modern materials. Features include a stickback seat, small rearboot, curved shafts and high dashboard. There are ball-race hubs and three spring suspension using manganese steel, claimed to be superior to the traditional ironwork of earlier periods.

Cut-under trap. American four-wheeled driving or exercise vehicle with cut-under of the forecarriage. Drawn by either a single horse in shafts or a pair in pole gear.

D

Dak. Vehicle formerly used for the transport of mails in the Indian sub-continent. Usually a strongly constructed, four-wheeled van or wagon, with slatted sides. There were also Dak river boats.

Danish farm wagon. Scandinavian farm wagon with pole gear rather than shafts. Wheels were well-dished and near equirotal, able to turn in quarter lock only. Loosely fitted side-planks gave the bodywork a characteristic 'V' shape. Unsprung or dead axle.

Danish mail coach. Large coach with ovoid or spherical bodywork, said to resemble a large pumpkin. Passengers were not usually carried and the guard shared a cross seat with the driver in an elevated position. Widely used throughout the 19th century, especially in country districts. Drawn by pairs, or larger teams, of powerful coach horses.

Daresbury phaeton. Specially designed driving carriage for modern cross-country events in the competitive sphere. Drawn by either a pair of horses or a four-in-hand team. The undergear is of hollow steel-section throughout, but the main bodywork is in a traditional wood-finish. Other contemporary features include coil springs or shock-absorbers, hydraulic disc-brakes and a spare wheel.

Daumont, à la. Type of coach or carriage without a driving seat, the horses guided by postillions. Generally considered a Continental rather than a British mode of transport, partly accounting for the fact that in most European countries traffic drives on the right rather than the left of the road. A postillion riding one horse and driving its fellow, prefers to ride the left-hand or near-side horse, keeping it to the crown of the road, most people being naturally right-handed and the whip-hand being on the right or off-side. The first vehicles driven in this manner were owned by the French Duc d'Aumont, of which Daumont is a corruption.

Dayton wagon. American pleasure wagon of the 19th century, with either one or two cross seats. Further noted for its prominent splashers or side raves. Hung, like the average American Buggy, on crosswise elliptical springs. Drawn by a single horse or large pony.

Dead axle drays. Various types of long, low drays for carrying large items of merchandise in the streets of American towns and cities. Some had rearward bolsters and side stakes, while others had chain-linked stanchions. Drawn by large teams of heavy horses, either led on foot or driven from an elevated (sprung) seat. Commonplace until the mid-1920's.

Dead axle wagon. Farm or commercial wagon without suspension of any type.

Dealer's cart. Open or slat-sided gig frequently used by cattle dealers, especially in the South-East of England and the Home Counties. A typical example would be the Whitechapel Cart. *See* Whitechapel Cart.

Dealer's trolley. Small dray or trolley normally having a headboard but minus side and tailboards. Drawn by a single horse or cob. Mainly used by street hawkers and dealers in a small line of business. Most had screw-down brakes. Hung on sideways semi-elliptical springs, front and rear.

Dearborn wagon. Boxlike American Buggy or road wagon with a standing top. Said to have been designed for military purposes by the American General Dearborn, after whom it was named. It later increased in size and weight, to be hung on crosswise elliptical springs and used for general haulage or delivery purposes. Although originally intended for a single horse, a number of more recent versions – towards the end of the 19th century – were drawn by pairs harnessed to a coach pole.

Decomeo. The original version of the cut-under type of American Buggy or road wagon.

Delivery wagon. Panel-top, closed or headed delivery wagon with panelled top and sides.

Demi-barouche. Alternative name for the cut-down Barouche or Barouchet.

Demi-coach. Name widely used, during the late 19th century, for a cut-down or coupè coach, normally seating two passengers facing forward.

Demi-Landau. Alternative name for a small Landau or Landaulet.

Demi-mail phaeton. Cut-down version of the larger and heavier Mail Phaeton. Drawn by a single horse or large pony.

Demi-tonneau. Popular farmer's gig of the late 19th century. Frequently had double seats, with access from the rear. Mounted on a three-spring system of suspension.

Democrat wagon. Square, boxlike American Buggy, having two or more crosswise seats on the same level as the driver's seat. Its name derives from the practice of jamming large numbers of people together, all in much the same state of discomfort.

Dennett gig. An English Gig appearing during the early 1800's.

It resembled the Stanhope Gig but with what was then a unique form of suspension. The Dennett was hung on one crosswise set of springs and two lengthwise springs, joined by 'D' links. Each set was said to be named after one of three Dennett sisters, renowned on the London stage for their beauty, wit and nimble dancing.

Depot wagon. An American family carriage, used – during the second half of the 19th century – as a station wagon. There were several different types, all of which may have been inspired by or developed from the Dearborn Wagon. *See* Dearborn Wagon. Drawn by either one or two horses, according to size. Noted for either two or three rows of crosswise seating, on which passengers faced in the direction of travel. Similar to the Rockaway but with a straight rather than a curved underside. A removable rear seat could be converted to luggage space.

Derbyshire wagon. Farm wagon of the East Midlands with a short wheelbase and high, fairly straight sides. A type of box wagon. The platform and bodywork were inclined downwards towards the fore-end. Spindle-sided and without raves or side rails. Some had fixed end-ladders known locally as 'gormers'.

De Tivoli's knifeboard omnibus. A patent omnibus of the mid-19th century, drawn by a pair of horses in pole gear. While the upper deck was of the conventional knifeboard pattern, the lower deck had separate compartments for corresponding classes of passenger. First class – in the forepart – was entered from the side, while second class was entered through the rear. Hung on sideways semi-eliptical springs at the front and Telegraph springs further back.

Devon buckrowe. Panel-sided Box Wagon of Devonshire and the South West of England. Noted for its short wheelbase and forward projection of the bodywork, well in advance of the forecarriage. The upper line was slightly curved, especially at the fore-end. Able to turn in quarter lock only. Fitted with iron rather than wooden naves.

Devon chest wagon. Small, neat farm wagon of the box-type, used in both Devon and parts of East Cornwall, up to the period of the Second World War. Could be purchased, during the 1900's, for about £10 each. Noted for well-chamfered woodwork, spindle sides and rearward or end-rollers – the latter fixed under the tailboard for attachment of lashing-down ropes. Drawn by a single horse in shafts.

Devon harvest trolley. An economy farm vehicle, used during the depression years, in place of more costly wagons. Similar to the

West Midlands Trolley but having fixed, outwardly inclined ladders at front and rear, also rearward rope rollers. Forewheels were able to turn in full lock, being much smaller than rear wheels.

Diable. French – devil. A semi-open carriage of coupè of the mid-19th century, its door standards cut down to the centre or waistline. It was fairly light and well-sprung, driven to a pair of fast horses at dangerous speeds.

Dicky coach. 1. Coach or carriage in which the boxseat was separated, or appeared to be separated, from the main bodywork.

2. Slang name for any passenger vehicle with a rear or rumble seat, sometimes known as the 'dicky'.

Digby. Alternative name, used in Northumberland and the North East of England, for a Governess Car or Tub Cart.

Diligence. Late 18th century name for a French public coach working on long distance routes. So-named from its reputation for promptitude and good time-keeping, as with the English Mail Coach. Although normally well-sprung and enclosed, seating eight or more passengers, some types had a semi-open seat, for three or more passengers, shared with the driver. This latter was known as the banquette. Although most vehicles were coachman driven, others were in the care of postillions. The number of horses varied according to difficulties of the route. Three, or a unicorn team were not unfamiliar, especially on the flatter roads of the north west. In Germany, Austria and some parts of Switzerland the Diligence was known as the Post Coach or Malle Post. *See* Malle Post.

Diligence coupé. A smaller or cut-down version of the Diligence, used on shorter than average routes. Usually drawn by a pair of horses in pole gear.

Diophramaxa. Open carriage of English origins but widely used in the United States of America. Also known as a Wagonette-Break. Seats were made to revolve or change position so that passengers could face away from sun and wind at will.

Diphron. Greek war chariot, with a high front shield. Entered from the rear. Drawn by two or more horses harnessed abreast.

Dioropha. London designed Landau, exhibited at the Great Exhibition of 1851. Low-slung and easier to enter than the average vehicle of this type. Patented by a carriage builder named Rock.

Disinfecting cart/wagon. Utility vehicle used either in civil or military life, for sanitary spraying. Introduced during the 1880's. Usually unsprung or dead axle. Either two or four wheeled. Drawn by a single horse at walking pace. Led rather than driven.

Disobliger.   Also known as a Disobligent. A cut-down coach or coupé, large enough for one passenger only.

Dogcart.   English sporting cart used as a conveyance for gun dogs and general purposes. The dogs were carried in a slatted underboot beneath the driving seat. There were both two and four-wheeled types, drawn by one or two horses, those harnessed to the former type being in tandem. The four-wheeled dogcart is more correctly known as a Dogcart Phaeton. Both derived from the earlier shooting gig of the late 18th century. Passengers on both vehicles sat back-to-back or dos-à-dos, one (next to the driver) facing forward and two facing backward, their feet – in the latter case – supported by an angled footboard on letting down chains. Shafts of the single type or two-wheeler were made from springy wood to counter the effect of a jogging motion felt more by the rearward passengers than the driver and fore-passenger. Wheels on the original single were at least 55″ diameter, although smaller on later and lower types, especially pony sizes.

The Dogcart was a useful vehicle on a large farm or small estate and made exempt, in 1843, from taxes levied on pleasure vehicles. In later years the two-wheeled dogcart developed into a smart show vehicle, especially when driven to a high-stepping tandem pair. The inner compartment was then seldom used and the slats mere dummies or painted slits. There were numerous regional styles and designs such as the Leamington, Worcester, Malvern, Nottingham Cart, etc. They were hung on sideways elliptical springs, although some also had a balancing device, adjusting the position of the bodywork, on parallel rods or rails.

Dogcart phaeton.   Four-wheeled dogcart, first appearing about 1860, having a double row of crosswise seats, which were sometimes reversible. Drawn by a single horse in shafts, or pair harnessed to a carriage pole.

Dolgusha.   Long-bodied, four-wheeled shooting break of Russian origins. Also known as a hunting wagon. Usually dead axle but sometimes used side braces of toughened leather. Drawn by a troika or three horses abreast.

Dormeause.   Long distance travelling chariot, widely used in France and other countries of Western Europe from the 1820's onwards, although less popular after the introduction of railways. There was a forward extension of the body that might be used for conversion to a sleeping compartment. Drawn by four horses in pole gear. Hung on cee-springs or sideways elliptical springs.

Considered to be a parallel development of the larger Britzska of
Eastern Europe.

Dormeuse chariot. Alternative name for the Dormeuse.

Dorsay. Contraction of Coupé Dorsay. A type of Brougham,
often appearing with an underperch or double suspension.

Dorset wagons. Usually a small, forward inclined version of the
box wagon. Slightly larger in the southern or coastal regions than
in the northern part of the county. The so-called Bridport version,
had a longer loading platform and sturdier wheels than inland
types.

Dos-à-dos. French back-to-back. Passenger vehicle such as a
docart, in which the occupants sat back-to-back, their feet
supported on an angled tail of footboard.

Double chair. American riding chair, wide enough for two
people, or driver and passenger, seated side-by-side.

Double suspension coupé. A Brougham or Dorsay with double
suspension.

Doughty wagon. An overland wagon hung on side springs rather
than thoroughbraces. First used in the City of St. Louis, Missouri,
U.S.A., but also widely adopted in the far West. There was
crosswise interior seating for six passengers. The driver sat on the
same level as other occupants but well in advance of them. Drawn
by two or more horses in pole gear. A later version, mounted on
platform springs, was used by the elite Signal Corps of the
American Army, from the 1870's to the 1930's.

Dowlais gig. Strongly-built, straight backed gig of the 19th
century. So-named on account of local make and distribution.

Drag. 1. An elegant version of the road coach, used for private
or park driving. This was usually painted in family colours, driven
by amateurs, with grooms on the rearward seats (on top) wearing
family liveries. It was traditional for passengers, usually guests of
the owner/driver, to ride on the upper seats or gammon boards.
The interiors were never used. Such vehicles frequently appeared
at race meetings, polo matches and other sporting events, serving
as mobile grandstands. At one period several regiments and corps
of the British Army owned drags, the only survivor still in use now
belonging to the mounted Household Cavalry Regiment.

2. Any type of awkward, heavy vehicle.

Drag-phaeton. A type of privately owned, medium-sized break.
Hung on semi-elliptical side springs. Drawn by two or more horses
in pole gear.

Drag wagon. American version of the English Neb or Pair of Wheels, used for conveying logs or large balks of timber by dragging them over the ground, attached under an arched axletree and extending in a rearward direction. Drawn by two or more horses.

Draper's delivery cart. 1. A version of the Coburg, used by drapers and haberdashers for door-to-door deliveries.

2. Light, two-wheeled delivery vehicle, usually headed, with double side panels and straight shafts. Hung on sideways semi-elliptical springs. Had either rearward double doors or half-doors and a tailboard. Up to loads of 15 cwts. Cost £30 during the 1890's.

Dray. Heavy commercial or freight vehicle, usually drawn by a team of powerful draught horses. The first known type in Europe, used during the 17th century, was a mere framework on two wheels, having neither floors nor side planks/boards. Later and larger types may have been hung on side or cross springs and usually had four wheels. All were flat, without sides or raves, although some had removable side stakes, especially those for transporting barrels. While some had a raised seat for the driver other teams were led or controlled from a standing position. With an early brewer's dray the driver frequently sat on the first barrel. Known in American cities as a Transfer Dray.

Dress Landau. Alternative name for a formal or state Landau.

Driving wagon. A road wagon or large American Buggy, usually driven for business or professional purposes.

Droitzschka. Droitska. A German pleasure or passenger carriage adapted from the Russian Drosky. *See* Drosky. Later used in England, after the Napoleonic Wars, as a low-slung vehicle easy to enter and safe to drive, favoured by the elderly and invalids. The crosswise passenger seat, with room for two facing forward, was only a few inches above the rearward axle. There was also room for two outside passengers on an enlarged box seat, shared with the driver. Most would be furnished with a falling or half-hood. Hung on sideways elliptical or semi-elliptical springs. A number of early types, however, favoured cee-springs. Drawn by either one or two horses, with heavy draught on account of the low centre of gravity.

Droitzschka-chariot. 1. An alternative name for the Brougham.

2. A Continental version of the Brougham.

Droshky. Four-wheeled passenger carriage of Russian origins. Originally ridden by two or more persons seated on an upholstered cross-plank. The seating was eventually changed to a well-padded bench, but near to road level. Protected by a falling or half-hood.

Drawn by three horses abreast, decorated with silver bells. The centre horse, between shafts and under a wooden arch or 'douga';did most of the hauling – at a smart trot, while the outer horses cantered, with outward turned heads, for show.

Dry goods wagon. American delivery wagon with a cab-type front and inward curved bodywork. Hung on either crosswise or sideways elliptical springs.

Duc. French – Duke. A formal park or show vehicle without boot or luggage space, described as a cross between a pony phaeton and a Victoria. Driven by the sole occupant, but frequently accompanied by a gentleman outrider or liveried groom. Usually hung on sideways elliptical springs, although a few early types were mounted on cee-springs.

Duc-phaeton. Same as a Duc but with a rearward seat or rumble for a carriage footman/groom.

Dump cart. Alternative American name for a tip cart.

Dump wagon. An enlarged four-wheeled version of the dump or tip cart. Used by American builders and contractors from the mid-19th to the mid-20th centuries. Adapted for either sideways or rearward tipping, although some unloaded through bottom planks, like hopper wagons. Tipping could be controlled by gears on the shafts. Usually unsprung or dead axle. Drawn by either a single heavy horse, or a pair in pole gear. A sprung driving seat would be in an elevated position above the fore-axle.

Doubus. Patent cab, used mainly in the streets of London, during the mid-19th century. Similar to the Boulnois Cab but larger and more comfortable. *See* Boulnois Cab.

Dual purpose appliance. A light, four-wheeled dray or trolley of the Victorian Fire Service, drawn by a pair of swift horses. Hung on sideways elliptical springs. Usually carried six firemen and extra gear, including an extending ladder mounted on large wheels. On reaching its destination the ladder was lowered to ground level and manhandled into the required position.

Duquesa. Spanish – Duchess. Large Victoria, usually drawn by a pair of horses in pole gear. Protected by a falling or half-hood. The box-seat was wide enough to seat two. Used in Spanish cities as a driving carriage for ladies. There was frequently a rearward or rumble seat for carriage servants.

Duquesita. Diminutive of Duquesa. Small or cut-down version of the Duquesa. Drawn by a single horse or large pony. Minus the rumble seat.

Dutch brewery dray. Type of four-wheeled delivery dray first used in Holland but later in the United States of America. Noted for its long wheelbase and rearward sloping platform, useful for off-loading heavy barrels to street level, assisted by a demountable ladder carried on the underside. The driving seat, on branched irons, was elevated above the forecarriage, which latter turned in full lock. Brakes, acting on the rear wheels, were operated by turning a screw-handle. Hung on semi-elliptical springs, front and rear. Drawn by a pair or larger team in pole gear.

Dutch Tilbury. A slightly more ornate version of the English Tilbury, the side panels appearing in two contrasting tones or colours. The hood was normally kept in a raised position, as with the Cape Cart. Frequently used by medical doctors and other professional men, driving themselves. Some had a small rearward compartment for a medical bag or other luggage. Shafts were less curved than on either the original or later versions. *See* Tilbury.

E

East Anglian wagon. High-wheeled Box Wagon of the Eastern counties, familiar in Norfolk, Suffolk and parts of Essex. Noted for its prominent wooden strouters or side supports and semi-permanent end-ladders, the rearward ladder fitted low-down to replace the tailboard. There were waisted sides for improved lock.

East Frisian market wagon. Panel-sided wagon from the northern provinces of Holland. Fairly high above road level. Fitted with crosswise seating which could be reached by clambering over the side, using a mid-way step iron. Hung on semi-elliptical springs at the rear and full elliptical springs at the front. Drawn by a single horse in shafts or pair in pole gear.

East Yorkshire cattle cart. This resembled a permanently headed version of the two-wheeled horse ambulance. Low-slung on cranked axles, entered over either lowered front or rear ramps. A regulating, screw-adjusted mechanism kept the bodywork level on all gradients. Usually dead axle, although some later types may have had sideways semi-elliptical springs. Drawn by a single horse in shafts.

East Yorkshire wagon. Farm or harvest wagon used in the East Riding of Yorkshire or what is now part of Humberside. Usually plank-sided with prominent out-raves. Could be used with either shafts or pole gear and swingle trees, harnessed to one, two, three (unicorn) or four horses. The near side wheeler may have been ridden by the wagoner-in-charge.

East Williston cart. Driving cart or gig as used on Long Island (U.S.A.), in country districts, during the 1890's and 1900's, until replaced by motor transport. Noted for its long, straight shafts, extending from the sides of the bodywork. Entered from the rear. Dual backrests folded-down to allow better access.

Eccentric carriage. Vehicle in which the fore-axle was designed as slightly off-centre to assisting turning. Wheels were thus enabled to pass beneath the underbody or fore-carriage without damaging this part. Intended to shorten the under-carriage.

Eight-spring caleche. Large, heavy version of the Caleche, hung on a combination of four cross and four lengthwise semi-elliptical springs. Drawn by a pair of horses in pole gear. *See* Calèche.

Eight-wheeled log truck. Large American timber carriage. Able to carry between ten and twelve tons of felled timber. Consisted of front and rear dead axle gears (limbered), with bolsters, attached by a reachpole. Each limber had four sturdy wheels with broad treads. Drawn by teams of six or more heavy horses.

Eilwagen. Passenger-carrying mail coach, of a type widely used in Germany and Austria, throughout the greater part of the 19th century.

Ekka cart. Two-wheeled driving cart of India and the Far East, usually having room for one person only. A single shaft rested on the back of the horse or pony in draught. Either driven by the occupant or led on foot by a servant. Usually hooded or screened for the sake of greater privacy.

Elevating grader. American elevating wagon that not only scooped-up earth and clay as it moved forward (excavation), but deposited it in other wheeled vehicles travelling alongside. Drawn by pairs or much larger teams.

Elliptic hearse. American all-black hearse, with silver-white interior trim. The side windows were of elliptical design, while the underpart of the bodywork was ogee curved or canoe-shaped. First introduced in 1865. Usually drawn by a pair of horses in pole gear.

Elysian chapel cart. Pleasure or driving cart mounted on high wheels and a three spring suspension system. Drawn by a single horse or large pony. Mainly used and constructed in Scotland during the second half of the 19th century.

Embalming wagon. American wagon of the buggy-type, used by undertakers. Provided with a large rear-boot, suitable for materials used in the craft of embalming, especially when this was done at a private address or nursing home some distance from the funeral parlour.

Emergency wagon.   Service wagon, usually sprung, with a long wheelbase. Drawn by a pair of medium-heavy horses in pole gear. Driven from an elevated box seat. Mainly used by street tramway and trolleybus operating concerns, containing equipment for emergency repairs.

Emigrant wagon.   Any type of large covered wagon, as used by pioneers in the American West. Usually straight-sided and dead axle.

Encamping cart.   Similar to an ordinary farm cart but with higher sides, headed by means of a canvas hood drawn over hoops. Contained two crosswise bunks. Used in British Colonial countries during the second half of the 19th century.

Encamping wagon.   Larger version of the Encamping Cart, mounted on four wheels. Drawn by a pair of horses in pole gear. Either sprung or dead axle.

End spring, drop-fronted phaeton.   Light America Phaeton, with a dropped or cab front, usually having basketwork sides and dashboard. Hung on one rearward and two sideways elliptical springs. Drawn by a single horse in shafts.

English quarter Landau.   Square or angular Landau with a dropped centre.

English spider gig.   An even higher and lighter vehicle than the French Spider Gig, hung on elliptical or semi-elliptical side springs. The outside shafts were fitted high on the sides of the bodywork, having to be stepped across to reach the interior.

Enspijk pleasure wagon.   An ornate Dutch family wagon, frequently driven to church and market. The rearward inclined tailboard was remarkable for its decorative carvings and painted surfaces. Usually drawn by a pair of medium heavy horses in pole gear.

Epiredum.   Covered passenger wagon of Ancient Rome. Drawn by a pair of horses or a larger team.

Equipage.   1. Name used to describe a carriage or other vehicle of superior design and construction.

2. A term often related to servants, escorts and various other persons or items pertaining to a carraige procession, in state ceremonial.

Equirotal.   Latin – wheels of equal size. Several vehicles have been designed with wheels of the same size (front and rear) although it was considered more elegant for the rear wheels to be at least slightly larger than the fore wheels. An equirotal phaeton was designed by the experimental engineer W. Bridges Adam, during the 1800's, which he claimed to be safer, lighter and of easier draught than the ordinary carriage. It was made in two separate but connected and articulated parts. Seldom popular with more fashionable clients although at least one was purchased by the first Duke of Wellington.

An equirotal carriage has been introduced for cross country driving during recent years, under FEI rules, although several snags have been encountered. They appear to have been too long and 'caused steering difficulties when put to a four-in-hand'.

Equirotal phaeton.   English driving phaeton with all four wheels of equal size. *See* Equirotal.

Eridge car or cart.   Low-slung but well-upholstered type of four-wheeled dogcart, the fore-carriage seeming detached from the rest of the vehicle, connected by strong but slender side irons of a skeletal structure. Designed by Lord Abergavenny, during the late 19th century. Considerable controversy surrounds its design, while it appears that only a few were ever made. Hung on full elliptical side springs throughout. Drawn by a single horse or large pony. A low-slung two-wheeled vehicle for two, also bears the same title.

Escort wagon.   All-purpose military wagon, used in the American Army from about 1878. Drawn either by horses or mules. Replaced by the Combat Wagon in 1917, during the First World War.

Esseda.   Lightly constructed chariot, entered from the front, used by the Ancient Britons for warlike purposes. Drawn by a pair of horses or large ponies in pole gear, with neck yokes.

Essex cart.   Country driving cart mounted or high wheels, with a broad cross-seat. Used by farmers and cattle buyers or dealers in the eastern counties. The high position of the driver enabled an interested person to see over hedges and the walls of stockyards, viewing cattle for intended purchase, without having to dismount. The seat had a backrest in the form of a broad leather strap. Lamps were placed high, on both sides, to prevent the glasses being cracked by small stones thrown-up when driving over badly made farm roads.

Essex plank-sided wagon.   Heavy, plank-sided farm wagon, usually found in the eastern part of the county. Noted for its prominent wooden strouters or supports and end-ladders, the latter set fairly low to replace the tailboard. Made with waisted sides for improved lock.

Essex trap.   American four-wheeled trap of the 1880's. Low-slung and slightly smaller than the average vehicle of this type. Seating was on the dos-à-dos plan, as with a dogcart. Rear seats could be reached from either front or back. Drawn by a single horse or large pony.

Eszterhazy. Hungarian (phaetonlike) carriage, semi-open, drawn by a single horse. Harness was frequently decorated with silver bells and colourful tassels. The rearward seat, for two passengers facing forward, was protected by a half-hood. Hung either on cee-springs or elliptical side springs. Named after a noble family of Hungary and Eastern Europe, by whom many of these vehicles were used, especially on their country estates.

Eventing and exercise carts. Modern vehicles for ponies or horses, usually of metal construction, running on either two or four wheels, depending on the type of event in which they take part. Of light, almost skeletal structure, often with shallow or flattened naves/hubcaps. Used in obstacle or cross-country driving.

Excavator. An American self-loading Dump Wagon. *See* Dump Wagon. Drawn by a pair of heavy horses in pole gear. Widely used by contractors from the mid-1870's to the 1900's.

Excursion wagon. Type of passenger wagon, with rows of crosswise seating, mainly used in the Western states of North America, from the mid-19th century to the 1900's. Seats were individually sprung, although the vehicle was dead axle. Headed with a fixed or standing top. Drawn by two or more horses in pole gear.

Exhibition float. A stylish version of the ordinary dairyman's float, used for advertising or display purposes. Noted for its curved shafts, prominent (front and side) nameboards and movable seatboard. Made from superior materials with high standards of workmanship. Appeared in both cob and pony sizes, with cranked axles. Introduced during the early 1900's.

Express wagon. Light-weight delivery wagon, having raves or flare-boards above the wheels to support and protect an over-hanging load. Hung on either ordinary sideways elliptical or platform springs. Normally used to carry luggage and parcels to and from railway depots, in North America. Drawn by a single horse or large pony between shafts. Either an open or semi-open type, its canopy head supported by corner posts or standards.

Extension Surrey. American driving wagon of the Surrey-type, with an extra row of seating and a forward extension of its canopy top. Usually drawn by two horses or large ponies harnessed in pole gear.

F

Fairville cart. Australian gig, hung on a three spring or Dennett system of suspension. It also featured detachable shafts.

Family chariot. Also known as a Travelling Chariot. A strongly built and less ornate version of the State Chariot, but designed on the same principles. Usually constructed with a rearward or rumble seat for servants, in place of a dummy board. Drawn by four horses either driven from the box or in the care of postillions. Originally hung on cee-springs but later on elliptical or semi-elliptical side springs.

Farmer's dogcart. Strongly constructed version of the two-wheeled dogcart, used for general farm and market purposes. Seating was dos-à-dos, but it frequently appeared without the slatted underboot.

Farmer's float. General purpose float, strongly constructed with cranked axles and semi-elliptical side springs. Raised side gates or rails above the splashers made it ideal for taking sheep, pigs or other small animals to market. Cost about £25 each.

Farm wagon. General name for any type of high-sided, four-wheeled vehicle used for agricultural purposes. Essentially a harvest wagon. Most traditional types, especially in Britain, had regional characteristics. Early wagons were without springs or brakes while the majority had limited lock or turning circle. Towards the end of the 19th century wagons ceased to be made by village craftsmen and were increasingly mass-produced or factory products, some acquiring a primitive form of suspension. All types could be drawn by one or more heavy horses, according to loads and gradients. In Essex and East Anglia double shafts may have been used (less frequently in other parts), while in East Yorkshire (formerly the East Riding, now Humberside) there was a preference for pole gear. The majority of wagons, however, were drawn by a horse between single shafts with an additional or chain horse in tandem, saving space when passing through barn doors or narrow gateways.

The main general distinction lay between bow-wagons with lower sides and bowed protection over the rear wheels and higher-sided box wagons with a shorter wheelbase. Size of wheels, usually well-dished, depended on the nature of the soil, clay, etc., over which local wagons were normally worked, also the width of wheel treads. Although ring tyres, shrunken on to the wheels, were widely accepted by the late 18th century, some wagons continued to use double strakes or strips of metal, nailed into position, until the mid-19th century. There was a general decline in the use and building of wagons from the 1930's in favour of low-slung drays and trailers on pneumatic tyres, drawn by both horses and tractors. The remaining traditional wagons, during the Second World War, were frequently drawn-up at the side of a country road to be used as a defence block in the event of an enemy invasion, later exposed to the elements and left to rot. New Farm wagons cost £30 to £46 each, in the larger sizes, more than double the cost of a cart.

Fiacre. The hackney coach of Paris, named after St. Fiacre, an early patron of hospitals and the suffering poor. This Celtic saint was said to have organised a crude ambulance service, using four-wheeled vehicles – during the early Middle Ages – that may have been ancestors of the modern cab. From the mid-17th century a number of cabs stood for hire outside an inn known as St. Fiacre, in the centre of Paris. For one or other of these reasons French Hackney Coaches or Cabs adopted their present name.

From the mid-19th century the Fiacre was similar to the Brougham or Clarence, types eventually seen in most parts of Europe and the Near East for over a century. Early types seated six and were drawn by a pair of horses but in later years the number was reduced to four and sometimes two, with a single horse between shafts.

Fiakr. A public cab or carriage, especially in Austria, Bohemia and other parts of Central Europe. It closely resembled the later version of the Fiacre, drawn by a single horse. *See* Fiacre.

Fine harness buggy. American show buggy with a traylike body, mounted on side bars rather than conventional springs or thoroughbraces. The single driving seat may have been sprung. Shafts and framework were of hollow metal tubes. Wheels were wire spoked, frequently equirotal and mounted on pneumatic tyres. Designed for the so-called Fine Harness Classes at horse shows and state fairs.

Fire engines. Fire engines have been known in various guises since pre-Roman times, although mobile versions on special carriages or trollies were not widely evident until the late 17th century. The earlier wheeled types varied very little for over a century and were known as Parish Pumps, mainly sponsored by local authorities and manned by half-trained volunteers. They were unsprung and mounted on disc-wheels, pulled or pushed manually, although a few may have been adapted for pony draught. They were little more than portable hand-pumps, the levers worked by parallel side bars, squirting jets of water through leather hose pipes.

On some large country estates the fire engine or pump, operated by domestic servants or farm workers, was more sophisticated and drawn by a medium-heavy horse between shafts. Water would be from local streams or ponds and not infrequently from ornamental fountains. Pump handles could be worked by men, women and even older children, usually six per side, in relays. In later years, towards the end of the 18th century, hand-manual pumps became much larger, owned, in town and country, by Fire Insurance Companies. They would be manned by ex-seaman, experienced in ladder techniques through long years of climbing the rigging. Each company had its own brigade with distinctive badges and uniforms. The vehicle on which the pump was mounted appeared as an oblong, boxlike construction, drawn by two or more horses, although a few were two-wheeled and drawn by a single horse.

In 1829 a former Swedish army officer named Ericsson, working in London as the partner of an English inventor and engineer named Braithwaite, patented a revolutionary fire-engine, its pump – although horse-drawn – driven by steam. This was mounted on an iron carriage, with iron-spoked wheels, having a vertical boiler or steam-raising plant well to the rear. Although proving its worth at several fires in the London area – turned out for trials and publicity purposes – it was not appreciated on home ground, first adopted in the City of New York and other foreign centres. Engines of this type were not accepted in Britain until the constitution of properly trained and established brigades, after the passing of the Fire Brigade Act in 1865. From that period onwards the manual type began a steady decline, although its vehicles were frequently converted to Chemical Engines used in a secondary role.

Two firms became established in Britain for the manufacture of fire engines and their fittings, these being Shand Mason and Merryweather. The most popular type of engine in Britain and Europe, was known as 'The London Vertical' on account of its compact vertical boiler. It had a forecarriage turning in full underlock and sideways-on seating for six firemen (three per side), a driver and senior officer riding on the box seat, plus an engineer-fireman – on a rear platform – tending the machinery. All mobile appliances were hung on elliptical or semi-elliptical side springs, with mail coach hubs and axles. Horses were in teams of two or three (unicorn), according to local gradients, stabled at the fire stations but frequently hired from job-masters such as Thomas Tillings of Peckham, by whom many of the London buses were also horsed. Fire horses wore a strong but light harness, which hung above their stalls and was automatically lowered into position at the sounding of an alarm bell. Such teams and vehicles, which sometimes moved at twenty miles per hour over good roads, were in widespread use until the period of the First World War, although the first self-powered fire engine, driven by steam, came in 1899.

In North America, throughout the second half of the 19th century, there were four main types of horse-drawn fire engine, known respectively as the 'Gould', 'Button', 'Silby' and 'Amoskeag'. The first three had short wheelbase and full lock beneath an arched cut-under of the forecarriage, perhaps better adapted for small towns and rural areas. Ladders and hose pipes were conveyed on separate carriages or back-up vehicles. The Amoskeag, as adopted by the New York City Fire Department, was such larger and longer, frequently carrying its own crew and equipment. A distinctive feature of all engines was the fire bell, rung by an officer riding on the box seat or fore-part of the machine.

A few horse-drawn types were still used in Britain, on large estates and in naval dockyards until the mid-20th century. A few were also used by main line railway companies, for fighting fires in large goods yards, or by private firms with a large acreage of commercial property or stockpiles.

Fish cart.   Two-wheeled vehicle, used by fishmongers for door-to-door deliveries. Sometimes an enclosed version of the butcher's cart, but frequently open and low-sided. A large type, often with side raves, was used by merchants and wholesalers, driven along the quayside at fish docks or even on to the beach (at low tide), where ever the catch might be landed. A single horse, according to tides and weather, might be driven some distance out to sea, standing up to its hocks in salt water. A similar cart, was sometimes used for inshore fishing, especially dredging for shrimps on the Lancashire coast. *See* Shrimping Cart.

Fishmonger's cart.   Low-slung flat cart with an open fore-end and hinged tailboard, the latter slightly higher than the single side planks. Shafts were curved rather than straight. There were splashers above the wheels on most types. Up to a ton capacity, in the larger horse sizes.

Fishmonger's and poulterer's cart. A light cart or low van, hung on sideways elliptical springs. There was a seat above the fore-part of the enclosed bodywork, which latter inclined in a rearward direction. Entrance to the inner compartment was through rearward opening doors. Shafts were slightly curved in an upward direction. Sides would be slatted while there were usually nameboards above wheel level.

Fitton garry. Light, open carriage similar to the Victoria, usually driven to a single horse. Fitted with a rearward half hood for limited protection against the weather. Large numbers of these ply for hire in cities and ports of India, North Africa and the Middle East. The name is a corruption of Phaeton-Garry.

Five glass Landau. Landau in which there were five glasses or windows. These were in the fore-part of the vehicle, behind the box seat. Frames hinged together to form a top or head for a fully enclosed interior. Rearward side springs of the vehicle were hung from dumb-irons or rearward projections.

Flanders wagon. Type of military wagon, drawn by a pair of horses in pole gear. Popular in most European armies throughout the 17th and 18th centuries. Usually open although sometimes having a canvas top, drawn over hoops/tilts. Without brakes, apart from dragshoes, and usually dead axle or unsprung. Developed from a simple farm wagon originating in Flanders and the Low Countries during the late Middle Ages.

Flat. Popular name frequently used in Scotland and the North of England for a dray or trolley.

Fleming carriage. American cab or public carriage, similar to the Rockaway. Introduced about 1850. Named after its designer J. R. Fleming of Harrisburg, Pennsylvania.

Float. 1. American goods wagon or dray, widely used in cities during the second half of the 19th century. Either sprung or dead axle, sometimes having a sprung seat. Drawn by a single horse.

2. Type of dray used for publicity or advertising purposes.

3. English two-wheeled, low-loading vehicle, used for both agricultural and retail delivery purposes. Usually, but not always, mounted on cranked axles. From the late 1890's it was frequently associated with daily milk rounds.

Floater. A primitive type of dead axle float, used in America for commercial purposes. *See* Float 1.

Florida passenger wagon. American passenger vehicle with a flat, canopy top and large rearward boot. Suspended on side or thoroughbraces of toughened leather. Normally seated six passengers facing forward, on cross benches. Drawn by a pair of horses in pole gear.

Floyd Hansom. A luxury vehicle of the cab type, designed for private owners. Fitted with an inner luggage rack, umbrella-holder and silver-mounted looking glasses. A hood or screen could be lowered to cover the normally open space between roof and dashboard.

Fly. Originally a type of sedan chair on wheels, also known as a 'Fly-by-night'. From the mid-19th century it also referred to a small station cab, as used in country districts. Drawn by a single horse of the cob-type.

Flying ambulance. Name given to a light, swift ambulance, well-sprung and running on four wheels. Popular during the second half of the 19th century.

Flying machine. Slang name for a comparatively swift stage coach of the late 18th century, especially in the American colonies.

Forage cart. Two-wheeled military vehicle with fixed end-ladders and side raves, used for conveying fodder for horses and mules, on the line of march. Unsprung, drawn by a single horse or mule in shafts.

Forest cart. Narrow military supply vehicle, intended for use on forest tracks. Unsprung and low-sided. Drawn by a single horse, pony or mule.

Forest of Dean wagon. Compact, panel-sided wagon of the box type. Used both for farmwork and as a road wagon for local coal mines. Drawn by a single horse.

Forge cart. Portable blacksmith's forge, mounted on two wheels. Mainly used for military purposes, attached to artillery and horse transport units. Other similar vehicles were either limbered or mounted on four wheels, better known as Forge Wagons or Travelling Forges. When at rest the cart was supported by propsticks at front and rear. Drawn by a single horse, led rather than driven.

Fourgon. 1. Type of luggage van or wagon, well-sprung and running on four wheels, that preceded a travelling carriage. Most were fitted-out with a row of crosswise seats for personal servants.

2. French luggage or goods van. Now usually a luggage van at the fore-end of a passenger train.

Four-passenger, standing top phaeton. American passenger phaeton with a fixed or standing top, supported by corner pillars or standards. Hung on crosswise elliptical springs at the fore-end and sideways elliptical springs at the rear-end. Drawn by a single horse in shafts.

Four-wheeled cattle van. High, plank-sided van with large equirotal wheels. Not usually headed. The shafts, for a single horse, could be attached at either end. Mounted on cranked axles and semi-elliptical side springs. Usually led rather than driven. Factory-made, during the 1890's and 1900's.

Four-wheeled dump cart. Alternative but inaccurate name for a tip wagon.

Four-wheeled governess car. Rare type of governess car or tub cart, mounted on four wheels and entered through the front rather than the rear.

Four-wheeled hansom. Hansom Cab of Continental origins, the fore-end mounted on a pair of small wheels. Also known as a Court Hansom. *See* Court Hansom.

Four-wheeled Ralli car. A neat four-wheeled dogcart, with cut under of the forecarrige. It resembled a Ralli car in having its sides curved upwards and outwards above the wheels.

Frame bed dump cart. Small American tip cart drawn by a single horse or mule. The panelled sides or frames were much lower than the wheel tops.

Freight wagon. High-sided commercial vehicle, drawn by one or more horses. A name popular in North America from the early 19th century.

Freight and baggage wagon. American medium delivery wagon/van. The forepart would be hung on two platform springs, with ordinary semi-elliptical springs under the rear-body. The driving seat was fitted above a combined tool and book box, the interior partitioned. Drawn by two or more horses in pole gear.

French butcher's cart. Two-wheeled hooded or headed delivery van, drawn by a single horse in shafts. Noted for its high dashboard. Hung on sideways semi-elliptical springs. Some had a rearward, racklike compartment in which pigs or sheep could be taken to and from the market area.

French Derby cart. French dogcart phaeton of the late 19th century, designed for lightness and speed combined with strength. Cheap and easy to construct they were manufactured in large numbers on a system of mass-production, but without sacrifice of quality or appearance. Side planks or boards were of varnished wood in the rustic or country style. All ironwork and metal parts were jet black. Each plank would be about three quarters of an inch thickness. There were splashers or mudguards of curved wood, over the rear wheels only.

French phaeton. High phaeton hung on sideways elliptical springs, front and rear. There was space for two on the driving seat with two rearward cross seats in a semi-open compartment, reached through side doors. There were also slatted compartments for gun dogs under both passenger and driving seats. Drawn by a single horse in shafts or a pair in pole gear.

French produce van. A French wagon or open van of the early 1900's. About 15 feet in length and over 6 feet wide, used in taking fresh fruit and vegetables to and from market centres. The rearward body was in the form of a well, at least 7' 8" long. Upper parts were ledge-sided, having generous outraves. Drawn by teams of two or more horses in pole gear. Hung on sideways semi-elliptical springs, front and rear. The elevated driving seat and footboard were mounted on curved brackets. Small but sturdy wheels were near equirotal. Able to turn in full lock.

French spider gig. Light, high-wheeled gig,hung on a three-spring system of suspension. Noted for its high, outward curving dashboard. Fitted with curved rather than straight shafts.

French wine van. Four-wheeled, ledge-sided van with a fairly long wheelbase. Used by French wine merchants from the mid-19th century until the 1920's. Fully headed or enclosed with decorative rounding boards at roof level. Hung on full sideways elliptical springs at the front and sideways semi-elliptical springs at the rear. Drawn by two medium-heavy horses in pole gear. There was an elevated driving seat at roof level.

Fresian sjees. Light gig with richly ornamented bodywork, not unlike a Continental Chaise. A Dutch vehicle driven by farmers of the northern provinces, especially at festivals and holiday periods. Drawn either by a single horse or pair of horses, the latter harnessed in a type of curricle gear. Popular from the late 18th century to the present day. There is room for the driver and a single passenger on the elevated cross seat-protected by a falling or half hood. Hung on a combination of cee-springs and side braces.

In some districts the Sjees was used for a version of 'tilting at the ring', the passenger – usually female – armed with a lance or spear for this purpose.

Fringe top Surrey. American canopy-top Surrey with deep side fringes.

Fruiterer's cart. Strongly made, open-fronted cart, used for street deliveries by fruiterers and green-grocers. A cross seat could be supplied for the driver, at a small extra cost. Many such vehicles, however, were led rather than driven. Hung on sideways semi-elliptical springs. Frequently supplied with mail hubs and axles. The rearward tailboard was hinged. Made in three sizes between 10 cwts. and 20 cwts. capacity.

Furniture wagon. American name for a horse-drawn furniture van, especially those used for deliveries of furniture rather than house or office removals. Drawn by a medium-heavy horse in shafts.

G

Gadabout. American pleasure cart of the late 19th century. Able to carry four passengers facing forwards on crosswise seats. Hung on cross or sideways semi-elliptical springs. Drawn by a single horse or large pony.

Gallymander. Limbered vehicle, with large wheels, supporting a pulley, boom and winch. Used in the granite quarries of New England to move blocks of stone. Drawn by large teams of either oxen or horses.

Gambo. Roughly made farm cart of Wales and the Marches. Used mainly for harvesting and field work in hilly districts. Often a mere platform between two wheels, the latter either spoked or solid discs. Sometimes boarded-up at the ends and having protection above the wheels for an over-hanging load. A similar vehicle was also used in the Cotswolds and the South West of England.

Game cart. Delivery van, with boarded-up top and sides, adapted to carry game and poultry for house-to-house deliveries. Hung on sideways semi-elliptical springs. Outstanding features were slatted vents under the eaves at side and rear. There were rearward opening doors for entrance to the carrying box and either curved or straight shafts for a single horse. Cost about £85 – during the 1890's.

Game van. Panel-sided, four-wheeled van, having full cut-under of the forecarriage. Drawn by two horses in pole gear. The front part of the canopy-roof was extended forward and downwards in a pronounced curve above the driving seat. Hung on sideways elliptical springs, front and rear. The rear body sometimes had a well floor and cranked axles, for low-loading. Used to collect the day's bag after shooting on a country estate.

Garbage cart/wagon. Two or four-wheeled wagon used by

municipal authorities in the collection and disposal of household waste. Later types, noted for both sideways and rearward tipping gear, were lined with sheet metal and made waterproof throughout. Drawn by one or two horses, the latter in pole gear.

Garden seat omnibus. London horse bus which gradually replaced the Knifeboard type, during the closing decades of the 19th century. Passengers on the upper deck sat in a double row of forward-facing seats, on either side of a gangway. Legs and knees were protected, in wet weather, by waterproof aprons.

Garry. Also spelt Gharry. An open carriage of India and the Middle East. *See* Gharry and Fitton Garry.

Gar tar van. Square-shaped van with iron sides and a manhole-shaped top filler. Mounted on two wheels with straight shafts. Drawn by a single heavy horse, although a few may have had double shafts for a pair. There were both side spring and dead axle types. Up to a capacity of 300 gallons, usually gar tar or ammoniacal liquids.

Gelderland wagon. Dutch farm wagon, to the interior of which cross seats might be added. Used for both harvesting and taking the family to church or market. The upper parts were covered by a canvas sheet on hoops or tilts. Panel-sided but much higher at the back than the front. Drawn by a single horse or pair, according to size. An even more decorative version, known as the Gelderland Speel Wagon, was reserved for festivals and ceremonial occasions.

General service wagon. Pair horse military wagon, although sometimes drawn by larger teams. Used for general cartage and distribution purposes, usually controlled by the Army Service Corps of the British Army. Also an essential part of regimental transport, used by most units either in the field or under training.

Replaced versions of the Flanders Wagon and even more primitive types in 1862, when army transport was being reorganised after the blunders and wastage of the Crimea. It survived in eleven marks, some still in use after the Second World War, especially for saving motor fuel at base, in the days of rationing and restricted imports. While some experimental versions had leaf springs of the elliptical type and full underlock, these were found to be less reliable and harder to repair in field conditions than dead axle types with larger wheels and limited lock. The driving seat, however, was usually sprung. Most had side raves and at least five tilts to support a protective cover. Mounted on so-called artillery wheels with strong spokes wedged into metal hubs. The naves of the wheels were protected by dust caps or excluders, with eyes for

drag ropes. There was rearward braking operated by levers from
the driving seat, while some had additional braking under the
control of a second man. Towards the end of their service a few
experimental types were fitted with pneumatic tyres.

George IV phaeton. Pony phaeton with low bodywork and easy
access, said to have been designed for the ageing and overweight
George IV, in 1824. It had a cabriolet-body but very small wheels,
seeming badly proportioned, although redesigned and greatly
improved during the early Victorian era. Drawn by either a single
pony in shafts or a pair in pole gear.

Germantown rockaway. Also known in America as a German
Town. Type of public carriage designed about 1814 by C. J.
Junkwurth of German Town, Philadelphia. A possible development of the Coachee, having several features in common, although
an entrance for passengers was from the sides rather than the rear.
The front row of seats was protected by a storm hood. Further
noted for a rear panel with ogee curves. Bodywork was hung on
crosswise elliptical springs, front and rear. Drawn by a single
horse.

German town. Alternative name for the German Town Rockaway.
See Germantown Rockaway.

German wagon. Alternative name for the Barouche, as imported
from Germany to Britain during the mid-18th century.

Gentleman's driving phaeton. An American version of the Mail
Phaeton, although perhaps lighter and more sophisticated than the
original type. Intended for pleasure or park driving.

Gentleman's wagon. Alternative name for the American Coal
Box Buggy.

Gharry or Garry. 1. Open four-wheeled carriage drawn by a
single horse, driven from an elevated seat. Similar to the Victoria.
Frequently used as a cab or sight-seeing vehicle in parts of India
and the Middle East.

2. Large, oblong public carriage, fully headed or enclosed, used
by natives throughout the Indian sub-continent. There were no
proper windows, only apertures guarded by slats. Driven from a
roof seat. Usually dead axle.

Gig. A shortened version of 'whirligig' – meaning something
light and fanciful. Normally a two-wheeled passenger vehicle used
mainly in country districts, but – in later years – for town driving.
Usually owner-driven. Noted for the ease with which it might be
turned in a confined space. At first a roughly made chaise or
driving cart – cheap to make and not taxed very high – but later

improved with various types of cross-seating, height of wheels and forms of suspension. The so-called Lawton and Liverpool Gigs have been retained as show vehicles and for cross-country driving.

All gigs were enclosed at the back but having ample luggage space below the cross-seat known as the buck. Most were fairly high above road level, to be entered by step irons hung from the shafts. An exception to the rule was the Cab-fronted Gig of the mid-19th century, which had a dropped or well-like front. The Chair Back Gig was designed with seating in the style of a spindle-backed kitchen chair, while Straight and Stick Back Gigs are self explanatory. There were both horse and pony sizes of all types. The average cost would be £25.

Gig, curricle.   Light gig used with either shafts for a single horse and pole (with curricle gear) for a pair. Shafts and pole were interchangeable.

Gig, fantailed.   American gig with a rearward extension of the bodywork that resembled a spread or fantail, as of a fantailed pigeon. Popular during the first half of the 19th century.

Gig, Gorst.   Strongly built, high-sided gig, designed by a Liverpool builder of the mid-19th century.

Gig, suicide.   Type of High-Cocking Cart popular in Ireland during the late 18th and early 19th centuries. Driven to either a single horse or tandem pair. Dangerous to both drive and mount, especially in heavy traffic.

Gig, tub-bodied.   Tub-bodied American gig, rounded or tub-shaped. Popular during the first half of the 19th century.

Gill.   Large pair of wheels used for moving logs or lengths of timber, especially in lumber yards. Also known as a Neb, Nib, Logging Wheels, etc. The log would be suspended beneath an arched framework, raised into position by means of a windlass at the rearward end of the shafts. Drawn by a single horse, although frequently assisted by chain horses in tandem or trandem.

Ginny carriage.   Basketwork Phaeton with cane sides and low wheels. Considered safe for children to leave and enter.

Gladstone.   Low, four-wheeled carriage or coupé with a skelton driving seat and rearward or rumble seat. Protected by a rearward falling or half-hood. Popular in Britain and North America during the second half of the 19th century. Mounted on sideways elliptical springs. Drawn by a single horse in shafts.

Glass coach.   Usually a large family or state coach with large glass lights or windows in place of ordinary side panels.

Glass-fronted Landau. Landau in which the upper fore-quarters were represented by glass lights or windows.

Goabout. American driving wagon of the mid-19th century. Lightly but strongly made, for its type, with a folding rumble or rear seat. Of boxlike or angular appearance. Hung on crosswise elliptical springs, front and rear. Drawn by a single horse.

Go-cart. 1. A light village or rustic cart of the mid-19th century.
2. Type of two-wheeled public carraige on cranked axles, that plied for hire in the London Borough of Lambeth, south of the Thames, during the first quarter of the 19th century.

Going-to-cover cart. An English version of the Dogcart, with high-sloping sides and a straight, deep backrest. The lancewood shafts were light and well-curved. Seated two, or driver and passenger, side-by-side. Drawn by a single horse but sometimes a tandem pair.

Golf wagon. Sporting passenger vehicle of the late 19th century. An open wagon with two or three crosswise seats, in parallel. Hung on sideways elliptical springs, front and rear. Drawn by a single horse in shafts.

Gondola. Large public carriage with lengthwise interior seating. Made and used in Paris during the late 18th and early 19th centuries. A predecessor of the revived omnibus, which latter was considered more compact.

Gondola-of-the-streets. Slang name for the London cab, especially the Chapman and Forder versions of the Hansom Cab, appearing during the second half of the 19th century.

Gondola Landau. Alternative name for the rounded or canoe-shaped Landau.

Goods delivery cart. Panel-sided cart with high raves and a forward projection above the horse for a overhanging load. Either dead axle or hung on sideways elliptical springs. Up to a capacity of 35 cwts. Drawn by one or two horses, the latter usually in tandem.

Goods delivery wagon. Larger, four-wheeled version of the Goods Delivery Cart.

Gospel wagon. Large, low-slung covered or headed wagon, the curved roof supported by numerous standards. Frequently used for outdoor religious services and revivalist meetings. The interior was furnished with several longitudinal benches, a pulpit or lectern and even a small organ or harmonium. Centre-side boards could be lowered and extended to form a platform-stage. An American vehicle first constructed by Pearce and Lawton of Washington

D.C., in 1887. A few may have been exported overseas in connection with missionary movements of the late 19th century. Sometimes known as 'a church-on-wheels'. Hung on sideways semi-elliptical springs or a three spring suspension system. Drawn by two or more horses in pole gear.

Gouda cheese wagon. Small Dutch country wagon, used in the bulk transport of farm-made Gouda cheeses. A low-sided wagon driven from a crosswise seat above the fore-axle. Hung on sideways elliptical springs, front and rear. In wet weather the load would be protected by a tarpaulin or wagon-sheet. Drawn by a single horse in shafts.

Governess car. A small, two-wheeled vehicle of a rounded or tub-shape, mounted on cranked axles. Entered through the rear by means of an outward opening door and low step iron. It was considered safe for young children in the care of a nursery-governess. Drawn by a single pony or even a donkey. Seating was in a sideways-on position, even for the driver, a continuous seat following the interior perimeter of a well for the feet. There were two mid-way driving positions, one on each side of the vehicle, designed with scooped-out portions in which the driver might twist his or her body for better control of the reins. Hung on sideways elliptical springs, bearing under a rearward ledge of the bodywork or a continuation of the curved shafts. Bodywork was stained and grained, although a few were cane/basketwork. A small minority were headed. Introduced about 1880.

Grantville cart. Popular Australian gig, hung on a three spring system of suspension.

Grasshopper chaise. Early 19th century gig or whisky. Two-wheeled and low-sided. Hung on shallow, lengthwise grasshopper springs. Drawn by a single horse or pony.

Greek chariot. Low-slung racing or war chariot of the Ancient Greeks. Frequently drawn by a four-horse team or quadriga (four abreast). Noted for its comparatively small wheels, medium-high front-board and curved sides, mounted with top rails. Horses were attached to a pole and neck yoke by harness of rawhide, without buckles or clasps. The rearward end of the centre pole curved under the bottom-front of the chariot.

Green-grocer's cart. Alternative name for the Fruiterer's Cart. *See* Fruiterer's Cart.

Green machine. Slang name for a green painted carriage of any type, but usually a green-painted Brougham.

Grocer's delivery cart. Deep, panel-sided cart, used in the wholesale grocery trade for buying in bulk quantities. Hung on both crosswise and sideways elliptical/semi-elliptical springs. Drawn by one or two horses, the pair usually in pole gear. Made in three sizes, the largest up to 30 cwts.

Grocer's van. The traditional English type, used from the 1870's to the 1930's, ran either on two or four wheels but was always headed or boarded-up on the inside. The interior – when used for house-to-house deliveries, would be furnished with a number of shelves and containers for such dry goods as tea, coffee, flour and salt – then sold by weight rather than in ready-packed quantities. Scales for weighing were an important accessory. Driven from a crosswise seat or bench above the rearward end of the shafts. Usually hung on sideways elliptical and/or semi-elliptical side springs. Drawn by a single horse. Cost between £15 and £30, according to size.

Grosvenor phaeton. Small phaeton designed by a member of the Grosvenor family (Dukes of Westminster), during the mid-19th century. The passenger compartment was entered from the rear, by means of a small door and step iron. Sides of the compartment were rounded rather than straight or angular, being slightly wider than the driving seat, as with the 'T'-Cart Phaeton. Drawn by a single horse between curved rather than straight shafts.

Guaga. Small public carriage, running on four wheels, used in the towns and cities of Cuba throughout the 19th century. Entered from the rear. Drawn by four ponies abreast.

Gurney cab. Two-wheeled street cab, able to seat four passengers. Invented by J. T. Gurney of Boston, Massachusetts, in 1882. Entered from the rear and fitted with internal, lengthwise seating. Passengers faced inwards. The driver sat on a low seat above the shafts, his back resting on the bodywork at the fore-end. Drawn by a single horse.

Gypsy cart. Country cart or gig of no particular design, sometimes made to the specifications of its would-be owner. Usually lined-out and decorated in an ornate style not appreciated by either the gentry or more conservative farming communities – as being garish and over-elaborate.

Gypsy wagon/van. Also known as a Vardo, Living Van or Caravan. A house-on-wheels, widely used by Gypsy families from the mid-19th century to the 1950's. There were a few Continental types mounted on two wheels, especially in Spain and Portugal, although most ran on four-wheels. Drawn by a single horse in shafts, although in hilly districts a second horse or 'sider' may have been used, hitched to the off-side.

In Britain there were several types of Gypsy Wagon or Van, ranging from the simple Open Lot and Bow Top to the more elaborate Ledge and Reading Vans. The latter were fully enclosed and constructed from either matchboards or panels, supported by hard-wood standards. Entrance was through a front porch and doorway, over demountable steps, let down between the shafts. At the rear of each vehicle would be external racks, cratches and cupboards, used for forage and cooking utensils, etc. Some vans, especially the Ledge type, had a small fowl pen or coop built on to the side of the bodywork. Horse-drawn types were less frequently used after the Second World War, replaced by motorised vans or trailer caravans. Only four per cent of the Gypsy population now depend on this type of vehicle.

H

Hack.   1. Contraction of Hackney Coach.

2. Term applied to an inferior type of horse used in drawing a cab.

Hackney coach.   The name is derived from the French 'haquenée', meaning an ambling, work-worn horse. They were public service vehicles that plied for hire in the streets of London, Paris and other cities, during the 17th and 18th centuries. Often discarded coaches of the nobility, patched-up for a few years extra service, before passing to the scrap heap, drawn by a similar type of horse. At one period they appear to have posed a serious traffic problem, also threatening the livelihoods of licenced watermen and sedan-chair carriers. As a measure of control owners were limited both regarding the number of horses and road-worthy vehicles they owned.

Some Hackney Cabs were drawn by a single horse but many of the larger types had a pair of horses in pole gear, sometimes with a postillion riding the near-side horse. They continued this service throughout the 18th century, replaced by smaller, better regulated vehicles during the early 19th century.

Hackney cabriolet.   A version of the gentleman's Cabriolet, used as a Hackney Cab. This had an off-side seat for the driver, next to the solitary passenger, between the bodywork and off-side wheel. Greater privacy was attained by raising the half hood and drawing a leather curtain. Designed by David Davis of Albany Street, London, about 1805.

Hack passenger wagon. Oblong-shaped vehicle with a long wheelbase, mounted on thoroughbraces. A version of the American Concord Coach. The bottom line was in the form of a dropped or well-shape. Seated eight inside passengers, with two on the box seat. Drawn by four or more horses. There was also a large roof rack and sloping rearward boot.

Hacquet. Type of flat wagon or dray used by the military train of most European armies, to carry pontoons or temporary bridging equipment. Drawn by teams of four or more horses with mounted drivers.

Halberline. The German name for a Berlinet. A half Berlin or cut-down version of this vehicle.

Half platform wagon. Cut down version of the Platform Wagon. *See* Platform Wagon.

Hammock coach/carriage. Type of litter or hammock slung between four wheels. Known to both the Ancient Romans and Anglo-Saxons. Drawn by a single horse or pair of horses.

Hampshire wagon. A light, low-sided farm wagon. Noted for its numerous side rails and spindles, also for a complex pattern of chamfering. Used with both single and double shafts.

Hannam's harvest cart. Patent hay cart of the mid-19th century. Low-slung and noted for extensive side-raves. It featured long, straight shafts, continuous with the bodywork, and metal rods or spindles bowed above the wheels. Wheels were fairly small, having iron naves. Factory rather than craftsman made.

Handy cart/wagon. Small, light vehicle, used by American farmers during the second half of the 19th century. Mainly adapted for harvesting and general purposes, although some might be converted to lumber wagons.

Hansom. A popular contraction of Hansom Cab. *See* Cab, Hansom.

Harma. Hunting or war chariot of the Ancient Persians. Drawn by teams of two, three or four horses harnessed abreast. Entered from the rear.

Harmamaxa. Four-wheeled carriage of Ancient Persia, frequently used by ladies of the harem. Protected by a canopy top supported on tall pillars or standards. Surrounded by decorative hangings or draperies for extra privacy. Drawn by either horses or mules, but led rather than driven.

Harness buggy. A lighter version of the Fine Harness Buggy, frequently with a high seat and dashboard. Made with full cut-under of the forecarriage. *See* Fine Harness Buggy.

Harness race cart. American Sulky with small wheels and a safer, more permanent seat than the ordinary sulky. Used when driving long-gaited horses for racing and other sporting purposes.
Harness racing sulky. Modern, two-wheeled racing sulky. Its curved shafts, in a continuous (bowlike) formation, from an extension of the meagre underframe. Mounted on wire-spoked 'bike' wheels with pneumatic tyres. The minute skeleton-seat is only 27″ from ground level, the whole vehicle appearing to slope in a rearward direction. Still manufactured in large numbers, especially in the United States of America and Australia, where harness racing is widely popular.
Haulier's spring float. Strongly made, general purpose float, used by road haulage contractors and the cartage departments of main line railway companies. Panel-sided, mounted on cranked axles, with sideways semi-elliptical springs. There was usually a forward cross seat for the driver. Drawn by a single horse. Up to 2 tons capacity.
Hawker's cart or van. Low-slung trolley or small dray, either headed or open. Used in the London suburbs and back streets for the sale of fruit and vegetables, either door-to-door or at the kerbside. The driver's seat or crossbench, with only a minimal footboard, was placed fairly high at the front of the vehicle. Most types were hung on sideways semi-elliptical springs, having full underlock and pedal brakes – acting on the rear wheels. Some had screw-down brakes. The lower part of the bodywork was protected by spindles, having arched-tilts or standards supporting a curved top. Usually driven to a large pony or small cob, there being upward curving shafts. A few still survived in the older suburbs until the early 1980's.
Hay bogie. Low, two-wheeled trolley used in the hayfields of Scotland and the northern border counties, for carting pikes or cocks of hay. The hay was collected into small piles for better drying, then transferred to the bogie as transport between field and stackyard. The bogie would be backed-up against the side of each pile, a chain or rope fastened round the base and the pile winched into position by means of a windlass on the shafts. Drawn by a single horse or cob. Most Hay Bogies were enabled to tip their platforms in a rearwards direction, to assist with loading. Found to be more economical than the larger, lumbering harvest wagon.
Hay wagon. 1. Any type of four-wheeled harvest wagon used in carrying the hay crop from field to stackyard. Usually furnished with side raves and end-ladders to protect an overhanging load.

2. A harvest wagon, known in America as a Hay Rig. About 18′ long.

Headed or improved dairy cart.   Cab-fronted dairy or milk float on cranked axles, used mainly for daily milk rounds. Entered through the front but having a low tailboard and rearward inclination for back-end loading. Sometimes issued with a framed hood or top of waterproofed material, adjusted according to weather conditions. Further noted for its curved dashboard and curved shafts. Most types had prominent wings or splashers. Popular during the early 1900's.

Hearse.   Four-wheeled funeral vehicle designed to convey a coffin to the graveyard or place of burial. Usually light and well-sprung with transparent glass side panels. The coffin was inserted through an end-door at the rear of the vehicle. Corners of the flat roof were ornamented with dyed ostrich plumes, while the centre of the roof might be crowned with floral tributes. Driven from a high box seat, although the hammer cloth was frequently a dummy of carved wood. Harnessed to a pair of black (Dutch or Belgian) horses in pole gear, but less frequently to a single horse in shafts. Seldom appeared before the mid-19th century and replaced by motor vehicles during the late 1920's and early 1930's. Hung on sideways elliptical springs at the front and sideways semi-elliptical springs at the rear.

Heavy carriage.   Passenger vehicle of the larger type, with a fixed head or standing top, also one in which the driver rides a box-seat separated from the main bodywork. Mainly answers to the description of a coach.

Hecca.   Two-wheeled passenger cart of India. Usually had a movable or canopy top. Unsprung with little or no metalwork in any part of its construction. Shafts met at a point above the withers of the single horse or pony in draught, which gave the vehicle a pronounced rearward inclination. The driver sat cross-legged on a small platform of the fore-part.

Hel-cart.   Alternative spelling of Hell Cart. *See* Hell Cart.

Hell cart.   Slang name, during the 17th century and earlier periods, either for a large passenger coach or passenger vehicles in general. A term of frustration used by pedestrians when splashed with mud or forced into the gutter by lumbering, ungainly coaches.

Herdic.   American public carriage or omnibus of a type designed by Peter Herdic of Pennsylvania. This was frequently used in the streets of Philadelphia during the 1880's and 1890's. It ran on cranked axles and was much lighter than the conventional omnibus, also easier to enter. A single-decker, limited to eight passengers, although the number was later increased to ten. Hung on elbow springs at the front and semi-elliptical springs at the rear. Drawn by a single horse in shafts. A few experimental types, were drawn by a pair in pole gear. Experiments were also made with a two-wheeled version, but these proved unsuccessful.

Herefordshire wagon. Medium-sized bow wagon of Herefordshire and the Welsh Marches. Plank-sided, marked with deep grooves rather than mid-rails, at the waistline. The fore-wheels were well-dished and turned in quarter lock. Noted for its broad wheel treads.

Hermaphrodite. A cross between a wagon and a cart, used on many English farms from the early 19th century to the 1930's. Although having the rear body of an open cart or tumbril, this could be fitted with a forward extension at harvest time, supported by an extra pair of wheels. Used as either vehicle, according to load and season, but costing far less than a full-sized wagon. Usually drawn by a single horse, although a second or chain horse might be harnessed in tandem.

Hertford miller. Large Miller's Wagon with double shafts. Usually headed with a canvas top supported by hoops or tilts. Hung on semi-elliptical springs, in a sideways position, front and rear. Further noted for an elaborate pattern of chamfering, a high front or forehead and row of straight spindles above deep side planks. A type first made at Welwyn in Hertfordshire during the mid-19th century.

Hertfordshire cart. Farm tip or dump cart with panel sides and a front board or forehead inclined forward at a steep angle. Further noted for high topboards above the side raves.

Hertfordshire wagon. Vehicle with fairly high sides and a cross rather than lengthwise-boarded loading platform. There were two mid-rails and five strouters or outer supports. Used both on the farm and for road work or market delivery purposes. Drawn by a single horse or pairs of horses, according to load.

Hide and skin van. Light open van or cart, hung on sideways semi-elliptical springs, front and rear. Used by butchers and leather merchants, especially those in the wholesale trade. Drawn by a single horse. There were spindle sides, usually with deep nameboards at front and sides, but having a low tailboard. Slightly higher at the front than the rear. Up to loads of 30 cwts. Cost £40.

High dogcart. Show dogcart running on a pair of high wheels, the driving seat being much higher than the rearward-facing passenger seat. A slightly lower and smaller version was for ponies and known as the Tandem Cart.

High flyer. Nickname given to a four-wheeled driving phaeton of the late 18th century. This had extremely large wheels, those at the rear being up to 8' diameter. Mainly driven by young men of fashion, including the Prince of Wales, later George IV. There were also a few notable lady drivers or whips, including Lady Archer and Lady Lade. Horses were either singles or pairs, although a few might be driven four-in-hand or to a team of six. In the latter case the near-side leader would be ridden by a postillion.

Hooded gig. Light gig of the early 19th century, protected by a falling or half-hood, usually kept in a raised position. Revived in popularity during the second half of the century, as a driving vehicle for ladies. Sometimes known as an English or Hooded Buggy.

Hoodlum wagon. A light farm or ranch wagon used in the American West. Sometimes a water wagon bringing refreshment to spare hands at round-up or harvest time. Frequently used to carry the bedding and personal gear of hired men, to and from the nearest rail road depot.

Hook and ladder truck. An American horse-drawn fire tender, mounted on four wheels and crosswise elliptical springs. Designed to carry extra gear needed in fire-fighting, for which there was insufficient room on the engine.

Hoopoe. Slang name for a Gypsy Wagon or living van, used in parts of North America to serve the needs of tourists or holiday-makers.

Hop tug or wagon. Long wheelbased wagon used in the Kentish hop fields. It carried not only sacks of garnered hops but also hop poles and other gear in due season. The much smaller fore-wheels could turn in half lock. There were raves above the rear wheels and either tall end-ladders or corner poles. The forepart was frequently open or semi-open (slatted) at the sides.

Horse-box. Square-shaped, well-sprung vehicle, usually headed, drawn by a single horse or pair of horses. The crosswise driver's seat would be at roof-level with an angled footboard. Entry was by means of a rearward ramp forming the tailboard. Used before the days of railway travel or to take valuable horses (blood stock) to the nearest station.

Hose carriage. Vehicle used by a fire department to carry spare reels of fire hose. Usually mounted on four wheels with mail hubs and axles. Drawn by a pair of swift horses in pole gear.

Hose cart.   Smaller, two-wheeled version of the Hose Carriage. Drawn by a swift, single horse in shafts.

Hospital van.   Type of military ambulance used in the American Army for invalids and walking wounded. Fitted with reclining chairs rather than stretchers. First used at the National Military Hospital, Fort Leavenworth, Kansas, in 1888. Large numbers were eventually supplied by the Studebaker Company. Drawn by a pair of horses in pole gear.

Hotel coach.   Type of private omnibus, usually a single-decker, running on four wheels. Used in conveying passengers between railway stations and hotels. In North America a small version of the Concord Coach was often adapted for this purpose. Usually drawn by a pair of horses.

Hourly.   Short distance stage coach or omnibus of the late 19th century, that operated to an hourly schedule.

Howell gig.   Type of gig-phaeton first used in 1872, the prototype designed by a gentleman named Howell, residing in New York City. Much lighter than the original gig, adapted to suit the undergear of a sporting phaeton.

H.R.H. The Duke of Edinburgh's phaeton.   Competition phaeton for cross-country driving, designed and built to specifications of H.R.H. the Duke of Edinburgh. Made with an all-steel frame and plywood bodywork. Doors to the rearward passenger section are removable. Wheels are also of steel with flattened hubcaps. Drawn by a pair of horses or a larger team.

Hug-me-tight.   Slang name for an American Buggy with a narrow, crosswise seat and generally narrow proportions. Once favoured by American courting couples.

Huntingdon miller.   Miller's Wagon with a bowed fore-end, headed and fully enclosed. Drawn by a single horse in shafts. The sides were made of open spindles although with a solid mid-rave. Tyre treads were narrow.

Hunting wagon.   American four-wheeled wagon of the phaeton-type, used throughout the 19th century for sporting purposes. Seated six people on crosswise benches, facing forward. Hung on crosswise elliptical springs with deep cut-under of the forecarriage. Drawn by a single horse in shafts.

Hurdle cart.   Slang name for an English sporting dogcart, usually painted yellow and black. Drawn by a single horse or pair in tandem.

Hybrid.   Vehicle of any type made up from different parts of other vehicles. Delivery vans were frequently constructed on the underworks of an unwanted wagonette.

I

Ice cart. Two-wheeled American vehicle, used for the delivery of ice blocks, especially before domestic refrigerators became popular. Hung on crosswise elliptical springs. Drawn by a single horse.

Ice cream cart. Low-slung vehicle for the kerbside sale of ice cream and similar products. There were both two and four-wheeled types, each protected by an overhanging canopy-top or awning. The latter was striped in alternating colours, supported by corner poles of polished brasswork in barley-sugar twists. Drawn by a small horse or large pony in shafts, led rather than driven. Either sprung or dead axle. The upper parts of a few later types were protected by glass panels with a sliding hatch for serving purposes.

Ice or meat van. Two-wheeled vehicle – fully enclosed – of English design. The interior was lined throughout with zinc panels to improve insulation. Used in the delivery of ice blocks or bulk quantities of meat. Designed with a single roof seat. There was a large roof rack with protective side rails, also screw-down brakes. Wheels usually had iron naves. Hung on sideways elliptical springs.

Ice wagon. Large to medium-sized van or wagon, designed to carry ice for domestic purposes, on a street delivery basis. An enlarged version of the American Ice Cart. *See* Ice Cart. Fairly common in both urban and suburban areas throughout the second half of the 19th century. Frequently a type of box wagon but sometimes a covered van with a canopy top, having considerable overhang of the bodywork at front and rear. Hung on platform elliptical springs. The high-panelled sides of the exterior were frequently covered with painted canvasses, showing Arctic or Alpine scenes, used both as a decoration and to improve insulation. Drawn by a pair of horses in pole gear.

Improved trade van. Light-weight, four-wheeled van drawn by a single horse. Hung on two sideways and one crosswise (rearward) set of semi-elliptical springs. The enclosed bodywork had cut-under for full lock of the forecarriage, while the driving seat was under an arched canopy. Versions of this type were popular in both Europe and America throughout the second half of the 19th century.

Indian cart. 1. **Alternative name for the Tonga.** *See* Tonga.

2. Any type of light cart used in India, especially those of native origin.

Invalid carriage. Type of small phaeton, hooded and well-sprung. Usually hung on cee-springs or a combination of cee and elliptical springs. In many cases this vehicle was little more than a Bath-chair, adapted for pony draught. Sometimes driven by the occupant but more frequently led on foot by a groom. Some are known to have made use of three wheels only.

Italian gig. Early type of gig dating from the second half of the 18th century. Noted for its high wheels and elevated driving seat, the latter sometimes well in advance of the axle. Shafts were long and straight but highly resilient, partly responsible for suspension. There were also rearward braces and, at a later period, cee-springs. Mounted by means of a stirrup-shaped shaft-step, near the highly ornate dashboard. Suitable for one person only.

J

Jack cart. Primitive flat cart in small horse, cob and pony sizes. Without sideplanks or spindles but having hoop-raves above the wheels. A smaller version of the Jack Wagon or wain, used in hilly districts of the south west of England.

Jack wagon. Primitive dray or low-sided harvest wagon, the wheels surrounded by a sideways overlap of the loading platform, protected by side bows or hoop-raves. Drawn by a single horse.

Jagger wagon. Early type of square-shaped American Buggy, mainly apearing in New York State during the 1830's and 40's. At first unsprung or dead axle, but acquiring crosswise suspension, also a canopy top. Later known as a Spring Wagon.

Jaunting car. Also known as an Irish Jaunting, Jaunty Car or Side Car. A two-wheeled passenger vehicle with back-to-back, sideways-on seating. Developed from the earlier Trottle Car of Northern Ireland. *See* Trottle Car. First appeared in the streets of Dublin, as a means of public transport, about 1813. Bodywork was hung on shallow platform springs of the sideways semi-elliptical type. Two rows of seats had a common backrest and footboards. The driver's seat, where this appeared, was much higher than the passenger seats, directly above the shafts. In many cases the driver's feet would be supported by a small, separate footboard. At other times his feet might be braced against the shafts, which were of the outward curving or lyre-pattern. Some cars would be driven from one of the side seats, usually on the off-side. They normally carried two passengers on each side. A well or parcels rack sometimes appeared between the driving position and passenger seats. A few are still used and preserved as a tourist attraction, but were little needed for general passenger transport after the early 1930's.

Jaunting wagon. A four-wheeled version of the Jaunting Car, which came at a slightly later period. Similar to the Bian. *See* Bian. Popular in the United States, for private driving and sight-seeing, especially at holiday resorts, from the 1890's.

Jenny. Small, open carriage, either two or four-wheeled, drawn by a small pony or donkey. Usually hung on sideways semi-elliptical springs.

Jenny Lind. Light American Buggy with a canopy top, hung on crosswise elliptical springs. Named after the Swedish opera and concert singer Jenny Lind (the Swedish Nightingale), by whom it was frequently driven during her successful concert tour of the United States.

Jersey milk float. Dairyman's float of the early 1900's with a cranked axle, hung on sideways semi-elliptical springs. Usually panel-sided with curved shafts. Noted for high, curved splashers raised well-clear of the wheels, and curved front and side boards. Up to a capacity of 15 cwts. Usually drawn by a cob or large pony.

Jersey van. Type of wagonette, with a long wheelbase, used as public transport on the Island of Jersey, throughout the greater part of the 19th century. Now almost extinct.

Jersey wagon. Alternative name for a Coachee. *See* Coachee. A later type was more akin to the Depot Wagon. *See* Depot Wagon.

Jigger. American slang for a small single-decker tram or street car, drawn by a single horse.

Jingle. Country name, widely used in the south west of England, for a light driving car or cart, usually a tub cart.

Jinker. Headed or open driving cart of either small horse or pony size, mainly used in towns or cities of Victoria State, Australia. The name appears to be a corruption of Jingle.

Job wagon. Type of passenger wagon hired-out by job masters or the owners of livery stables. A name frequently used in England during the late 19th century.

Jockey carriage. Single-horse pleasure carriage, once fairly common at British seaside and holiday resorts, especially Scarborough. It resembled a Victoria but the single horse in shafts was ridden by a liveried postillion, known as a 'Jockey'. Mainly active between the 1880's and 1900's.

Jogging cart. Low-slung exercise cart, used for training and exercising trotting horses, especially for road work.

Jolt wagon. Primitive dead axle wagon, used in the Western states of North America during the second half of the 19th century. A version of the American Farm Wagon.

Juggernaut. 1. Temple on wheels dedicated to the Hindu god Vishnu. Although having the appearance of being drawn by horses these were usually carved representations, motive power being manual.

2. Any type of large, cumbersome vehicle, claimed to resemble Juggernaut 1.

Jump seat carriage. Any type of passenger vehicle with movable or jump seats. Frequently known in America as a Shifting Seat Carriage/Wagon.

Jump seat wagon. 1. American passenger wagon in which the rear seat can be jumped, reversed or inverted.

2. An alternative name for the Jump Seat Carriage.

K

Kalesch. The German name for a Calèche. *See* Calèche.

Kansas-Nebraska wagon. High-sided American farm wagon used in the Middle West of the United States, especially during the second half of the 19th century. A dead axle type but having a sprung driver's seat. The track or gauge between the wheels was narrower than with other types of farm wagon. Usually drawn by a pair of horses in pole gear.

Karid. Danish version of the Norwegian Cariole. *See* Cariole.

Karjol. Norwegian gig with a low, well-front, hung on semi-elliptical side springs. Frequently used for mail deliveries, especially in country districts.

Karozzin. Four-wheeled passenger carriage of Malta, drawn by a single horse or large pony. Seated four passengers vis-à-vis, under a high canopy roof or top. Hung on four sideways elliptical springs. Further noted for its high clearance above road level.

Kentish hop wagon. Same as a Hop Tug or Wagon. *See* Hop Tug or Wagon.

Kentish pole tug. Timber tug or trolley with a long wheelbase and narrow platform above the coupling pole (reach pole). There were also low side or out-raves. Usually dead axle. Drawn by two or more horses in tandem.

Kent wagon. A compact farm wagon of the box type, having panelled sides. Usually painted light buff with red wheels. Able to turn in quarter lock only.

Kibitka. Roughly made posting wagon used in Russia and other parts of Eastern Europe from the late Middle Ages. It was frequently a wooden framework held together by strands of rope, supporting hay-filled cushions or bundles of straw, in place of passenger seats. Sometimes protected from the weather by a canvas sheet secured over tilts or bows. Drawn by teams of various numbers.

Kirkbrik. Dutch – Church Break. Light wagon used by Dutch farmers in taking their families and neighbours to church. A fully enclosed vehicle that resembled a private omnibus, having cut-under of the forecarriage and hung on sideways elliptical springs. There were separate arrangements of seating for either catholics or protestants. Protestant types had separate seats for children. Drawn by a pair of medium-heavy draught horses in pole gear.

Kittereen. 1. Light, two-wheeled passenger cart, said to have been used in the town of Kettering, during the mid-19th century.

2. Four-wheeled passenger carriage used in Jamaiaca during the first half of the 19th century. Similar to an American Buggy with crosswise suspension and a falling hood.

Knacker's cart/van. Also known as a Dead Horse Cart. Used by knackers or horse butchers for recovering dead or fallen horses, often when killed in street accidents. The ample tailboard let down as a support and ramp over which the carcass might be winched. Sides of the bodywork were curved and surmounted by rows of metal or wooden spindles, each side having a prominent name-board. There was a crosswise seat for two, in the centre of the vehicle with a common back rest/rail. Hung on sideways semi-elliptical springs. Usually had straight rather than curved shafts. Drawn by a single black horse.

Knifeboard omnibus. Popular type of London omnibus intro-duced about 1851, although based on a similar vehicle first used in Paris. A double-decker, passengers on top were seated back-to-back, on longitudinal centre-seats, facing outwards. The only protection was a form of low side rail, not high enough to prevent numerous accidents, especially if passengers did not have enough time to find their seats before the vehicle started. Access to the upper deck was by means of an almost vertical ladder. Mounted on sideways semi-elliptical springs. Drawn by a pair of horses in pole gear. Replaced, from the 1880's, by the Garden Seat Omnibus. *See* Garden Seat Omnibus.

L

Ladder wagon. Continental-style farm wagon in which the sides were in the form of outward sloping ladders.

Ladies driving phaeton. Light or park phaeton, hung on sideways elliptical springs, front and rear. Usually had a low skeleton seat at the rear for a groom. Drawn either by a pair of horses in pole gear or a singe horse in shafts. An American version had a forward inclined dashboard and parasol top. Popular during the 1880's and 90's.

Ladies road wagon. American light road wagon, of a type frequently driven by ladies. The interior would be provided with a small looking glass and receptacle for vanity bags and other toilet requisites. Usually a headed or canopy-top vehicle, mounted on crosswise elliptical springs. Drawn by a single horse. Popular during the 1880's and 90's.

Lady Suffolk sulky. American metal-framed exercise cart, running on two wheels. Named after the famous trotting mare 'Lady Suffolk'.

Lancashire cart. Low-sided farm cart used in gathering the potato harvest and other root crops, especially in flat countryside of the Fylde. There was an upward curving centre line or midrail on both sides of the bodywork, supported by an inner row of spindles and an outer row of strouters or wooden supports. The frontboard or forehead inclined well forward above the shafts. Side raves were prominent and well-chamfered.

Lancashire coal cart. Strongly constructed coal delivery vehicle, drawn either by a single horse in shafts or tandem pair. Panel sided with a rearward inclined mid-rail and removable top or extension boards. Up to a capacity of two tons. Nave-band brakes, for holding back the load on steep hills, were operated in a rack on the near side of the vehicle. Led rather than driven.

Lake District cart. Typical horse-sized tumbril usually fitted with a semi-permanent rack or raves to support an overhanging load. The forward part of the rack extended as a ladder, well in advance of the forehead, above the hind-quarters of the horse in draught.

Lance truck. American military wagon, usually dead axle, with a long wheelbase. Used by the Signal Corps to carry poles or lances on which overhead (air) lines could be strung. Drawn by a pair of horses or larger teams.

Landau. Four-wheeled open or semi-open carriage, said to have been designed and first used in the Bavarian town of Landau, during the late 16th century. It came to England during the mid-18th century, but in a greatly improved and more compact version. Usually had two half-hoods of harness leather, protecting two opposite cross seats for four passengers, vis-à-vis. When raised the hoods would meet at the top to form an enclosed inner compartment. Various treatments were used to make the leather more flexible, but these sometimes gave-off an offensive odour. As the hoods would not lie flat they also began to look untidy, after a certain amount of wear. After about fifty years a greatly improved double-hood was introduced that lay flat when not required, taking up far less space than the earlier arrangement. There were eventually two main types of Landau, these being the square type with angular bodywork and the more elegant rounded or canoe-shaped vehicle. Both were hung first on cee-springs but later on sideways elliptical and semi-elliptical springs or a combination of both. Usually drawn by a pair of horses in pole gear, although a few smaller types were drawn by single horses in shafts. Most were driven from a box seat although a number of the larger, so-called State Landaus, had the box removed and were controlled by postillions. Purchased from £200 upwards.

Landaulet. A coupé version of the Landau, seating two passengers facing forward. A square type, the rear part protected by a falling hood or half hood. Drawn by either a single horse in shafts or a pair in pole gear. Hung on sideways elliptical and semi-elliptical springs.

Landship. English name for the Spanish or Latin American Barco-de-Tierra, as used in the Spanish colonies. *See* Barco-de-Tierra.

Land yacht. Name frequently given to early pleasure caravans, during the second half of the 19th century. Caravanning for persons of wealth and leisure was made popular by a travel book on this subject written by Dr. Gordon Stables, an ex-naval officer, by whom a tour of Britain was made in a purpose-built living van, known as 'The Land Yacht, Wanderer'. The privately-owned vehicles chosen by amateurs of the road, had a much longer wheelbase than the average Gypsy wagon, divided into two or more rooms. Usually drawn by a pair of medium-heavy horses in pole gear. The original 'Wanderer' is now the property of the Caravan Club, on semi-permanent loan to the Land Transport Gallery of Bristol Museum.

Laundry vans. The majority were four-wheeled in two main types. Both were hung on elliptical or semi-elliptical side springs. The earlier and more traditional type, especially in the London area and Home Counties, had a square, panel-sided body, headed by a canvas top on bows or tilts. A later type, seen mainly in the provinces, was more like a conventional delivery van with rear access, having a low tailboard and two small or half-doors above. The roof of the second type was either flat or arched, curved down at the front, but there were numerous variations. There may have been a footboard or toeboard on either vans, but seldom a proper dashboard. Drivers-in-charge sat on a crosswise bench large enough for two. Most vehicles turned in full underlock while lever or pedal brakes could be applied to the rear wheels. Cost from £45 to £50.

Lawrence wagon. Low-slung American Buggy of a type designed by James Lawrence of the Brewster Carriage Company of America, during the mid-19th century. More a maker's name than an actual style or type. A large vehicle, usually headed.

Lawton gig. A superior type of Liverpool gig, constructed by the English firm of Lawton, during the second half of the 19th century.

Lawton show phaeton. Elegant but strongly constructed Phaeton produced by the English firm of Lawton, intended for showing and park driving. Hung on sideways elliptical springs, front and rear. Drawn by a single horse.

Leamington cart. Light but elegant version of the English two-wheeled dogcart, named after the Warwickshire town of its origin. Hung on semi-elliptical side springs.

Leather quarter Landau. Early type of Landau in which the upper quarters were guarded by half-hoods of supple harness leather.

Ledge van. Medium-large Gypsy Wagon or Caravan. Its main feature was an overhanging section of the upper bodywork, which resembled the first story of a Tudor house or cottage, much wider at roof than floor level. Also known as the 'Cottage Van'. It contained the usual fittings of corner stove, cross bunks and bow-fronted cupboards. The bodywork was of matchboarding, richly carved and gilded. Many of this type were further noted for horizontal projections supporting the overhang of the porch, known as featherings. Hung on sideways semi-elliptical springs, front and rear. Provided with screw-down brakes operated from the porch. Some had a small hen-coop under the fore-part of the ledge.

Leeds cart.   Farm or road cart of a type widely used in the North East of England during the second half of the 19th century. A plank-sided tip cart, frequently fitted with semi-permanent end-ladders. Made in several different sizes for either one or two horses, the latter in tandem. The largest would be up to 35 cwts. capacity. An unsprung or dead axle cart.

Life boat carriage.   Low-slung carriage or set of limbered undergear, mounted on artillery wheels, used as a carrying frame. It appeared in many European countries, from the mid-19th century, for the purpose of launching coastal life boats. Pulled out to sea by a team of eight or more horses and slipped into the surge of its own volition, when the water was high enough. Horses were replaced by tractors during the period between the world wars, although a horse-drawn carriage is still used on the island of Ameland, in Holland.

Lift van or trolley.   Flat dray or trolley, either sprung or dead axle, used in handling container traffic, especially in dockland areas. The small, sturdy wheels were usually equirotal, able to turn in full lock. Either led rather than driven or with an elevated driving seat fixed to brackets on the front board. Drawn by a pair of heavy horses in pole gear. The demountable container could be hoisted from the loading platform by crane-power, then lowered into the hold of a ship. Widely used, especially for overseas house removals or furniture deliveries, from the 1880's.

Light carriage.   Usually an open or lightly built carriage, drawn by a single horse or pony in shafts.

Light drop-fronted phaeton.   Light-weight American Phaeton of the 1870's. Hung on crosswise elliptical springs, front and rear. Frequently appeared with an umbrella or parasol top. Drawn by a single horse.

Light spring cart.   Light, cheap version of the market cart, made in both cob and pony sizes, at a cost of between £15 and £20. Able to seat four passengers dos-à-dos. A narrow tailboard let down at the rear, useful for loading market wares and to support the feet of rearward facing passengers. A slightly later type of the 1890's was higher and with straight rather than curved shafts, this being known as an Improved Light Spring Cart.

Light spring float. Pony-sized float, used by dairymen in a small line of business, from the 1900's to the 1950's. Usually mounted on cranked axles with sideways elliptical under-springs. Shafts would be well-curved. Cost from £22 to £25.

Light spring milk cart. A milk delivery van or cart more in the style of a butcher's two-wheeled delivery vehicle than the conventional float. There were two main types, both with straight (patent) axles and straight shafts. On both types the driver mounted via shaft steps or step irons. The slightly more popular version made in pony, cob and full-horse sizes, had a body of double panelling, with fully enclosed sides, front and rear. There was a crosswise seat for the driver but neither back nor arm-rests. Churns or cans of milk were placed in a rearward part, behind the movable seat. There would be an aperture in the tailboard, through which the tap of a large, vertical milk churn might project for filling jugs at street level. Hung on sideways semi-elliptical springs, both front and rear.

The slightly cheaper Spring Milk Cart was usually a cob-drawn vehicle, having a semi-open front with a toeboard rather than a footboard. The sides were partly open or slatted and the upper side board or panel, on each side, curved above wheel level, sometimes with additional name board and hand rail. The driver's seat also had a low back rest. Both types were frequently constructed with mail hubs and axles. Popular during the 1880's and 90's.

Light spring milk van. Compact, four-wheeled milk delivery van, similar to the so-called Station Milk Van. *See* Station Milk Van. Made in cob and full-horse sizes. Sides were semi-open or slatted, topped by curved name boards and hand rails. The cross seat for the driver, unlike that of the Station Milk Van and the Light Spring Milk Cart, had a high back rest. Hung on a three-spring system of suspension. Used for town deliveries rather than country or station work. Up to 25 cwts. capacity. Cost from £30 to £34.

Light spring parcel van. Light, square or oblong-sided delivery van as used by drapers, confectioners, grocers and in a variety of other trades. Noted for its short wheelbase but fairly high wheels. The cross bench or driving seat was usually shared by the driver and his assistant or delivery boy. The main part of the fully enclosed and headed bodywork was slightly higher than the driving seat and inclined in a rearward direction. An iron hand rail surrounded the head or roof. Able to turn in full lock. Hung on sideways elliptical or semi-elliptical side springs, front and rear.

Loaded to a capacity of between 15 and 20 cwts. Drawn by a single horse.

Light spring tipping cart.   Small luggage and/or tip cart, used for general delivery purposes. The interior cross seat had a high back rest. Small end-ladders and outraves could be fitted to support an overhanging load. Made in four sizes, but mainly for cobs or small horses. Hung on sideways semi-elliptical springs. Up to a capacity of 20 cwts.

Limbers.   Two-wheeled ammunition or tool carts, made in pairs for military service. The ammunition type could also be used to support the trail of a field gun, for both horse and tractor haulage. When hooked together both parts combined to form an articulated unit, more flexible in open country than the General Service Wagon, which it partly replaced from the 1900's. Although taking up more room and carrying a smaller load than the General Service Wagon, limbers could move at greater speed over rougher terrain, in the care of mounted drivers. This made them ideal for supporting cavalry and horse artillery, rather than the slower moving infantry. While usually appearing together each limber of a pair could be detached and used separately. Similar vehicles of the articulated type, in civil life, were also known as limbers.

Lincolnshire cart.   Medium-sized, low-sided tip cart, mainly used for harvesting potato and other root crops. Sometimes spindle-sided. Unsprung or dead axle. Drawn by a single horse in shafts.

Lincolnshire wagon.   Box wagon with high, spindled sides and a short wheelbase. Frequently used with corner poles rather than end-ladders. Usually dead axle. Drawn by one or two horses, the latter in tandem. Turned only in quarter lock.

Limousine.   Cut down version of the American Rockaway, seating two people only, or a passenger and driver. Headed or covered with a standing top on corner pillars. Hung on crosswise elliptical springs.

Lineika.   Russian carriage similar to the Droshky but much larger, seating four passengers vis-à-vis. Open or semi-open with a falling hood. Drawn by a troika, or three horses abreast.

Liverpool float.   Dairyman's float of the 1900's. Hung on sideways semi-elliptical springs and a cranked axle. Curved shafts were fixed to the front boards by means of metal brackets. The wheels frequently had mail hubs. Entered through the rear by means of an outward opening door and step iron. Supplied with a crosswise rear seat, but often driven in a standing position. Up to 15 cwts. capacity, usually in cob sizes.

Liverpool gig. Fully enclosed, square-sided gig, elegant although sturdy and workmanlike. Without rearward access to the luggage space but with a large buck under the cross seat. First made and used in Liverpool, but later widespread throughout the British Isles, from the mid-19th century.

Liverpool market cart. A slightly larger and more robust version of the Manchester Market Cart. Panel-sided with a low tailboard on letting-down chains. Seated four, dos-à-dos. Shafts were slightly curved. Made in full-horse sizes only. Hung on both sideways and rearward-crosswise, semi-elliptical springs. Up to 20 cwts. capacity. Cost £25.

Liverpool market gig. Lighter and slightly smaller version of the Liverpool Market Cart, without rearward seating. Usually made with plain rather than panel sides.

Livery hack. 1. Alternative name for the American Mountain (Passenger) Wagon.

2. Type of vehicle hired by members of the general public for casual or pleasure driving, usually from a livery stables.

Logging wagon. American name for an articulated, four-wheeled log or lumber wagon. Logs or lengths of felled timber carried were supported at either end by bunks or false bolsters, plus true bolsters and stanchions. Drawn by two or more horses in pole gear.

Logging wheels. Large pair of wheels, similar to the Nib or Neb, for which this was an alternative name. The diameter of the wheels was about 8′. Used for transporting logs, which were hung from the arched under-side but allowed to trail at the rear. Drawn by a single heavy horse or pair of horses.

London brewer's dray. Typical brewer's dray of London and the Home Counties. It appeared in several sizes, the largest up to a load of 12 barrels, about 15′ in length. Long metal rods, down both sides of the loading platform, were useful for the attachment of skids, down which barrels were slid to ground level. Each dray carried a pair of demountable skids under the hind-carriage, secured in a special rack. Driven from an elevated seat on vertical irons, having a book box, for paper work, under the footboard. An off-side lever brake acted on the rear wheels. Usually drawn by a pair of horses in pole gear.

London builder's cart. High-sided tip cart with side raves and a prominent forward extension to support an overhanging load.

Wheel treads were at least 6″ wide. Up to loads of 25 cwts. although certain types, used with chain horses in tandem, could handle over 2 tons. Cost about £16.

London builder's van. Short-wheelbased builder's van or wagon, frequently used in the London area from the 1880's to the 1920's. Panel-sided of oblong-boxlike appearance. Fitted with prominent side or out-raves to cope with an overhanging load. Driven from an elevated cross seat, mounted on vertical irons. A lever brake acted on the rear wheels. Either dead axle or hung on sideways semi-elliptical springs. The loading platform was about 8′ long. Up to a capacity of 3 tons. Usually drawn by a pair of horses in pole gear, although sometimes adapted to a single horse in shafts.

London butcher's cart. Metal-lined cart, of light but sturdy construction and almost streamlined appearance. Noted for its fully enclosed but curved and sloping fore-end, beneath the crosswise driving seat. Hung on both side and crosswise semi-elliptical springs. Made in both cob and pony sizes. Cost £20 to £25.

London butcher's van. A larger version of the London Butcher's Cart but running on four wheels. Hung on sideways elliptical or semi-elliptical springs, both front and rear. Made in both cob and full-horse sizes. Cost about £40.

London carman's trolley. A strongly framed trolley for conveying bar iron, small girders and lengths of timber, etc. Noted for its outward inclined side raves and movable crosswise bolsters. Either dead axle or hung on a combination of lengthwise and cross springs. Fitted with either shafts or pole gear. In later years a few were fitted with drawbars for mechanical haulage. About 12′ long and up to a capacity of 5 tons. Usually drawn by large teams of heavy horses.

London dairy van. Four-wheeled, open van with low sides. Hung on sideways elliptical or semi-elliptical springs, front and rear. The driver's seat was the full width of the bodywork. Although a few appear to have been made without brakes the majority had pedal brakes acting on the rear wheels. The fore-carriage turned in full lock. Drawn by a singe horse or cob in shafts.

London forage cart. Large but light-running cart, used in taking bulk loads of hay and straw from wharves or station yards to either commercial stables or cattle markets, in the London area. There were both forward and sideways projecting raves to cope with overhang. Hung on sideways semi-elliptical springs. Made in three sizes, the largest up to a capacity of 25 cwts.

London hay cart. A larger version of the London Forage Cart, having a long, almost vertical ladder at the fore-end, extending above the hind-quarters of the shaft horse. The extremities of this ladder or support ended in a graceful upward curve.

London mineral water van. Open, four-wheeled delivery van used by manufacturers of mineral waters and bottled soft drinks. Well-stayed with heavy side irons supporting a slatted wooden framework. Similar in many aspects to the construction of certain railway cartage vans. Hung on sideways semi-elliptical springs, although some also had crosswise elliptical suspension. Drawn by a pair of medium-heavy horses in pole gear. The largest or full-horse type would be up to 3 tons capacity.

London parcels van. Strongly constructed delivery van running on four wheels. The sides were often of double thickness mahogany panels, boarded-up inside the head or roof. There were rearward double doors, while the semi-enclosed driver's seat had side lights or small windows. Hung on sideways semi-elliptical springs at the rear and full elliptical side springs at the front. Turned in full lock. Drawn by a single horse or cob. Cost between £50 and £55.

London railway delivery van. Usually a four-wheeled, pair-horse van, fitted with either double shafts or pole gear. A similar type was also used by independent road haulage companies, although frequently acting as agents for the main line railway companies. The arrangement of side planks was partly open or slatted, alternating between horizontal planks and iron rods. Wooden out-raves protected the wheels from an overhanging load. Hung on sideways semi-elliptical springs, front and rear. The driver's seat above the fore-end, was mounted on 'Y'-shaped irons. Made in 11'/12' lengths, although a few smaller types were only 8' long. Similar vans in the provinces tended to have solid rather than slatted sides.

London timber trolley. Long-wheelbased trolley, the low plank sides much higher at the front than the rear. Hung on sideways semi-elliptical springs, front and rear. Resembled the London Coal Trolley or Carriage but minus side spindles and bowed front. Fitted with either shafts or pole gear for single horses or pairs. About 12' in length, the largest sizes being up to 4 tons capacity.

Long hay or harvest cart. Low-slung, plank-sided cart, the platform of considerable length. Designed to carry trusses or bales of hay. Drawn by a single horse.

Long shaft or timber lob. Similar to the Timber Neb or Nib, but having much longer shafts, well-dished wheels and rearward projecting boom or derrick for raising felled timber. The derrick would be operated from a windlass at the rear-end of the shafts, able to slew through 180 degrees.

Long wagon. Travelling carriage of the dead axle type, without underlock. Versions of this vehicle were used in Britain and other European countries throughout the 13th and 14th centuries. Headed or protected by canvas covers on hoops, with rich embroidery work. Inner seats were slung on the hammock principle. Drawn by teams of six or more horses, controlled by postillions. Also known a the 'Whirlicote'.

Lonsdale wagonette. Also known as the Lonsdale Break. Vehicle said to have been designed and first used by the then Earl of Lonsdale, towards the end of the 19th century, but may have been based on an earlier type of the 1860's. Among its characteristic features were two lengthwise hoods or heads that let-down in a sideways-on position, meeting in the centre when raised. Each hood had a small window or light of oblong-oval shape. Hung on sideways full or semi-elliptical springs. Drawn either by a single horse in shafts or a pair in pole gear.

Lorry. Name used in country districts, especially the North of England, for an open truck, dray or trolley. Large numbers were formerly used by the railway cartage departments for general haulage and delivery purposes. Frequently unsprung with equirotal or near equirotal wheels. Up to a capacity of 8 tons. Drawn by a single horse in shafts but more frequently by large teams of chain horses. Driven from the fore-end of the plaform in a standing position. During the Second World War a number of smaller types were fitted with pneumatic tyres – and, being cheap and easy to construct – considered valuable (as an economy measure) in a time of grave material shortages.

Low down milk wagon. Alternative name for the Parson's Milk Van or Wagon. Noted for its mid-way, well-like driving position. Reins to a single horse or large pony, passed through apertures in a windscreen, at the fore-end. Difficult to drive or control, especially in heavy traffic, but much easier to load and enter than the former high-platform milk wagon. Hung on sideways semi-elliptical and/ or full elliptical springs. Mainly popular in the United States and Canada from the 1900's to the 1940's. A similar type was used in Britain during the 1930's.

Lumber buggy. Slang name, mainly used in North America, for any type of vehicle used when 'logging' or transporting timber.

Lumber wagon.   An unsprung or dead axle (often articuated) vehicle, used for hauling logs or lumber. The fore and hind parts were detachable, similar to military limbers. *See* Limbers. Both parts were connected by means of a coupling or reach pole. Drawn by teams of three or more heavy horses in chain gear, although the wheeler would be in shafts.

Luggage cart.   Either a two or four-wheeled vehicle, with or without double rows of crosswise seating. Used in the conveyance of luggage/parcels, etc., to and from country houses and hotels. Not usually headed, although protected by a waterproofed canvas cover, in wet weather, sometimes on hoops. Either sprung or dead axle. Drawn by a single horse. Four-wheeled types usually had lever brakes acting on the rear wheels.

Lunch wagon.   American name for a horse-drawn snack bar or coffee stall. One side would be open, when in business, normally protected by folding shutters. There would be a long counter, with storage shelves and cooking facilities to the rear. Entered through an end door by means of removable wooden steps. Hung on sideways semi-elliptical springs, front and rear. Some had a driving seat either at roof level or fixed on brackets, but most were led rather than driven. Popular from the 1890's to the 1940's. Drawn by a single horse in shafts or – less frequently – by a pair in pole gear.

Lurry.   Alternative name for Lorry, especially in the North of England. *See* Lorry.

M

Madras cart.   Two-wheeled vehicle for military service, usually a small arms ammunition cart of a type first used in India. Shafts were fixed to the wheel hubs, over which they looped – secured by external through-pins. Drawn by a single horse or mule.

Mail cart.   Light, two-wheeled cart, formerly used to collect and deliver mail, especially in the outer suburbs and country districts. Made in horse, cob and pony sizes, but sometimes drawn by a donkey, especially in Cornwall and the south west of England. Usually hung on sideways semi-elliptical springs although the prototypes may have been dead axle.

Mail coach.   *See* Coach, Mail.

Mail delivery truck.   Square-bodied American Mail Van, hung on crosswise elliptical springs, front and rear. A glass panel or windscreen could be made to open at the upper-front, for better control of the reins. Entered through side doors – one on each side, via low step irons. The interior had a small compartment for sorting letter post. Drawn by a single horse in shafts.

Mail jerker. American passenger wagon, suspended on thoroughbraces. A smaller version of the Concord Coach. Fitted with two or three rows of crosswise seats facing forward. At first semi-open although later types had a fixed top. Also known as a Western Passenger Wagon. Drawn by two or more horses in pole gear.

Mail phaeton. Massive Phaeton of the 1820's, that resembled a stage or mail coach minus the enclosed passenger compartment. Frequently used for exercising coach horses, leisure driving and delivering local mails. Drawn by two or more horses harnessed in pole gear, using chains rather than leather traces. Fitted with mail hubs and axles, also having a strong underperch and hung on sideways semi-elliptical or Telegraph springs. The high front seat was hooded while the rear or groom's seat (rumble) was contained within a traylike (open) compartment entered through side doors by means of step irons.

Mail wagon. Type of square, panel-sided delivery wagon, of the late 19th century. Hung on sideways elliptical springs, front and rear. Versions were used in both Britain and North America for delivering parcels mail. Drawn by a single horse.

Mallee jinker. Australian driving sulky named after a part of Victoria State where they were first made and used, during the early 1900's. Well-upholstered and sprung, considered an improvement on the Sydney or Stock's Sulky of a slightly earlier period. Drawn by a single horse or pony in curved shafts.

Malle post or mail post. German or Austrian name for a Diligence or public mail coach, as used on Alpine routes.

Maltese cart. Small military cart usually drawn by a pony, cob or mule, but sometimes adapted as a hand cart. First used in the British Army, for imperial service, during the 1860's. Later employed for base work in most camps or barracks, especially where a large vehicle – either horse-drawn or mechanical – would be inappropriate. Usually a mere carrying frame of cross members, used for ammunition boxes, entrenching tools and general supplies. When coal, coke or builder's materials needed to be moved the floor could be boarded-up, forming a loading platform of the conventional type. Front and tailboards could be inserted as required. Dead axle or unsprung. There were five marks, some later types used until the end of the Second World War.

Malt wagon. High-sided, dead axle wagon, usually lined and waterproofed, used in the delivery and distribution of brewer's malt. Drawn either by a single horse or pair of horses, the latter in double shafts or pole gear.

Malvern cart. Light, elegant version of the two-wheeled dogcart. First used and constructed in Great Malvern, Worcestershire. The bodywork was lower than the usual vehicle of this type and easier to mount. Seated four, dos-à-dos.

Manchester fish cart. Low-sided cart suitable for either the retail fishmonger or the poulterer. Made in full-horse or cob sizes, both with straight shafts. There was a simple crosswise seat with low dashboard, mounted via stirrup loops rather than ordinary shaft steps. Hung on sideways semi-elliptical springs. The tailboard was secured by letting down chains.

Manchester goods cart. Panel-sided cart used for general town cartage and delivery purposes, usually in the Manchester area. The sides were semi-open with protective front and side rails. Hung on two sets of sideways elliptical and one set of crosswise elliptical springs. Well-stayed with strong ironwork. Made in three sizes, the largest up to 45 cwts. capacity.

Manchester market cart. Popular market cart of the 1860's although widely used throughout the second half of the 19th century, being in the medium price range. A sturdy but well-finished type, first appearing in the Manchester district and the north-west. Panel-sided with a heavy oak framework. Shafts were either straight or curved, but usually the former. Seated two or four, dos-à-dos. Drawn by a small horse or cob.

Mangonel. Type of large sling-engine or catapult running on four wheels, used in siege warface. Versions mounted on crude travelling carriages were known throughout the Middle Ages. Drawn by large teams of horses or oxen as part of the military train.

Mantelet. Type of mobile shield or shelter running on four wheels, forming part of the military train, throughout the Middle Ages. Used to protect pioneers when digging saps or trenches, especially in siege warfare. Drawn by teams of either horses or oxen.

Mantua single cart. An Italian gig or sulky with room for one person only.

Manure or muck cart. Tipping cart with lengthwise rather than crosswise floorboards. Used in distributing farmyard manure on arable land. Lengthwise boards made it easier for unloading and scraping-out. The frontboard or forehead was slightly higher than the tailboard. Also known as a Dung Cart.

Margitson and Hek tip wagon. Four-wheeled garbage wagon of a patent type, first manufactured by the Britol Wagon and Carriage Company from the 1880's. Named after its patentees and used in various municipal boroughs until the mid-1950's. High-sided and able to tip in either rearward or sideways directions. Drawn either by a single horse in shafts or pair in pole gear, the driver standing on a narrow front platform. There were three sizes, the largest up to a capacity of 2½ cubic yards. Hung on sideways elliptical or semi-elliptical springs.

Market cart. Two-wheeled vehicle used in country districts and town suburbs by tradesmen and small dealers. Popular from the 1850's to the 1920's. Strongly built with panelled sides, crosswise seating and a rearward space for market produce. Usually without a footboard or dashboard. In some versions there might be a rearward seat for extra passengers. In most cases the seating plan would be dos-à-dos. A compromise vehicle between a smart gig and ordinary goods cart.

Market and station cart. High-wheeled Market Cart, frequently used in rural areas, for station deliveries and collections. Hung on sideways elliptical or semi-elliptical springs, also having mail hubs and axles. There were mudguards or splashers over both wheels, while the low front also served as a footboard. Normally carried up to 15 cwts. Drawn by a single horse or cob.

Market float. Farmer's float with cranked axles and spindles above side panels. Entered through the front by means of a shaft step or iron. The tail-board was deep enough to let down as a ramp. Small livestock such as pigs or sheep could be transported in the rearward part, secured under nets. Hung on sideways semi-elliptical springs.

Market wagon. A light, four-wheeled wagon, driven from an elevated seat of skeletal structure with angled footboard. Used for general delivery purposes in and around market areas. Either plank or panel-sided, hung on sideways elliptical springs under the forecarriage and sideways semi-elliptical springs under the hind-carriage. A pedal brake acted on the rear wheels. Drawn by a single horse or cob in shafts.

Martin's dogcart. Dogcart Phaeton with full cut-under of the fore-wheels. Hung on sideways elliptical springs, front and rear. Drawn by a single horse in shafts or pair in pole gear.

Matinee wagon. American show wagon of light but sturdy construction, drawn by a single horse or pony, according to size. The wire-spoked wheels were secured by double frames. Painted in white or light pastel shades. Usually appeared at shows in morning or afternoon classes. Darker vehicles were reserved for evening or more formal appearances.

Meadow Brook cart. Alternative name for the East Williston Cart. *See* East Williston Cart.

Medical Brougham. Small Brougham designed for the daily use of doctors and other professional men. A wheelbase of only 30 inches between front and rear wheels offered great advantages in parking and turning.

Medical cart. Small, two-wheeled military vehicle, with a hinged lid or cover. Used to carry medicines, dressings and surgical equipment in the field or line of march. Either sprung or dead axle. Drawn by a single horse, pony or mule. Led rather than driven.

Menagerie wagon. Also known as a Cage Wagon. *See* Cage Wagon.

Merchandise truck. American heavy dray hung on sideways semi-elliptical springs. The loading platform sloped in a rearward direction, for greater ease of loading. Sides were protected by upright stakes or pillars. Mainly used in the streets of New York, and a few other large cities, handled by teams of grey stallions, which served as an advertisement for the firm using them. Driven from an elevated seat directly above the fore-axle. Up to loads of between 6 and 8 tons.

Merchant's wagon. Near cube-shaped American delivery van, drawn by a single horse. The driving seat was semi-open, protected on both sides by roll-down blinds. Short wheelbased. Hung on sideways semi-elliptical springs, front and rear, although some also had rearward cross springs.

Midlands float. Large delivery float, also used for farm and agricultural purposes. Made with a cranked axle and hung on semi-elliptical side springs. The curved shafts were supported by diagonal brackets. Noted for a pattern of elaborate chamfering, especially along the waist or mid-line. Head and side boards had a series of fanciful curves. Much higher at the front than the rear.

Midlands trolley. High, flat trolley without either raised sides or outraves. Mainly used for general cartage work and harvesting. Wheels were near equirotal. Either dead axle or hung on sideways semi-elliptical springs, front and rear. Drawn by a single horse or cob in shafts. Usually factory made. Popular on the average mixed farm from the 1890's to the 1930's.

Miller's cart. High-fronted, panel-sided cart used for carrying sacks of flour. Hung on three sets of semi-elliptical springs. Up to a capacity of 30 cwts. Drawn either by one or two horses, the latter in tandem chain gear.

Miller.   Contraction of Miller's Wagon. Usually a covered or headed vehicle of which there were several regional types.

Miller's wagon.   This resembled the ordinary farm wagon of the box type, but with higher than average sides and loading platform. Used to convey sacks of both grain and flour. Usually drawn by a single heavy horse but sometimes a pair in double shafts or pole gear. Cost from £36 to £49.

Miller's wagon (London type).   Single or pair-horse wagon with panelled sides, rising towards the fore-end. Hung on sideways semi-elliptical springs, front and rear. The single driving seat, with angled footboard, was of skeletal structure on vertical irons, well in advance of the fore-axle. Adapted to either double shafts or pole gear.

Mill wagon.   High-sided builder's wagon or van, usually drawn by a single horse.

Milord.   Continental version of the Cab-Phaeton, drawn by a single horse. A vehicle representing a stage of development in the evolution of the Victoria. Early 19th century.

Mineral water trolley.   A smaller and lighter version of the London Mineral Water Van, although more in the style of an open dray. The near equirotal wheels had thick, strongly made spokes. Hung on sideways semi-elliptical springs, front and rear. The elevated driving seat was mounted on curved irons with a footboard projecting well forward. Approximately half the rearward part of the loading platform was protected by stanchions and decorative metal scrollwork. An off-side pedal brake acted on both rear wheels. Drawn by a single horse in shafts. Cost about £32.

Miniature Lanadau.   Small-sized Landau, frequently drawn by a pair of ponies. Easy to enter and suitable for elderly persons or invalids.

Minibus.   Alternative name for the Boulnoise Cab of the mid-19th century. *See* Boulnois Cab.

Missionary van.   Vehicle used by evangelical missions, frequently appearing at public gatherings or sporting events and in market places, from the 1880's to the 1920's. A type of living van with side bunks and a heating-cooking stove, also wardrobe space for one or two persons. The forecarriage turned in full lock under an enlarged front porch, the latter having access on both sides by means of removable wooden steps. Some had a clerestory section at roof level, for improved lighting and ventilation. There were windows on both sides and at the rear, protected by shutters. The front porch could be used as an improvised pulpit to address prayer meetings. Hung on several arrangements of sideways and crosswise elliptical or semi-elliptical springs. Drawn by a single horse, driven from the porch or led on foot. A larger type may have used a pair of horses in pole gear.

Mobile pigeon loft.   Four-wheeled military vehicle used by the Royal Engineers of the British Army. There were both inner and outer doors, with wire mesh release cages at top and sides. Drawn by two horses in pole gear, the driver's single seat being on the off-side of the main entrance, supported by letting-down chains. The forewheels were slightly smaller than the rearwheels, but turned in quarter lock only. Hung on sideways semi-elliptical springs at the rear and full elliptical springs at the front. Ladders were frequently carried in a horizontal position on both sides of the bodywork. The French Army use a smaller mobile loft in the form of a bow-topped cart.

Mock calèche.   Passenger vehicle in which the upper quarters were removable. The rearward end was fully panelled but without a folding or falling top.

Monachus.   Gig of Ancient Rome, higher and slightly larger than the Cisium.

Monalos.   Type of American Buggy first used in Boston and district, Massachusetts (U.S.A.), about the year 1866. A sulky intended for a single person only, usually the owner-driver. There were equirotal wheels and thoroughbraces rather than cross springs. Frequently mounted on cranked axles.

Monkey-tail post chaise.   Known on the Continent as 'Chais de poste à cul de singe'. Two-wheeled but fully enclosed version of the post chaise, frequently used in France and Germany throughout the second half of the 18th century. Suitable for only one passenger at a time, facing forward. Entered through a front door that opened on to a narrow platform, although shut-in by a hood-shaped dashboard. Drawn by two horses, one in shafts and the other attached to an extension bar of the near-side shaft, keeping the outer horse (controlled by a postillion) slightly ahead of its partner, especially when turning corners. Luggage was carried at both front and rear, between diagonal braces and/or whip springs of the suspension.

Monmouthshire wagon.   Often a smaller and simpler version of the Worcestershire Wagon, in turn derived from the Staffordshire

Wagon. Panel-sided and well-chamfered. Able to turn in quarter lock only. Usually drawn by a single horse.

Monocycle. A barrowlike truck with one wheel, drawn by a single horse. Invented by an English engineer named Hammond, about 1832. Tested for both agricultural and trade purposes but little used in either sphere. Claimed to be cheaper and easier to repair than the two-wheeled cart.

Moore's coal carriage. A high-wheeled, spindle-sided coal carriage or trolley of the late 18th century, invented by Francis Moore of London. Claimed to be the ancestor of the London Coal Wagon, Van or Trolley, used in street deliveries for over two centuries.

Moore's high-wheeled carriage. An unusual type of public carriage, mounted on an exceptionally high pair of wheels. Invented by Francis Moore of London (also inventor of the Coal Carriage) in 1771. It had several features in common with the much later Hansom Cab, but the passenger compartment for six or more people, tended to be cramped and over-crowded – even for its size. Driven from a seat fixed in the centre of the flat roof, which proved difficult to mount.

Moray car. Type of two-wheeled dogcart, slung fairly low. Usually drawn by a small horse or large pony. Bodywork was arched above the axle for greater ease in entering and leaving the vehicle, bringing the floor nearer to road level. The upper part on each side formed an ogee curve, while shallow side springs were clipped to the underside of the axle (leaf springs). Popular in most parts of Britain from the 1860's to the 1900's.

Moreg. Early type of threshing machine or box, mounted on either two or four wheels. Drawn between farms and holdings, in the Lowlands of Scotland, by a single horse in shafts. Mainly worked on a contract basis.

Morgan cart. Alternative name for the English Cab-fronted Gig. Named after its designer.

Morning cart. Light, hooded gig of the mid-19th century. Hung on cee-springs. Frequently driven by a lady to a single horse or pony.

Morovi car. A version of the Ralli Car with dos-à-dos seating. Shafts were usually inside the bodywork.

Mortar wagon. Type of low-slung military vehicle – frequently limbered – used in conveying a siege mortar, as part of the military train. Drawn by two or more horses, led rather than driven. Several versions and sizes were used from the late Middle Ages to the mid-19th century.

Motor back sulky. Australian sulky of the 1900's. The driving seat was high-backed and well upholstered, with arm-rests, in the style of an early motor car. A popular show vehicle for over fifty years.

Motor car lorry. A low-slung lorry or dray of the 1900's with small but sturdy, equirotal wheels. Suitable for the delivery of motor vehicles, which co'·'ld be winched on to the loading platform over a rearward ramp. Drawn by a pair of heavy horses in pole gear. Hung on sideways semi-elliptical springs, front and rear. Much larger and heavier than similar vehicles used for delivering carriages. Driven from a single, elevated seat, mounted on brackets, above the high frontboard. Some had single (vertical) side planks, supported on either side by a midway projection or earsbreadth.

Mountain passenger wagon. Type of American passenger wagon, used in mountainous regions of the far West, from the mid-19th century to the 1900's. Seated either two or four persons on crosswise seats, which were little more than crude planks. Fitted with a high, standing top and having ample rearward luggage space. Usually hung on thoroughbraces rather than cross springs. Drawn by a single horse or pair of horses in pole gear.

Mountain farm wagon. Also known as a Mountain Wagon. Heavy, high-sided American farm wagon, used in highland districts, especially in the far West. Noted for its powerful lever brakes, necessary on steep tracks. Drawn by a pair of horses in pole gear. Similar to the California or Rack Bed Wagon, but with a shorter wheelbase and lower capacity. Dead axle but with a sprung driving seat.

Mud wagon. What might be termed a poor relation of the American Concord Coach. A cheaper, slightly smaller version of this type, not usually entrusted with the mails or valuables. Open-sided with minimum protection from the weather, its passengers frequently splashed with mud and mire.

Murphy wagon. High-sided American freight wagon, used in the Western States, throughout the greater part of the 19th century. Designed by a Joseph Murphy of St. Louis, Missouri, in 1826. Usually dead axle but able to carry up to 3 tons. Drawn by a pair of medium-heavy horses in pole gear.

Mylord. Alternative name, frequently used in North America, for the Milord. *See* Milord.

N

New York butcher's cart. Low, panel-sided delivery cart, enclosed at the front but without dash or footboard. Hung on sideways elliptical or semi-elliptical springs. Fitted with straight shafts. Drawn by a single pony or cob. Popular throughout the second half of the 19th century.

New York delivery van. Light but strongly built four-wheeled delivery van, with inward curving sides and a semi-enclosed driving seat. Hung on a three spring system, both front and rear, with sideways and crosswise semi-elliptical springs. Drawn by a single horse or cob.

New Zealand Cobb coach. Version of the Concord Coach, widely used for long distance passenger transport and mail deliveries in both islands of New Zealand, until the coming of railways. A slightly modified version of an even earlier type used in the Australian outback, minus a forward facing rear seat for the guard. Seated 14 passengers. *See* Concord and Cobb Coach.

New Zealand rural mail carrier's wagonette-omnibus. Headed or semi-open wagonette-type vehicle, used for passenger carrying and mail deliveries, on short or country journeys, in both islands of New Zealand. Drawn by a pair of horses in pole gear, or a four-in-hand team, according to routes and gradients. Hung on sideways elliptical or semi-elliptical springs. Entered through a rearward door by means of two stepirons. Passengers (either six or four) sat facing each other on either side of a central gangway, as on the lower deck of a horse-drawn omnibus. Sides of the vehicle were unglazed but frequently protected by roll-down blinds or tarpaulins.

New Zealand settler's wagon. Light spring wagon with low sides and near equirotal wheels. There were also permanent out-raves, known as bars or outbars. Two sets of semi-elliptical springs were frequently mounted in an inverted crosswise position. Up to a capacity of 30 cwts. Drawn by two medium-sized horses in pole gear.

New Zealand spring cart. Light but strongly built gig or driving cart, drawn by a single horse or large pony. Hung on sideways semi-elliptical springs.

Nib or neb. Also known as a Timber Bob or Pair of Wheels. Used for trailing logs or lengths of timber beneath an arched framework.

Night biner. Slang name in New York City, for a cab or public transport carriage running at a late hour.

Night hawk. Slang name for an all-night cab, usually a four-wheeler.

Night owl. Alternative name for a Night Hawk. *See* Night Hawk.

Noddy. Two-wheeled public carriage popular in Scotland and Northern Ireland during the early 19th century. A type of chaise with room for three passengers on crosswise seating. Early types were drawn by a single horse, but – in later years – pairs were used, harnessed to a carriage pole. Frequently headed. Hung on sideways elliptical springs.

Norfolk cart. Type of shooting cart or two-wheeled dogcart, widely used in East Anglia from the mid-19th century. Frequently slat-sided with a grained and varnished finish of natural wood. Hung on sideways semi-elliptical springs. Shafts were either straight or curved.

Norfolk gig. Light but strongly built gig, favoured in country districts of East Anglia throughout the greater part of the 19th century. Later produced in many different parts of the country. Frequently made use of dos-à-dos seating, in the style of a dogcart, but minus the slatted under-boot.

Norfolk shooting cart. High-wheeled dogcart of a type used in East Anglia during the second half of the 19th century. Made with plain rather than slatted sides. Suitable for four occupants, dos-à-dos.

Norfolk wagon. High-sided, box-type farm wagon. Noted for its short wheelbase and spindled sides. Waisted for improved lock of the forecarriage. Frequently fitted with double shafts.

Northamptonshire wagon. Box-type farm wagon, with high spindled sides. Frequently used with corner poles, to support an overhanging load, rather than end-ladders. There was usually a curved or crooked axlebed. Able to turn in quarter lock.

Northumberland float. Dairyman's float of a type mainly used in Newcastle-on-Tyne and other urban districts of the north east. Made in both cob and pony sizes. Hung on sideways semi-elliptical springs. Panelled in the front and lower half but with open sections above the springs. The upper line was curved beneath semi-circular nameboards. Entered through the rear, having a rearward, crosswise driving seat.

Northumberland harvest cart. Large type of harvest cart, which often replaced wagons, in the north east of England, especially during the 18th and 19th centuries. Noted for semi-open or spindle sides and curved out-raves. Wheels were high and well-dished.

North Wales cart. Farm vehicle used in mountainous areas of North Wales. Plank-sided with outwardly inclined top boards or raves. Made in horse, pony or cob sizes, the largest being up to a capacity of 30 cwts.

Nottingham cart. Light, two-wheeled dogcart, as made and used in Nottingham, from the mid-19th century onwards. Frequently slat-sided.

Nottingham float. Small, neat delivery float, mounted on a cranked axle, with sideways semi-elliptical springs. Entered and driven from the rear. Introduced during the early 1900's, remaining popular in the East Midlands for about thirty years.

O

Obose. High-sided freight or goods wagon, of Russian origins. From the late 18th century it was frequently adapted as a dead axle stage wagon. Drawn by two or more horses in pole gear.

Octagon front coupé. Type of Clarence in which the fore-part of the bodywork consisted of three square frames or lights, making a total of eight upper panels.

Oil or tar cart. Tanker cart with cylindrical cross-section, drawn by a single horse. Mounted on a wooden frame or still. Constructed of mild steel or iron-plating, rivetted throughout. It ran on either wrought-iron or wooden spoked wheels. Hung on sideways semi-elliptical springs or dead axle. Up to a capacity of 200 gallons.

Oil tank van. Four-wheeled tanker on iron or wooden wheels, made from rivetted mild steel or iron-plating. Either sprung or dead axle, having straight shafts and a crosswise driving seat above the fore-end. Provided with an ample footboard and having pedal brakes, acting on the rear wheels. In later years some driving positions were protected by a half cab or canopy top. Up to 500 gallons capacity. Sometimes drawn by a single horse but more frequently by a pair in pole gear. Popular from the late 1880's until the 1920's.

Oil pipe gear. Limbered gear mainly used in the Texas oil fields during the early 1890's. Conveyed both pipes and drilling equipment to and from the nearest railhead. A mere coupling pole with end bolsters, between fore and rear-carriages. Could be

extended to a length of 16′, up to loads of 4 tons. Frequently
drawn by mixed teams of mules and horses, according to weight.
Oil wagon. American name for an Oil Tank Wagon, used in the
delivery of bulk quantities of oils and spirits, from the 1890's to the
1920's. A long, cylindrical tank, mounted on bolsters or a broad
platform and platform springs. The larger types were fitted with a
canopy-topped driving seat. Up to 1,000 gallons capacity. Drawn
by a pair of horses in pole gear.
'Old times' gig. A two-seater gig, produced with several slight
variations, during the 1890's. Box-bodied and fairly high, in a
traditional style. Ideal for fast driving and frequently chosen by
professional men such as doctors and surveyors or contract
engineers. Hung on shallow semi-elliptical springs. The square
sides frequently had false slats in the style of a dogcart, rarely with
an inner or under compartment, apart from the conventional
luggage space or buck.
Omnibus. The prototype of this public service (passenger)
vehicle, was invented by the French philosopher Blaise Pascal
(1623–1662), during the second half of the 17th century. It was
reintroduced over a hundred and fifty years later, becoming very
popular in the streets of Paris from the 1820's onwards. It may be
described as either a single or double-decker, running on four
wheels and drawn by a single horse, pair of horses or three horses
abreast (in the French and Russian style). It plied between short
stages or stops but was distinct from the short stage coach of the
outer suburbs. In most cases it was confined to the inner suburbs
and city centres.

Its re-invention was ascribed to experiments by Jacques Lafitte
of Paris, in 1819. Its name, however, was chosen by a man named
Baudy, nearly ten years later. Baudy ran a service, with improved
passenger vehicles, between the centre of Paris and a public bath
house on the outskirts of the city. This compact and highly
popular form of transport was noticed by an English coach builder
named Shillibeer, by whom a version was brought to London in
1829. A similar vehicle was also run in the streets of New York
City, a few months later. The horse-drawn omnibus dominated
inner-city public transport until the 1900's, when it was replaced
by motor vehicles.

Early types were entered from the rear, with either longitudinal
or crosswise seating, perhaps a combination of both. The double-
decker bus was more familiar than the single-decker, especially in
larger towns. Shillibeer's first London Omnibus ran between

Paddington and the Bank of England, being a single-decker, drawn by three horses abreast. This was later banned as dangerous, by the newly formed Metropolitan Police Authority, to be replaced by a smaller pair-horse bus.

Two main types to run in Britain, during the second half of the 19th century, were the Knifeboard and Garden Seat buses. Both were double-deckers, with open tops or upper decks, drawn by pairs of horses, although sometimes assisted on steep gradients by a third or cock-horse in unicorn formation. Upper seating on the knifeboard was outward facing on both sides of a longitudinal bench, reached by narrow steps. The garden seat bus had forward facing seats – on the top deck – with a safer spiral stairway and larger rearward platform. Drivers of both types sat on a forward projecting seat with angled footboard, mounted on curved or straight irons, slightly lower than the floor of the upper deck, above the hindquarters of the pair in pole gear.

Omnibus, French. Usually a knifeboard, double-decker type, with outward facing seats on the upper deck. Drawn either by a pair of horses or teams of three abreast.

Omnibus van. Small, enclosed van of a type familiar in English towns and cities during the second half of the 19th century. Similar in structure and suspension to the single-horse Brougham, with an elevated double driving seat. Usually drawn by a single horse or large pony, although a few larger types were handled by a pair in pole gear. Also known as a Brougham Van. *See* Brougham Van. Cost about £40.

One horse van. Light delivery van with a short wheelbase. The boarded-up top or head slightly overlapped the wheels in the form of a ledge. Normally plank-sided. Driven from a crosswise bench under the fore-part of the head. Hung on full or semi-elliptical side springs, front and rear. There were either single or double doors for rearward access. Up to a capacity of 15 cwts. Cost about £30.

One horse London road van. A light-weight, fully sprung delivery van, usually open with either plank or panel sides. Made with side raves, a tailboard on letting-down chains and a crosswise driving seat. Up to a capacity of 35 cwts.

Open delivery cart. A light, fully sprung cart, mainly used for parcels traffic. Straight and square or oblong, with side boards or raves above the wheels. Hung on two sideways and one crosswise set of semi-elliptical springs. Shafts were slightly curved at the extremities. Usually appeared in cob or full-horse sizes.

Open lot. Type of bow-topped caravan, the felt and canvas roof mounted above the body of a light dray or market wagon. Although some were boarded-up at the rear, the majority were protected by canvas curtains only, like tent flaps. Frequently remarkable for the beauty and variety of painted sides and carved or turned axle trees, lined-out in contrasting colours. The last type of Gypsy van produced in large numbers. Drawn by a single horse in shafts.

Opera bus. Small, private bus, as used for theatre-going. A single-decker vehicle, first appearing during the 1870's. Seating was longitudinal, reached through a rearward opening door and folding steps. Drawn by a single horse in shafts.

Ore Wagon. Heavy type of commercial wagon, widely used in the mining industry throughout the second half of the 19th century. Usually high-sided and dead axle. Drawn by two or more heavy horses in pole gear.

Outside car. Alternative name, frequently used in North America, for the Irish Jaunting Car.

Oval hearse. American hearse, appearing during the second half of the 19th century. Either the entire bodywork was oval or there were oval side windows/panels. Drawn by a pair of horses in pole gear.

Overland wagon. Type of American passenger wagon hung on thoroughbraces, drawn by teams of four or more horses. Used in the Western States as a possible rival to the Concord coach, during the mid-19th century. Not always confined to tracks or roads but able to travel across country. Sometimes carried the United States Mail. Several were known to have been built by the Abbott Downing Company.

Owl. Contraction of Night Owl. *See* Night Owl.

Oxford dogcart. High-wheeled, single dogcart, frequently driven by undergraduates of Oxford University.

Oxford bounder. Slang name for the Oxford dogcart. *See* Oxford Dogcart.

Oxfordshire wagon. Also known as the 'Woodstock Wagon'. An early bow-type farm wagon, with hooped raves above the wheels and a slight upward curve at the fore-end. Noted for its elegant proportions, making it seem one of the most attractive of all English farm vehicles. There were up to 18 spindles supporting the plank sides. End-ladders were frequently carried, but – in the Cotswolds – corner poles were often used in place of such supports. Sides were deeply waisted to improve underlock. In some parts of the county there were known to have been much smaller wagons, minus hoop raves. Drawn by a single horse in shafts but frequently assisted by a chain horse in tandem.

P

Panel boot Victoria. Large version of the Victoria, having a panel-sided box seat with rearward boot. There was also an extra (folding) seat for vis-à-vis passengers. Drawn by a pair of horses in pole gear.

Pannel. Two or four-wheeled military carriage used for mortars and their ammunition. Usually unsprung or dead axle. Drawn by two or more horses. Part of the military train, from the late Middle Ages until the late 18th century.

Pantechnicon. Large, four-wheeled furniture van, hung on sideways elliptical and semi-elliptical springs. Driven to a pair of heavy horses in pole gear, from a seat at roof level. Rear wheels were on cranked axles and fitted into side recesses of the bodywork, which bowed above them. Most types had the rear part in the form of a well, for extra headroom and greater ease of loading. Length was about 16', although there were a few smaller sizes, some drawn by a single horse in shafts. Extra carrying space on the arched or flat roof was created by the use of deep rounding boards. Fore-wheels were small enough to turn in full lock. Side planking was in diagonal form rather than horizontal or vertical. Popular for house removals from the 1880's to the 1930's. Many such vans were taken to the nearest railway station by horses and rolled on to a flat (carriage) truck, to be met at the town of their destination by a hired team. Cost between £100 and £120.

Parasol top runabout. American runabout or light road wagon, drawn by a single horse. The driving seat was protected by a rearward mounted parasol, the latter deeply fringed, its prop or handle attached to the seat rail.

Park phaeton. Any type of smart, light phaeton, adapted for park driving. Frequently had a rearward seat or rumble and a falling hood. Drawn by a single horse in shafts or pair in pole gear.

Park wagon. Alternative name for a Spring Wagon. *See* Spring Wagon.

Parson's milk wagon. Popular American delivery wagon for bottled milk. Noted for its low centre of gravity and central driving position. Hung on semi-elliptical springs.

Passenger wagon. American passenger vehicle with crosswise seating, usually drawn by a pair of horses in pole gear. Hung on crosswise elliptical springs.

Patrol wagon. Police wagon of a semi-open type, first used by the Chicago Police Department during the 1870's. Entered from the rear by means of folding steps, in the same manner as a Wagonette. Mounted on crosswise or sideways semi-elliptical springs. Frequently headed, with a canopy top. Drawn by a pair of horses in pole gear. Designed by a Major W. J. McGarigle, then General Superintendent of the Chicago Police Force.

Peabody Victoria. Light, low-slung Victoria of a type popular in the United States of America, during the second half of the 19th century. Drawn by a single horse in shafts.

Pedlar's wagon. Closed or box van mounted on platform springs, used as a mobile shop, especially in country districts. The interior would be fitted-out with numerous shelves, cupboards and containers. Hung on either sideways elliptical or semi-elliptical springs. Drawn by a single medium-heavy horse, in shafts. Popular throughout the greater part of the 19th century.

Peeler's cell. Slang name for an early version of the Brougham, considered by many to be stuffy and confined. The original Peeler's Cell was a lock-up at the police station.

Peking cart. A small, two-wheeled passenger vehicle of Chinese origins, frequently appearing in the streets of Peking until the second half of the 20th century. Unsprung or dead axle with either disc or spoked wheels. There were low panel sides and a bowlike arch or head, usually of felt. Shafts were long and straight, attached to the single pony or mule by rope rather than leather harness. Led on foot rather than driven, although the driver sometimes perched cross-legged on a front platform. Passengers sat further back in the vehicle, also cross-legged. Where spokes were used these would be up to 18 in number, round in section and profile. Wheels were straight rather than dished.

Perch carriage. Type of vehicle supported by an underperch, as part of its construction. Usually a large or heavy type.

Perithon. Type of wagonette in which the driving seat could be bisected for improved passenger access through the front or fore-part.

Phaeton. Swift, light vehicle used in Western Europe, especially for pleasure driving and exercise purposes, from the late 18th century. The name derives from Phaeton, in classical mythology, by whom the Sun Chariot was driven. At first characterised by its large wheels and high bodywork, seating one or two occupants at a time. Driven to a single horse, pairs or teams of four/six.

Later types were either much smaller or heavier and more substantial, adapted for pony draught, in one instance, and the exercise of powerful coach horses in another. Phaetons of the mid-19th century had rearward, crosswise seating – in addition to the driving seat – and improved suspension of sideways elliptical and semi-elliptical springs. Early types were hung on cee or elbow springs. The driver's seat was usually protected by a falling or half-hood.

Phaeton, basket.   Small, English Phaeton of the 19th century, drawn by a single horse or pony. The sides were made of basket or canework. Known in America as a Beach Carriage or Wagon. Basketwork was easier to clean and keep in good order than painted surfaces, especially when marked by the grubby fingers of young children. The American version was essentially a family carriage, some versions having an umbrella or parasol top.

Phaeton, crane-neck.   Early type of High Perch or Perch High Phaeton. This had crane-neck suspension for better cut-under of the forecarriage, having smaller front wheels able to clear the underworks without risk of damage. Easy, however, to overturn when driven at speed.

Phaetonette.   The combination of phaeton and wagonette. This vehicle carried two passengers in the fore-part of the phaeton-end and four passengers (seated sideways-on) in the wagonette or rearward end. Drawn either by a single horse in shafts or pair in pole gear. Hung on sideways semi-elliptical springs.

Phaeton, gentleman's.   Heavy type of Phaeton, large and often difficult to control. Drawn either by a pair or four-in-hand team. Similar to a Mail Phaeton. *See* Mail Phaeton.

Phaeton, high-perch or perch-high.   Sporting phaeton of the late 18th century, with room for passenger and driver on an elevated driving seat above the fore-axle. Noted for its high wheels, those at the rear being up to 8', while those at the front were about 6'. Balanced on both underperch and cee springs or whip springs. The perch was curved or raised at the fore-end for improved under lock.

Phaeton, ladies'.   Also known as a Park Phaeton. Usually drawn by a single horse in shafts. Much lighter and more compact than the Gentleman's Phaeton.

Phaeton, mail.   *See* Mail Phaeton.

Phaeton, Malvern.   Park Phaeton similar to the four-wheeled dogcart or Dogcart Phaeton. The sides were frequently of basket or canework. Drawn by a single horse in shafts. Named after Great Malvern, in Worcestershire, its place of origin.

Phaeton, park. General description for the lighter type of phaeton, suitable for park driving in fashionable areas, or for showing.

Phaeton, pony. Small, light phaeton, with a low centre of gravity. Frequently drawn by a single pony in shafts or a pair in pole gear. One such vehicle, designed for Queen Victoria, was drawn by four ponies controlled by postillions. An even smaller type, the fore-wheels only 18″ in diameter, was presented to her by the Mayor of Southampton, after a royal visit (before she came to the throne). This appears to have set a fashion and many of the smaller phaetons of the period were briefly known as 'Victorias', a name later used to describe a much larger carriage. Usually hung on cee springs but later with sideways elliptical and semi-elliptical springs. Most types were provided with a falling or half-hood, but this was normally kept in a lowered position.

Phaeton, Queen's body. Elegant phaeton of the 1860's, with a curved underside or bottom line. Fairly low and easy to enter, especially by ladies with flowing skirts and crinolines of the mid-19th century. Drawn by a small horse or large pony in shafts.

Phaeton, spider. Light phaeton of the 1860's, being a Tilbury body mounted on four rather than two wheels. The driving seat had a spindle-back. There was frequently a rearward or rumble seat for the groom. A notable feature was the almost skeletal structure and size of the wheels, reminiscent of much earlier types. Mounted on arched irons for improved cut-under and hung on sideways elliptical springs, front and rear. Driven either to a single horse in shafts or pair in pole gear.

Phaeton, Stanhope Light-weight gentleman's driving phaeton of the early 19th century. Noted for its detachable shafts, designed for greater ease of storage in a confined space, such as a town mews. There was a railed-up rearward seat for a liveried groom. Hung either on sideways elliptical or Telegraph springs. Driven to a small horse or large pony.

Phaeton, 'T'-cart. Light phaeton for a small horse or large pony. Characterised by having a driving seat much wider than the groom's rearward seat. Seen from above it appeared in the form of a capital letter 'T'. Popular in military circles and said to have been designed by a serving officer in the Brigade of Guards. Popular throughout the second half of the 19th century.

Phaeton, village. Square, angular phaeton with arched cut-under of the fore-carriage to improve its turning circle. There would be a slatted under-boot in the style of a Dogcart Phaeton. Hung on full elliptical springs, front and rear. Usually drawn by two horses or cobs in pole gear. Fitted with mail coach hubs and rubber tyres. Popular, as a rustic version of the Dogcart Phaeton, during the second half of the 19th century.

Phoongyes' car or chariot. Four-wheeled ceremonial car used as a processional vehicle in India. Usually dead axle or unsprung. Drawn by either horses or oxen.

Pickering float. Strongly made but elegant float with cranked axles, hung on sideways elliptical springs. There were both crosswise driving and passenger seats. Designed for general purposes but ideal for showing and private driving. Made in both horse and pony sizes. First used in the Vale of Pickering, Yorkshire, during the 1890's.

Pick-up cart. Same as the Timber Neb, Logging Wheels, etc.

Pie wagon. Oblong or square-shaped delivery wagon of American origins, drawn by a single horse in shafts. Used in the sale and delivery of hot pies, sometimes sold at the kerbside. The crosswise driving seat was semi-enclosed, reins passing through an aperture in the windscreen. Access to the rearward compartment was through sliding doors on either side of the bodywork. Both front and rear carriages were hung on two lengthwise and one crosswise set of semi-elliptical springs. Either lever or pedal brakes acted on the rearwheels.

Pilentum. 1. A travelling cart or carriage of Ancient Rome, running on either two or four wheels. Its canopy top would be supported by corner pillars. Used for ceremonial and religious purposes, especially as a chariot for the vestal virgins, or ladies of rank attending public functions.

2. A light, four-wheeled carriage of the early 19th century. An English version of the Droitzschka, with curved rather than straight bottom line.

Pill box. Slang name of the late 18th century for a small phaeton or chariot used by a doctor of medicine on his daily rounds. A sulky on four wheels, drawn by a single horse in shafts.

Pill box phaeton. 1. A larger and sturdier version of the Pill Box, with room for a passenger or groom. *See* Pill Box.

2. Type of Peddler's Wagon as used in the Atlantic Coast States of North America, especially during the colonial period. Used for the sale of patent pills and potions.

Pipe line gear. Pair of wheels, drawn by large teams, similar to

Logging Gear. Adapted for laying pipe tracks, especially in North America during the 1890's and 1900's.

Plantation cart. Open dump or tip cart used on the plantations of the American South. Sides were slightly lower than the wheel-tops. The body dumped itself in a rearward direction when a hook was released from its loop at the fore-end. Dead axle or unsprung. Drawn by a single horse or mule in straight shafts.

Platform spring dray. American dray with a long wheelbase and elevated driving seat. The fore-carriage turned in full lock. Swingletrees, attached to a sturdy doubletree, were chained to the fore-axletree. The undergear was hung on sideways elliptical springs, although the rear-carriage had sets of one crosswise and two sideways springs. Drawn by two or more horses in pole gear.

Platform spring grocery wagon. American delivery wagon or van, drawn by a single horse or large pony. Mounted on sideways semi-elliptical platform springs.

Platform wagon. American semi-open freight or passenger wagon, frequently serving both purposes. Mounted on semi-elliptical platform springs. Drawn by a single horse.

Plaustrum. Dray or wagon of Ancient Rome, mainly used in harvesting the grain crop. A few, however, were mounted with crosswise seats and employed as passenger vehicles. Drawn by teams of oxen, horses or mules. It sometimes had low, basketwork sides. Slow and ungainly but thought to be the ancestor of many later vehicles.

Pleasure carriage. Any type of vehicle used for pleasure or show, rather than practical purposes.

Pleasure wagon. Square-bodied, four-wheeled passenger vehicle, widely used in New England during the early 19th century. Hung either on thoroughbraces or sideways semi-elliptical springs. In some versions the seats could be lifted-out and inner space used for goods or luggage.

Pomeranian. Small coach or four-wheeled chariot of the early 18th century. It normally seated two facing forward. A type of vehicle first used in Prussia or Pomerania. Hung on strap suspension. Drawn by a single horse, although – less frequently – by a pair in pole gear.

Postellum. Light wagon or cart, used in Ancient Rome as a plaything for children. Drawn by a small pony, ass or goat.

Pole cart. Pair-horses cart, used for commercial purposes. Fitted with pole gear for a pair of horses or ponies.

Pole chair. American gig or riding chair drawn by a pair of horses harnessed in pole gear. Popular during the colonial period of the 18th century.

Polo cart. Alternative name for a Polo Gig. *See* Polo gig.

Polo gig. Sporting gig of the late 19th century, in which a polo pony could be driven, either to a match or for exercise. Notable features were crude disc brakes and a wickerwork basket for polo sticks. Large numbers of this type were made in Birmingham by the firm of Brittain and Sons.

Pontoon wagon. Military carriage with a long wheelbase used by the Royal Engineers to convey a punt or pontoon for temporary bridging purposes. Drawn by teams of six or more horses controlled by mounted drivers. Usually unsprung or dead axle.

Pony break. Light break of Australia, drawn by four or more small ponies for exercise purposes.

Pony chaise. Small, low-slung (four-wheeled) chaise or phaeton. Seated two occupants, driven from the interior. The passenger, frequently a child, sat on a tip-up seat almost opposite the driver. Hung on sideways elliptical springs, front and rear. Popular for country driving during the mid-19th century.

Pony dogcart. English, two-wheeled dogcart, suitable for a small pony.

Pony milk float. Pony-sized delivery float on a cranked axle, much smaller and lighter than other vehicles in this category. Frequently supplied with a 12 gallon churn with brass fittings, mounted on gimbles, fixed in the fore-part of the bodywork. Also featured a crosswise driving seat, high splashers or mudguards and prominent nameboards. Cost from £19 to £22.

Pony phaeton. *See* Phaeton, Pony.

Poor man's stage coach. Alternative name for a lumbering stage wagon of the 17th and 18th centuries. Slower but cheaper and safer than the stagecoach.

Poor man's Surrey. American road wagon, frequently without head or cover. The rear seats could be removed for carrying luggage or merchandise. Some later types eventually had a falling hood. Introduced during the early 1900's.

Portland wagon. Medium-sized wagonette hung on sideways elliptical springs. Drawn by a single horse in shafts.

Portuguese cabriolet. Lavishly carved and painted cabriolet used by noble and wealthy families of Portugal during the 18th and 19th centuries. The single or double (crosswise) seat was fully enclosed at the front by means of hinged flaps. Frequently hung on braces but sometimes on cee springs or a combination of both.

Drawn by a pair of horses, one ridden by a postillion, the second harnessed to the vehicle by an extension bar.

Post cart or float. Cranked axle delivery cart, usually with straight shafts, hung on sideways semi-elliptical springs. The upper part of the bodywork had a ledged effect, supporting scroll irons for the springs. Made for a rearward entrance, having a crosswise driving seat at the centre of balance. Similar types were widely used for wholesale newspaper collections (at railway stations) and mail deliveries in rural areas. Up to a capacity of 13 cwts. Drawn by a cob or large pony in shafts.

Post chaise. Type of four-wheeled travelling carriage or chariot used for public hire, operating between inns and post houses where fresh horses and drivers could also be engaged. Sometimes adapted for the carriage of mails, in remote areas. This system of cross-country travel, using the Post Chaise, was introduced to England, from Europe, by John Tull, a retired artillery officer, in 1743. Often a cut-down and discarded travelling carriage, the box seat removed and driven either to pairs in pole gear or four-in-hand teams guided by postillions. Large trunks could be carried at the rear of the vehicle and between the front wheels, with smaller luggage on a roof rack. Most had a sword case for dress or ceremonial swords attached to a rearward part of the bodywork. Hung on either whip or cee springs. In later years a few such vehicles were controlled from an improvised box seat. When returning empty, at a slower pace, the postillion frequently rode on a projection of the forecarriage. Frequently painted bright yellow or yellow and black, and known as a 'Yellow Bounder'.

Post chariot. Privately owned chariot that could be converted into a Post Chaise.

Postillion landau. The larger type of Landau or State Landau, hung on cee springs but minus the box-seat. Drawn by teams of four or more horses, controlled by postillions.

Post office van. A type of metal-lined van used by the General Post Office from the early 19th century until the Autumn of 1949. Hung on sideways semi-elliptical springs and eventually furnished with pneumatic tyres and hub brakes. There would be a semi-enclosed driving seat with a rounded or scuttlebox dashboard. Each vehicle was driven to a single, cob-type horse in shafts. Although mechanisation began during the 1930's its progress was halted by the Second World War and shortage of motor fuels. Both horses and vans were hired to the Post Office by the firm of

McNamara and Company. They were painted in the traditional colours of the Royal Mail or red, black and gold.

Post omnibus. Privately owned, single-horse bus, frequently chartered for the conveyance of passengers and mail in remote areas.

Pot cart. Two-wheeled vehicle, similar to a Bradford Cart. *See* Bradford Cart. Hung on sideways semi-elliptical springs although early types may have been dead axle. Used by hawkers and Gypsies for selling cheap pottery in market places and from house-to-house. At night the cart would be rigged up with a tent on hoops, as a miniature caravan.

Pot wagon. An enlarged version of the Pot Cart, running on four rather than two wheels. Hung on sideways elliptical springs. Claimed to be an ancestor of the Bow-Top and Barrel-top living vans, favoured by Gypsies throughout the second half of the 19th century. Drawn by a single horse of the cob-type.

Powel passenger wagon. Low-sided American passenger vehicle with crosswise seating and a flat canopy top. Mounted on side or thoroughbraces. Drawn by a pair of horses in pole gear.

Prairie schooner. American emigrant wagon of light/medium weight and dimensions. Headed by a canvas top supported on bow-shaped hoops or tilts. Either sprung or dead axle, up to a capacity of 3 tons. Lever brakes acted on both rear wheels. Drawn by either two or four horses in pole gear. First came to prominence during the gold rush period of the 1840's. Not to be confused with the much larger Conestoga Wagon. *See* Conestoga Wagon.

Prince Albert. Light or Park Phaeton with a single or double driving seat and rearward seat for the groom. Usually had a falling or half hood. Drawn by a single horse in shafts. Popular during the 1850's.

Princess cart. Type of Governess Car of the late 19th century. Entered from the front rather than through the rear. There was a small side door and step irons on either side of the fore-end. Mounted on a cranked axle and semi-elliptical side springs. Drawn by a pony in shafts.

Prison van. A version of the Black Maria. *See* Black Maria. Those used in America were frequently larger than the English or European versions, with a longer wheelbase. Usually panel-sided, driven from a roof seat. Able to turn in full lock. Hung on sideways elliptical springs at the front and sideways semi-elliptical springs at the rear. Drawn by two horses in pole gear.

Private jaunting car. Irish Jaunting Car, designed for private use. The driver's seat was further back than on the ordinary type. All seating was well-upholstered with button-back cushions and matching braid or trimmings. Designed by a carriage-builder named Killiger and displayed at the Dublin International Exhibition of 1865.

Private omnibus. Small, private bus, drawn by a single horse, although less frequently by a pair in pole gear. Some had an extra, crosswise roof seat for two, but more were for six or four inside passengers only, facing inwards on longitudinal seats. Many had a deep well or centre gangway for improved headroom. Hung on sideways elliptical springs at the front and semi-elliptical side springs at the rear. Entered through a rearward door with folding steps or a single step iron. Often used by families at remote country houses or by railway companies and country hotels.

Punch carriage. Four-wheeled carriage of the early 19th century, its coupè bodywork mounted in reverse and protected by a falling hood. Passengers faced away from the direction of travel and the combined effect of a falling hood and driving apron suggested the appearance of a Punch and Judy Show. Used by those disliking draughts and allergic to the odour of horses. Many found them easy to enter and leave, thus favoured by doctor's on their rounds, or the infirm and elderly.

Q

Quadriga.   1. Roman chariot or war-cart drawn by four horses abreast.

2. The team drawing a four-horse chariot.

Quaker chaise.   Alternative name for the Grasshopper Chaise. Mounted on shallow or grasshopper springs. *See* Grasshopper Chaise.

Quarter or Quartette.   American public carriage, also known as an Extension Top Phaeton. Able to carry four passengers on two crosswise seats, facing forward. Introduced during the mid-19th century, but seldom popular. Drawn by a single horse in shafts.

Quatrobus.   Four-wheeled London cab, similar to the Quarter. Designed by a man named Okey during the 1840's, but not a financial success. Made use of short couplings or connections for easier draught. Drawn by a single horse in shafts.

R

Racing biga.   Racing chariot of Ancient Rome, drawn by a pair of horses harnessed in a form of curricle gear. Noted for its forward inclined, bow-shaped front. The wooden wheels usually had eight spokes each.

Radnorshire wheel car.   Low-slung wain or two-wheeled dray, normally confined to the Welsh border counties. The forepart had a fitted or permanent end-ladder, beneath which were semi-permanent skid blocks, acting as crude brakes, especially when the vehicle was driven downhill. Unsprung or dead axle. Drawn by a single horse or cob.

Radnorshire wagon.   Smaller version of the Herefordshire Wagon. Mainly used in the Welsh Marches and border areas. Drawn by a single horse, although sometimes assisted by a single horse in chain gear. Limited to quarter lock.

Ragman's trolley.   Small version of the Totter's Cart or Van, drawn by a single pony. Widely used, especially in the East End of London, up to the mid-20th century, for the collection of rags, scrap material and assorted junk. The small fore-wheels turned in full lock. The driver crouched on a low cross-bench, minus adequate toe or footboard. Most had horizontal side or outraves, above the wheels, to protect an overhanging load. The lower bodywork was frequently panelled.

Railed cart or trolley.   Heavy commercial trolley of the late 19th century, frequently used by the cartage departments of main line railway companies. Noted for an elevated driving seat on vertical irons and full cut-under of the forecarriage. The loading platform was surrounded by a railed-in effect, its low top rail surmounting a row of outwardly curved brackets or spindles. There was also a low tailboard on letting down chains. Frequently drawn by two horses in pole gear. There were full elliptical springs under the forecarriage, supporting the wagonlike turntable. The rear carriage was hung on sideways semi-elliptical springs. A few early types were known to have been dead axle.

Railway cartage vehicles.   These were mainly concerned with deliveries from stations or depots to private homes, farms or factories. Mainly divided between heavy cartage and parcels traffic. A few ordinary carts and wagons were reserved for general maintenance and internal traffic, especially in large goods yards.

One of the most familiar types was the Single Horse Wagon, for medium deliveries, although sometimes fitted with pole gear and harnessed to a pair. This was about a ton in tare weight and up to a pay load of two tons. It had either a high skeleton seat on curved irons or a crossbench, forming partof the fore-end construction. Most had either foot-pedal or hand-lever brakes, with full underlock and a demountable top or head. Large wagons or vans of heavier construction and greater capacity were drawn by teams of four to six shires, known as 'waggoners', often the pride of the stable. Sides of vehicles, in both cases, were planks or panels, the low tailboards on letting-down chains.

Parcel vans were much smaller and lighter, running on both two and four wheels, drawn by large ponies, cobs or 'vanners' but sometimes by ex-hunter types, according to size. From the late 1930's a modern four-wheeled parcels van was introduced with pneumatic tyres, disc brakes and ball-bearing hubs, many of which survived the Second World War by about ten years. At one period British Railways, even in the nationalised era, were the largest commercial horse owners in the British Isles. Before the introduction of pneumatic tyres and disc wheels, many railway-owned vans and wagons ran on a type of artillery wheel with metal rather than wooden hubs. Most were hung on sideways semi-elliptical springs or full elliptical springs. Single or double shafts, and pole gear, were all used for different type of vehicle, frequently interchangeable. A fair proportion of railway road vehicles were built in their own workshops.

Railway parcels cart. Two-wheeled, headed delivery van with curved shafts. Made with a high dash and foot board. Mounted on patent axles and sideways semi-elliptical springs. Rearward access was through double doors with oval glass lights – one per door. An iron rail surmounted the outer part of the roof or head forming an exterior luggage rack. On most types the fore-part of the roof formed a canopy above the driver's seat, curving slightly downwards towards the dashboard. Made in three sizes, the largest up to a capacity of 20 cwts.

Railways parcels van. Light delivery van made in several types and styles, but those claimed to be prototypes, although seldom seen after the 1900's, were fully enclosed with a boarded-up top and arched canopy above the crosswise driving seat/bench. There was usually a high dashboard, roof rails or rack and side lights for the driving position. Mounted on sideways elliptical springs at the front and sideways semi-elliptical springs at the rear. Loaded through double doors at the rear. Usually drawn by a single horse in shafts, loading between 25 cwts. and 2 tons. Later vans were without a roof rack, having ledge-type upper works, overhanging the wheels at the same level from end-to-end. All vehicles had lever or pedal brakes and could turn in full lock.

Ralli car. Frequently misnamed Ralli Cart. Two-wheeled English passenger car, also nicknamed a 'clothes basket'. Small and light, drawn by a single horse, cob or large pony. Named after the family by whom it was originally designed. The rearward extremities of the shafts were either inside or outside the bodywork rather than under the vehicle or fixed to the front by brackets. Usually featured crosswise seating for two but sometimes converted to dos-à-dos, in the style of a dogcart. Hung on sideways semi-elliptical springs.

Ralli-dogcart. Sporting Ralli Car with dos-à-dos seating.

Ration cart. Two-wheeled military cart, used to supply troops with food and other necessities, either on the march or in the battle zone. Unsprung or dead axle. Drawn by a single horse or mule in shafts.

Reading cart. Panel-sided driving cart or market cart with a prominent row of spindles above the top line, surmounted by iron hand rails. Hung on sideways semi-elliptical springs. Widely favoured as Gypsy carts, from the 1860's to the 1920's.

Reading van. Gypsy living van of a type first constructed in the workshops of Dunton of Reading. Several generations of this family firm were involved in making horse-drawn vehicles for travellers, from the early 19th century to the period of the First World War.

Most Reading Vans were of horizontal matchboarding supported by vertical uprights or standards of chamfered hard wood. They had full underlock and were hung on semi-elliptical side springs, front and rear. The front or entrance porch would be decorated with carved scrollwork that also supported a forward projection of the arched roof. From the 1890's the roof usually had a clerestory or 'mollicroft' section for improved ventilation. Entered via movable steps, placed between the lowered shafts when the horse was shut out. There were also shaft or step irons. Screw-down brakes acted on both rear wheels, operated from the front porch. Carved under members or futchells, supporting the upper works, were curved rather than straight.

The Reading Van was considered the Rolls Royce of Gypsy wagons, usually owned by wealthy horse dealers and Romany Kings or tribal leaders. They were furnished with elaborate cross-beds, bowed sideboards with displays of Crown-Derby china and having the more expensive cooking stoves. Painted in bright colours with carved achanthus leaf motifs and lavish gilding. Their main fault was a tendency to sag in the middle, after a few years service, due to being overweight. Seen more on the flatter roads of the eastern and southern counties, rather than the extreme north or west. Drawn by a single horse in shafts, although sometimes with a second horse or 'sider' attached to a draught bar.

Red River cart.   An all-wooden cart, frequently homemade by early settlers in the Red River district of Manitoba, Upper Canada. Drawn by horses, oxen or mules, usually in pairs. First introduced about 1800. Built without nails, bolts or other ironwork, most parts held together by strips of knotted rawhide. Seldom lubricated, most vehicles making a harsh creaking sound at the slightest movement. Although seeming thrown together they outlasted many craftsman-made vehicles from the east.

Reefer.   Alternative name, used mainly in America, for a station or depot wagon.

Regimental coach.   Private coach or drag, owned by the officers of certain regiments or corps of the British Army. Driven to sporting events, especially race meetings, where they served as mobile grandstands. At certain horse and agricultural shows they competed in driving events reserved for this type of vehicle, in the four-in-hand classes, along with park drags and road coaches. Notable examples to survive the Second World War were owned by The Royal Horse Guards (now the Blues and Royals), The Royal Engineers, The Royal Artillery and The Royal Army Service Corps (now the Royal Corps of Transportation). The only remaining example still active is owned by the Household Cavalry Mounted Regiment.

Republican wagon.   Later version of the so-called Democrat Wagon. Differently named – in the United States of America – by supporters of a rival political party (Republicans). *See* Democrat Wagon.

Retail market cart.   Type of market cart used by prosperous farmers and country tradesmen. Fitted with dos-à-dos seating and able to double as a passenger vehicle. Boarded sides were open below horizontal upper rails. There was a low dashoard but no tailboard. A rearward iron bar, on the horizontal, sometimes acted as a foot rest.

Reversed seat carriage.   Deeply hooded version of the Punch Carriage. *See* Punch Carriage. Characterised by large splashers or mudguards and a rearward facing dashboard to which the canopy hood was attached by cords. Frequently used by those allergic to the odour of horses.

Rheda. Four-wheeled vehicle of Ancient Rome, used as either a freight or passenger carrier. Some could be adapted as carriages for overnight travel, having sideways suspended hammocks. Drawn by teams of horses, mules or oxen.

Rib-chair or rib-back gig. Gig or chair having its driving seat designed with a ribbed support or backrest.

Riding chair. Name used, during the 18th and 19th centuries, for a chair mounted on two wheels, drawn by a single horse.

Rig. Slang name for any type of horse-drawn vehicle, especially those inclined to be shabby or out of fashion.

Road breaker. An articulated four-wheeled vehicle of the mid-19th century, that resembled an Hermaphrodite. A rearward carrying box was loaded with large stones and scrap iron, its wheels shod with conical spikes. As the vehicle moved forward, the spikes broke up old road surfaces, necessary before repairs could be undertaken. Drawn by teams of four or more horses, the wheelers being in double shafts. Led rather than driven.

Road carrier. Large road wagon mainly used for commercial purposes. Featured open, slatted-sides and double shafts. Used mainly in Sussex and areas south of the Thames, during the late 18th and early 19th centuries. The sturdy, well-dished wheels had broad treads with a triple row of strakes rather than band tyres. Limited to quarter lock.

Road cart. Two-wheeled passenger vehicle drawn by a single horse or pony.

Road wagon. 1. Four-wheeled wagon better suited for carrying merchandise on busy roads, than for field work.

2. Vehicle similar to the American Buggy, especially when used for business, professional or trade purposes. Usually headed, well-sprung and drawn by a single horse in shafts.

Road sulky. Road cart with a single driving seat.

Robinson Hansom. Open-fronted, two-wheeled cab with a falling hood. Popular during the second half of the 19th century, especially at seaside resorts.

Rockalet. Vehicle of compromise between an American Rockaway and a Landaulet. Frequently a smaller version of the Rockaway. Drawn by a single horse in shafts.

Rockaway. American passenger vehicle appearing throughout the 19th century in a variety of types and sizes. It may have developed from the earlier public coach or Jersey Wagon, frequently used as a Depot Wagon, driven to and from the nearest railway depot. Public or private, usually headed but with semi-open sides protected by curtains or roll-down blinds. Hung on crosswise springs in the style of an American Buggy. The driver's seat was sheltered by a forward extension of the roof canopy. A later version of the Rockaway was a cut-down type or Limousine. *See* Limousine. Drawn by either a horse in shafts or pair in pole gear.

Rockaway Landau.   A vehicle of the late 19th century, combining the best features of Landau and Rockaway. There would be a falling or half-hood protecting the rear seats and a standing top above the fore-seats, including the driver's seat.

Rockaway Landaulet.   Alternative name for the Rockalet. *See* Rockalet.

Rolley.   Light, low dray, drawn by a single horse. Frequently hung on sideways semi-elliptical springs. Minus side planks, stakes or supports of any type.

Rolling cart.   English farm vehicle or implement, combining the work of a roller and manure spreader. The roller-part was in three sections and the body of a manure cart placed above them, fixed on an iron framework. Mainly used during the second half of the 18th century. Drawn by a single horse in shafts.

Roman travelling cart/wagon.   Four-wheeled, tray-shaped vehicle of Ancient Rome, drawn by a pair of horses or larger team of mules. Usually headed or hooded and well upholstered. The vehicle was minus suspension although hammock-like seats were slung on cords or braces. Length was about 10'. Fore-wheels were able to turn in full lock. Many were fitted with a device of small stones dropping through geared cogs to record the length and time of journey.

Romney Marsh wagon.   Farm wagon with a long wheelbase, having partly open or slatted sides, between the second and top planks. Corner poles were used in place of end-ladders. Unsprung or dead axle with limited lock. Drawn by a single horse in shafts. Used on Romney Marsh near the borders of Kent and Sussex.

Roof seat break.   Driving break with three rows of forward facing seats for six passengers, mounted on a level platform. Drawn by a four-in-hand team harnessd to pivoting swingletrees rather than hitched to a full-length splinter bar and roller bolts.

Roulette.   Alternative name for the Brouette. *See* Brouette.

Round back gig.   Gig with a rounded back rest for the driving seat.
Round cornered Landau.   Similar in style to the square Landau, but having rounded corners of the lower bodywork and less severe outlines. Usually hung on cee springs. Popular during the second half of the 19th century, especially in British India.
Round or bow-fronted Landaulette.   The fore-part or upper quarter of this vehicle was a rounded glass panel, which could be lowered or raised according to weather and seasons. Its forecarriage was hung on sideways elliptical springs, while the rearcarriage depended on rearward projecting arms known as pump handles.
Round-up wagon.   Same as a Chuck Wagon. *See* Chuck Wagon.
Runabout.   Any type of light driving wagon, not used on formal occasions.
Rustic cart.   Alternative name for a Country Cart or Country Driving Cart. Finished with a treatment of staining and varnishing rather than painted in solid colours.
Rulley.   The same as a Rolley. *See* Rolley.
Rutland wagon.   Box-type harvest wagon of the East Midlands. The fore-wheels were fairly large and well-dished, turning in quarter lock only. Drawn by two horses in double shafts.

S

Sack hauling spring wagon.   A vehicle similar to the London-type Miller's Wagon, used for carrying merchandise in sacks or bags. There were prominent outraves above the wheels, while the sides were made from alternate planking and iron rods, based on sturdy framework of oakwood. The fore-end, mainly of spindles, was slightly curved. Hung on sideways semi-elliptical springs, front and rear. Often featured a large nameboard at the front. Drawn by a single horse in shafts.
Salisbury boot coach.   Passenger vehicle of the late 18th century in which the box-seat was mounted above a turtle-backed or rounded fore-boot. This often appeared as though detached from the main bodywork, connected to the latter by curved irons only.
Saloon van.   Large, low-slung living van, used by the wealthier showmen, while on tour, from the 1900's to the 1940's. Usually had a side door and movable steps rather than an end door and porch. Drawn by two or more horses in pole gear, although – less frequently – by a single heavy horse in shafts. The greater part of its journey, however, would be on the flat truck of a passenger

train, as with the Pantechnicon. Horses were mainly used to take the Saloon Van to the nearest railway station with a carriage landing bay, or from station to show ground. Large numbers of this type of vehicle were produced by such firms as Savages' of King's Lynn – noted for both fairground and agricultural equipment – during the 1900's. Hung on sideways semi-elliptical springs, front and rear. The interiors were divided into two or more rooms with free-standing furniture. Wheels, of small diameter, were eventually fitted with pneumatic tyres. From the 1920's most Saloon Vans were drawn by motor lorries or tractor units, forming part of a road train.

Santa Fé wagon. Type of Murphy Wagon, as used by settlers travelling to the Far West of America, on the Sante Fé Trail. *See* Murphy Wagon.

Sarracum. Crude vehicle of Ancient Rome, mounted on either two or four wheels. Mainly used for light haulage work. Drawn by a pair of horses, mules or oxen.

Savanilla phaeton. Light carriage or phaeton, widely used in Bangkok, Siam (now Thailand). A semi-open cab operated as such from the late 19th century. Hung on sideways elliptical springs at the front and sideways semi-elliptical springs at the rear. Drawn by a single horse or large pony in shafts.

Sark van. Large wagonette-type vehicle, with a longer than average wheelbase. A popular form of passenger transport on the Island of Sark, where motor vehicles are forbidden. Drawn by a single horse in shafts.

Sawdust cart. Light American-type dump cart, used in saw mills and lumber yards for transporting large quantities of sawdust and off-cuts. Usually unsprung or dead axle. Drawn by a single horse, pony or mule in shafts.

Scavenger wagon. Alternative name for a Garbage Wagon or Dust Cart/Van.

Scirpea. Ancient Roman Chariot or driving cart, fitted with a crosswise seat. Drawn by a single horse or pair in curricle gear. Limited to city or town use.

Scoop. American Buggy of the 1860's, with a scoop-shaped body and side rather than cross springs.

Scorpion. Type of large catapult, used for military purposes, able to sling large rocks or lumps of iron in siege warfare. Mounted on four disc-wheels to form part of the military train, especially in Medieval Europe, until the widespread use of gunpowder. Drawn by large teams of horses or oxen.

Scotch cart. Agricultural cart of the early 19th century, lightly

but strongly built. At first made by village craftsmen and confined
to the Lowlands of Scotland. In later years they were factory-made
and distributed throughout the greater part of mainland Britain.
First introduced to East Anglia by thrifty farmers from Scotland
who bought up the bankrupt holdings of English yeomen, during
an agricultural slump of the mid-19th century.

Scottish tilt cart. Low-sided covered or tilt cart of a type first
used in the Lowlands of Scotland, during the early 19th century.
Noted for large, well-dished wheels and prominent side raves. The
large hubs were of outwardly expanded iron.

Sedan cab. Form of sedan chair mounted on two wheels, drawn
by a single horse or large pony. Used in the streets of London
during the first half of the 18th century. Much cheaper than the
Hackney Coach but less comfortable, used by the middle or lower
rather than the upper classes. Easy to manœuvre in a busy street or
narrow place. Revived as the Improved Sedan Cab, over half a
century later. With early types the horse was either ridden in shafts
or led on foot.

An American version of the Sedan Cab was patented in 1870 by
a Chauncey Thomas of Boston, Massachusetts.

Sediola. Type of large gig popular in France and Italy during the
18th century. Dead axle, its only suspension being from long,
highly flexible shafts. Round-backed with high wheels.

Sefton Landau. Alternative name for the rounded or canoe-
shaped Landau.

Sège. Two-wheeled passenger cart or cab, used in the Azores,
from the late 18th century, onwards. Semi-open, mounted on
either braces or whip springs. Drawn by a pair of horses in pole
gear, controlled by a postillion. Usually headed.

Semi-mail phaeton. Alternative name for the Demi-Mail Phaeton.
See Demi-Mail Phaeton.

Semi-state Landau. Slightly smaller, less elaborate version of
the State Landau. Usually had a rearward or rumble seat for
carriage servants.

Service cart. Small luggage or general utility cart, as used on a
large country estate. Frequently dead axle or mounted – in later
years – on sideways semi-elliptical springs. Drawn by a cob or
large pony in shafts.

Seven spring gig. Alternative name for the Tilbury or Tilbury
Gig. *See* Tilbury.

Sextet. American Extension-Top Phaeton, seating six occupants
on forward facing seats. A family vehicle of the late 19th century.

Hung on crosswise elliptical springs. Drawn by a single horse in shafts.

Shandry. A large, strongly constructed market cart,of a type widely used in the Lake District and North West of England, for business and pleasure. Seated up to six people. Hung on sideways semi-elliptical springs. Popular during the second half of the 19th century.

Shay. Colloquial name and spelling of Chaise, especially in North America, during the early 19th century.

Shebang. American-Irish name for an old or worn-out carriage.

Sheep cart. Farmer's float on a cranked axle and sideways semi-elliptical springs. The tailboard let down for use as a loading ramp. There were side rails or gates above the ordinary side planks. Used for taking sheep and other small animals to and from market.

Sheep wagon. Small, bow-topped caravan used by shepherds in the Rocky Mountains of North America. Either dead axle or hung on sideways semi-elliptical springs. The interior contained a single bed-bunk in a crosswise position, folding table and cooking stove. Used from the 1880's onwards. Drawn by a single horse in shafts.

Shelburne Landau. Version of the English Quarter or Square Landau, with angular lines and dropped centre.

Shifting seat carriage. American passenger vehicle with movable seats. Also known as a Jump Seat Carriage.

Shillibeer. Name given to the original London omnibus of the 1830's. Drawn by three horses abreast. Designed by George Shillibeer, an ex-naval officer and carriage-builder of London and Paris. Essentially a single decker with longitudinal seating. In the care of polite, well-mannered conductors, unlike the often bad-tempered cabbies and short stage coach drivers of the period. There was inner seating for twenty two passengers.

Ship-of-the-plains. Alternative name for the covered wagons used by gold-prospectors and pioneers in North America during the 1840's.

Shoeful. London slang for an imitation or counterfeit product. Frequently said of a two-wheeled vehicle – of which there were large numbers – attempting to copy or improve on the Hansom Cab.

Shooting break. Light break used by shooting parties during the mid-19th century. Similar to the Sporting Break. Carried six persons on crosswise seating. Hung on sideways elliptical or semi-elliptical springs. Drawn by a single horse in shafts or a pair in pole gear. Some types had both cross and lengthwise seating.

Shooting phaeton. Four-wheeled sporting phaeton of the late 18th century. Usually drawn by a pair of horses in pole gear. Noted for its traylike body and strong underperch, suitable for driving over rough tracks. There was a large boot above the rear axle. The elevated driving seat had room for two, with rearward cross seats for vis-à-vis passengers. The rearward seat was protected by a falling or half-hood. First hung on whip springs but later on sideways semi-elliptical springs.

Show cart. Vehicle for showing harness horses and ponies, according to size. Often has a light, tubular frame and wire-spoked wheels. Introduced in America during the 1890's and still manufactured in respectable numbers.

Show wagon. A four-wheeled version of the Show Cart. Slightly larger and heavier in build.

Shropshire wagon. Usually a lighter and slightly smaller version of the Staffordshire Wagon.

Shrimping cart. Cart or tumbril drawn by a single horse, used for shrimping in shallow, tidal waters on the Lancashire coastline. A typical example would have four-plank sides and straight shafts. It would be either dead axle or hung on sideways semi-elliptical springs. Nets were let-down at the rear and trawled. Most shrimping carts carried a compass in case of fog or sea-mist.

Siamese phaeton. Also known as a 'Siamese'. Pleasure phaeton, dating from the mid-19th century, drawn by a single horse. Fore and rear parts of the bodywork were of symmetrical design.

Side bar wagon. 1. American road wagon, its suspension depending on side bars.

2. Show wagon by Mills of London. Its driving seat was mounted on longitudinal steel bars.

Side car. Alternative name for the Irish Jaunting Cab.

Side-seated platform wagon. Traylike American passenger vehicle with longitudinal seating for nine or more passengers, one sharing the driving seat. Most were headed by a light, canopy top. Mounted on two sets of crosswise and four sets of sideways semi-elliptical springs. Between 9 and 10 feet long. Drawn by a pair of horses in pole gear. Used as a Depot Wagon, especially at holiday resorts.

Side-seated slat wagon. Similar to the Side-Seated Platform Wagon, its sides constructed with open-work slats.

Sight-seeing wagon. Large semi-open passenger wagon, drawn by teams of four or six horses. Used mainly at holiday resorts and show places on the Atlantic coast of North America, during the

1870's. Seated about twenty passengers on both lower and upper decks, those on the lower deck lengthwise on the knifeboard plan. Upper deck passengers faced in either direction – front or rear, on cross-seats reached by a near-vertical ladder. Front wheels were small enough to turn in full lock. Mounted on an underperch with both sideways and crosswise semi-elliptical springs. A dangerous vehicle to drive, mount or ride, as it was inclined to be top-heavy with a low centre of gravity. Declined in popularity after about five years.

Six passenger, canopy top phaeton. American passenger vehicle with a long wheelbase and full cut-under of the forecarriage. Hung on sideways elliptical springs, front and rear. Seating was vis-à-vis for at least six passengers, under a fringed canopy top. Drawn by a pair of horses in pole gear.

Six passenger Surrey. American Fringe-top Surrey, with vis-à-vis seating for three passengers per side. Drawn by a pair of horses or large ponies in pole gear.

Skeleton break. Training vehicle used by professional horse-breakers, especially during the second half of the 19th century. Merely a platform of longitudinal members with an elevated driving seat directly above the fore-wheels. Horses were driven in pairs, harnessed to pole gear, one being older or more experienced in harness work than the other. A groom frequently stood behind the driving seat, able to jump down and run to the head of the novice in times of danger.

Skeleton gig. Light but strongly made driving gig, without buck or luggage space.

Skeleton phaeton. A longer and heavier version of the Spider Phaeton, with smaller wheels in relation to its size. Hung on sideways elliptical springs, front and rear. Drawn by a pair of horses in pole gear.

Skeleton wagon. Trotting or show wagon mainly used in track events. Made with the lightest possible materials and construction, having wire-spoked wheels and a tubular framework.

Slab cart. Heavy, strongly made cart, sometimes able to tip or dump in a rearward direction. Used for carting both slabs and waste material in quarries, etc. Dead axle or usprung. Drawn by a single heavy horse in shafts.

Slice-of-an-omnibus. Slang name, in London, for the Boulnois Cab or Minibus. *See* Boulnois Cab.

Sliding bodied dogcart. Sporting, two-wheeled dogcart, the seat of which could be adjusted on small rails or brackets above the shafts. A type widely used from the 1880's, especially for show purposes. The laminated shafts were less well curved than on the original dogcart. Frequently driven to a tandem pair.

Sling cart. Two-wheeled military cart, used like a Timber Neb for transporting heavy gun barrels. The load was supported in chains or a sling, on the underside of an arched framework. Drawn by two or more horses according to weight of load.

Sling furniture van. Container-type furniture van of the 1900's, its oblong, boxlike body transferred from a flat dray to a railway wagon or hold of a barge or ship by crane power. Drawn by two or more horses according to size and weight. Either dead axle or hung on sideways semi-elliptical springs, front and rear.

Small arms ammunition cart. Two-wheeled ammunition cart, designed for service with the British Army from the 1870's to the 1920's. The interior was divided into compartments for different types of small arms ammunition. An arched, canvas covered top was bolted to side and headboards, while a tailboard, on letting-down chains, formed a rearward shelf or platform. Propsticks supported both front and rear while the vehicle was at rest. Usually drawn by a single horse or mule, it could be adapted for double draught – with pole gear. Shafts were connected directly to the hubs, as with the Madras Cart. *See* Madras Cart.

Small carosse. Smaller version of the large travelling coach of the 17th century. *See* Carosse. Drawn by a pair of horses in pole gear. Hung on strap suspension and/or braces, front and rear. Hinged doors and glass lights or windows appeared during the second half of the century. Seated four people vis-à-vis, with two footmen riding on a rearward dummy board. Popular until the mid-1720's.

Sociable. 1. English open carriage of German origins, first appearing about 1790. Broad in beam and gauge, able to take three adults on the same cross seat, but frequently driven from the interior of the vehicle. Some had a double row of crosswise seating, on the vis-à-vis plan. Others had three rows of seating, the driving position being part of the first row.

2. Public carriage with a fixed top and lengthwise or longitudinal seating, passengers facing inwards. Appeared in the streets of New York City about 1829/30. A forerunner – in America – of the omnibus. Drawn by a pair of horses in pole gear.

Soda water van. Square-shaped, fully enclosed delivery van, running on four wheels. There were high sides and either a rear door or half doors and tailboard. Hung on sideways semi-elliptical springs, front and rear. A driver's seat extended across the full width of the bodywork, having an off-side lever brake acting on both rear wheels. Drawn by a pair of horses in pole gear. Up to a capacity of 2 tons.

Solo. A sulky or riding chair. Usually a two-wheeled vehicle for a single person.

Somerset churn cart. Medium-sized, panel-sided cart hung on sideways semi-elliptical springs. Usually appeared with straight shafts. Mounted from the fore-end by means of shaft steps, clambering over the low front board. Frequently driven from a standing position. Used with both mail and common or drabble-type hubs/axles. Top rails extended down both sides of the bodywork, slightly curved above the fore-end and secured by spindles or iron bars. The interior was fitted with lengthwise iron rails or slats over which heavy churns could be slid, when loading or unloading. Short, straight splashers or mudguards were fitted above the wheel tops.

Somerset wagon. Farm wagon with a short wheelbase and high loading platform. Sides were much higher at the back than the front, tending to slope outwards. Rear wheels were protected by half-sized hoop raves. Usually drawn by a single horse in shafts.

South Gloucestershire pedlar's cart. Panel-sided cart with straight shafts. Hung on sideways semi-elliptical springs. Usually fitted with mail hubs and axles. Mainly used in parts of Gloucestershire bordering Wiltshire, also in the Cotswolds.

South Wales brewer's dray. Mainly found in urban/industrial centres of South Wales and Monmouthshire (Gwent). A slat-bottomed type, based on an oak framework stayed with cast iron. The single driving seat was mounted on vertical irons, having an off-side lever brake for the rear wheels. Hung on four sideways elliptical springs or semi-elliptical springs. Adapted to either shafts or pole gear.

South-west Wiltshire wagon. Farm wagon of a type widely used in the southern part of Wiltshire, bordering Somerset and Dorset. Short wheelbased and panel sided with prominent outraves. Able to turn in quarter lock only. Usually drawn by a single horse in shafts.

Spar wagon. Light passenger wagon, first used in the State of New Jersey, U.S.A. Introduced about 1812. Its suspension depended on flexible side bars or spars, from which its name derives. Drawn by a single horse or cob in shafts.

Speeding wagon. Sulky adapted as a park driving wagon. Introduced during the 1880's. Essentially an American vehicle, some parks in New York having special tracks or speedways on which such wagons could be driven 'flat out'.

Spider phaeton. *See* Phaeton, Spider.

Spindle-sided governess car. Governess Car or Tub Cart in which the upper parts above the waistline or mid-line consisted of spindles, apart from a short backrest on either side.

Spindle wagon. American Buggy having a spindle-sided body and driving seat.

Spinner. Light gig of the early 19th century, often with a slatted floor, used for training and exercising young horses. A version of the American Jogging Cart. Noted for its low centre of gravity and shallow, sideways semi-elliptical springs.

Sporting break. Large break, carrying at least six people, sometimes as many as eight. Usually made with a slatted underboot for gun dogs. Hung on sideways elliptical or semi-elliptical springs, front and rear. Drawn either by a single horse in shafts or pair in pole gear.

Spray wagon/cart. Either a two or four-wheeled vehicle used in both military or civil life for pest control and sanitary purposes. A type of horizontal cylinder mounted lengthways-on with a rearward sprayboard. Drawn by a single horse or mule, between shafts. Led rather than driven. Introduced during the early 1900's.

Spreading wagon. Dump wagon drawn by a single horse.

Spring cart. Any type of farm or commercial cart mounted on metal side/under springs.

Spring lurry or livestock wagon. A type of farm dray hung on sideways elliptical or semi-elliptical springs, drawn by a single horse in shafts. When fitted with detachable side gates or railings it could be used to convey small livestock such as sheep and pigs.

Spring hay van. Four-wheeled harvest truck hung on sideways semi-elliptical springs, drawn by a single horse in shafts. Fitted with demountable front-ladder and side raves. Able to double as a market wagon. Drawn by two horses in pole gear.

Spring wagon. Type of American passenger wagon with at least two rows of cross-wise seating, mounted on shallow semi-elliptical or platform springs. Drawn by a single horse in shafts.

Sprinkler. Water or spray cart making use of a rearward hose and sprinkler or spreadboard. Usually drawn by a single horse in shafts but sometimes by a pair in pole gear. Either sprung or dead axle.

Square-bodied float. Patent float of the late 1890's. Mounted on a cranked axle with sideways semi-elliptical springs. Originally designed for the delivery of sewing machines, but later adapted for general trade purposes. Noted for its square, flat sides and prominent splashers or mudguards. Spindle-sided above the midline. There was a removable cross-seat and low tailboard on letting-down chains. Made in either cob or pony sizes.

Square Landau.   The Shelburne or square-sided Landau.

Square town sociable.   Pair-horse sociable driven from a box seat. *See* Sociable 1. This type had angular lines and a dropped centre. Hung on sideways elliptical springs. Seated four, vis-à-vis.

Stable break.   Small exercise break seating four occupants, including the driver. Entered from the near-side by means of step irons. The rear-cross seat could be reversed and the tailboard let down as a foot rest.

Staffordshire wagon.   Large type of farm or harvest wagon, from which several others – in the West Midlands – appear to have derived. High-sided and, when fully laden, needing a large team – of four or more – for successful draught. The sturdy, well-dished wheels often had iron strakes in place of ordinary ring tyres. Treads were at least ten inches wide. Hubs were large and conical made of selected elmwood. Side raves and end-ladders were prominent to protect and support overhanging loads. Able to turn in quarter lock only.

Stage.   Contraction of Stage Coach or Stage Wagon, but usually the former. A name frequently used in North America throughout the 19th century.

Stage coach.   Public passenger coach operating between stages or stopping places, both in the ancient world and modern Europe/ America. Revived in England during the late 16th or early 17th centuries, although a nationwide system was not organised until 1658. Considerable improvements came during the 18th century with the turnpike system and better engineering of public roads. Always a headed vehicle, fitted with roof seats or gammon boards, from the early 19th century. In the early days poorer class passengers crouched in an open basket or rumble, between the rear wheels. Drawn by four or six horses, usually the former, except in hilly districts where extra horses were needed. Driven from an elevated box seat, its footboard supported by brackets. At first unsprung or dead axle, but later hung on braces, elbow and finally Telegraph springs, as with the Mail Coach. *See* Coach, Mail. Forced from its main trunk routes by railway competition from the late 1830's, although some lingered in remoter areas until the 1850's. In North America a few Concord Coaches survived until the first half of the 20th century. Most stage coaches were named and painted in special liveries.

Stage wagon. Lumbering passenger and freight wagon, its bowlike canvas cover (top) supported on hoops or tilts. Although mainly for boxes, barrels and packages, a number of passengers also crouched between items of merchandise. There were neither springs nor brakes and many found it more comfortable to walk part of the journey on foot, keeping close to the wagon for safety, as they were seldom challenged by highwaymen in open country. Wheels were well-dished with broad treads, helping to level-out the ruts for other traffic. Speed was seldom more than a slow walking pace, the team of eight or more heavy horses, controlled by drovers or wagoners walking alongside armed with cart whips. The wagoner-in-charge frequently rode a nimble pony or cob. Wheel horses or 'wheelers' were in double shafts rather than pole gear. On the credit side Stage Wagons were beneath the attention of armed robbers and – unlike Stage Coaches – were impossible to overturn. The main danger was from fire, when over-heated axles or sparks from pipe smokers caused a needless conflagration.

An American Stage Wagon of the late 18th century, was of similar construction but, in later years, hung on thoroughbraces or having sprung seating. Unlike the British wagons, with their traditional bowtops, the canvas head was eventually supported by corner pillars, which made the interior less stuffy and restricted.

Stake-sided dray. Heavy but low-sided goods wagon, used in many towns and cities of North America from the mid-19th century to the 1920's. Drawn by matching teams of Percheron or Belgian horses (usually stallions) with good action. The finest of these were to be seen in New York City during the 1890's and early 1900's. Controlled from an elevated, skeleton driving seat, sprung if the vehicle was dead axle. Side stakes or strakes were connected and secured with hanging chains that also steadied the load.

Stanhope. 1. Contraction of Stanhope Gig. *See* Stanhope Gig.

2. A late 19th century version of the Stanhope Gig, having a straight back rest or rail instead of the usual rounded or stick back.

Stanhope gig. English gig designed and first driven by the Hon. Fitzroy Stanhope, a keen amateur whip of the early 19th century, about the year 1814. The prototype was open, without a hood or top of any kind. Main bodywork was in the form of a buck or luggage compartment, above which was a driving seat balanced on two crosswise members, hung on double side or Telegraph springs. The stickback seat was also known as a Tilbury seat, after the builder of the Stanhope Gig. It was a double seat with room for both passenger and driver, side-by-side. Shafts were strongly reinforced with ironwork, fixed to the axles by independent brackets. Wheels were about 56″ in diameter.

Stanhope phaeton. *See* Phaeton, Stanhope.

Stanhope wagonette. Small version of the wagonette, seating six people. The driving seat had a stick or spindled backrest, half of which was made to lift, for improved access. Drawn by a single horse in shafts. Hung on full elliptical springs, front and rear.

State, Bismarck barouche. Ornate German-style barouche, hung on cee springs or a combination of cee and sideways elliptical springs. Drawn by a pair of horses in pole gear. Popular during the second half of the 19th century.

State canoe barouche. Shallow-bodied, canoe-shaped barouche, popular during the second half of the 19th century. Hung on a combination of cee and semi-elliptical side springs. Controlled either by postillions with a team of four, or driven from a box seat with hammer cloth.

State chariot. Formal or dress chariot that frequently replaced the earlier and bulkier State Coach, from the 1820's onwards. Seated two passengers facing forward, separated from the box-seat by a glass panel or windscreen. Hung on cee springs with a neat underperch, raised for an improved turning circle. In later years semi-elliptical springs were also used, sometimes combined with cee springs. Driven from a box seat with elaborately fringed hammer cloth. Two liveried footmen rode on a rearward dummy board. Drawn by a pair of horses in pole gear. One of the most attractive designs of its era.

State coach. 1. Coach frequently used by a monarch, head of state or noble personage, for ceremonial purposes. Usually drawn at walking pace by a team of six or more horses. Most were mounted on a combination of strap suspension and thoroughbraces.

2. Formal town coach used by the nobility and wealthier classes when attending important functions. Heavy and often cumbersome, driven from a box-seat with a fringed hammer cloth. At least two footmen would be poised on the rearward dummy board. Seated four passengers vis-à-vis. Drawn by a pair of matching coach horses, usually bays with black tails. Declined in popularity during the second half of the 19th century, although a few were still in use until the period of the First World War. Hung on cee springs but later with the addition of elliptical and semi-elliptical side springs. An underperch was always present.

State Landau. Large, canoe-shaped Landau, used on state or formal occasions. Usually drawn by four matching horses, controlled by postillions, with mounted out-riders. Those at the Royal Mews have a rearward or rumble seat for two footmen. Much heavier than the average vehicle of this type. Hung on cee springs with a strong underperch. Later types also had sideways elliptical springs.

Station bus. Small private bus, usually a single-decker, that plied between stations, hotels and country houses. Frequently owned by the main line railway companies. Drawn by a single horse in shafts or pair in pole gear.

Station fly. Small, four-wheeled cab or carriage used in station service, especially in remote country districts, throughout the greater part of the 19th century.

Station milk van. Four-wheeled van or small wagon with a short wheelbase, used for conveying milk in churns between farm and railway depot. Hung on sideways elliptical springs at the front and sideways semi-elliptical springs at the rear. Able to turn in full lock. Made in horse and cob sizes. Cost about £40 – late 19th century.

Station wagon. Same as a Depot Wagon. *See* Depot Wagon.

Steppe carriage. High-wheeled primitive carriage or truck, used in the migration of tribes from Central Asia to Eastern Europe during the Dark Ages.

Stick-back gig. Gig having a back rest for the driver supported by straight sticks or ribs, inclined in a rearward or outward direction.

Stick back slat wagon. American road wagon featuring near equirotal wheels and a stick-back driving seat. There was also a slatted floor. Hung on both crosswise and sideways semi-elliptical springs. The latter were fairly long and resembled the thoroughbraces of a Concord Coach, sometimes known as Concord Springs.

Stivers wagon. This name applies to a whole range of American Buggies and road wagons, designed by a carrigae-builder known as Stivers. An outstanding example would be the Piano Box Buggy.

Stocks sulky. The same as a Sydney Sulky. *See* Sydney Sulky.

Stolkjaerre. Two-wheeled driving cart of Norway, with room for at least four persons facing forward. Usually driven from a low seat at the rear. Suspension was originally from flexible shafts alone, but – in later years – sideways semi-elliptical springs were added. Drawn by a single horse or large pony.

Stone cart. 1. Low-sided cart used on arable land for collecting stones turned-up in cultivation. Drawn by a single horse in shafts. Dead axle.

2. Low-slung cart on cranked axles, with a bow-shaped front. Used for delivering blocks of quarried stone to a building site. Usually dead axle. Drawn by a single horse in shafts.

Straight raved wagon. Factory built farm wagon with iron naves. Popular in most parts of Britain during the mid-19th century. Flat side raves were at an angle of sixty degrees above the wheel tops.

Straight-sided spring cart. Cheap road cart used for delivery purposes, constructed in both cob and pony sizes. Used in large numbers, for delivering parcels and other small items, throughout the second half of the 19th century. The single cross-seat with back rest was near the centre of the vehicle, which had an enclosed front and rear. Hung on two or three sets of cross/sideways elliptical springs or semi-elliptical springs. Panel-sided with straight shafts.

Stratford cart. Small type of country driving cart, popular during the 1890's. Seated two people side-by-side or passenger and driver. Hung on a three spring or Dennett system. The trace hooks were also sprung.

Stratton's Northampton cart. Low-sided tip cart, used either for farm or road work. Dead axle or unsprung. The shafts were slightly curved.

Stratton's liquid manure cart. Low-slung tank-vehicle with rearward spreadboard. Shafts were usually curved. Drawn by a single heavy horse. Flow of liquid manure was controlled by a longitudinal lever with an upward curved handle. Widely used on English farms from the 1860's to the1900's.

Strawberry cart. A light, four-wheeled spring van, although usually known as a cart. Used in the harvesting and marketing of strawberries and other soft fruits. Frequently painted a bright red or deep crimson colour. The rear carriage had a three spring system of semi-elliptical springs one being a crosswise, reverse or damper spring. The forecarriage had a pair of sideways semi-elliptical springs, placed well forward. Shaft steps were bolted to the splinter bar. Broad outraves covered the wheel tops. A crosswise driving seat, within the bodywork, had an inclined back rest. Drawn by a medium heavy horse in straight shafts. Lever brakes acted on both rear wheels.

Studebaker aluminium wagon. Patent American farm and road wagon. Dead axle but driven from a low, sprung seat. All metalwork, except tyres, was made of aluminium.

Studebaker wagons. Any type of farm, military or commercial wagons built by the Studebaker Company of South Bend, Indiana, U.S.A. They frequently won gold medals at international exhibitions, being exported to all parts of the civilised world, from the mid-19th century until the 1930's. The same firm, like the Bristol Carriage and Wagon Company of England, produced everything on wheels from barrows and carts to coaches and motor cars. A special show vehicle, advertising the company, known as the 'Studebaker Wagon', was widely exhibited at fairs and exhibitions throughout America, inlaid with medals awarded over a period of sixty years.

Suffolk wagon. Box-type wagon of East Anglia, frequently appearing with double shafts. Fore-wheels tended to be well in advance of the front boards or forehead. There was a pronounced waisted effect for improved lock of the fore-wheels.

Suicide gig. *See* Gig, Suicide.

Sulky. 1. Any type of vehicle or farm implement with room on the driving seat for one person only, rather than having a shared or double cross-bench. Said to have been chosen by unsociable people fond of their own company or fits of sulking.

2. English post chaise or chariot, the narrow interior wide enough for only one passenger at a time.

3. Type of American gig or riding chair, used almost exclusively by male owner-drivers.

4. Modern exercise or show wagon/cart, with a tubular frame and wire spoked wheels.

Sulky saddle. Two-wheeled American driving or exercise cart of the mid-19th century. The driver was seated on a type of riding saddle placed between the rearwards ends of the shafts.

Sumpter truck. American name for a heavy freight or goods wagon of any type, running on four wheels.

Sundown. A light, open carriage on four wheels, having two or more crosswise seats. Made without a hood or head of any type. Used both in the Far West of the United States of America or the outback of Australia.

Surrey. American passenger vehicle or family carriage, drawn by either a single horse or pair of ponies in pole gear. Usually had room for at least four persons on double cross-seats, although a few later types held six. Early Surreys were made with rearward folding half-hoods, while later and larger versions had umbrella, canopy or extension tops. A notable example was the Fringe Top, first appearing during the 1880's. Mainly hung on crosswise suspension, as with the American Buggy.

Surrey cart. A version of the English or two-wheeled dogcart. Very little is known concerning this type, which may have been experimental. There is no connection between it and the American Surrey.

Surrey wagon. Type of farm wagon also appearing in parts of Sussex and Hampshire. Noted for spindle sides and elegant strouters or side supports. Of medium/long wheelbase. Both loading platform and upper line had slight, inward curves. Able to turn in quarter lock only.

Sussex timber wagon. Near equirotal Timber Carriage or Wagon, mainly used in the county of Sussex. Noted for an extensive circular reachpole and rearward, screw-down braking. Drawn by teams of variable sizes, although the wheeler was in single shafts. Most carried a dragshoe, hung on the hind carriage.

Sussex wagons. Farm wagons noted for their high-sided or boxlike appearance and short wheel base,having large fore-wheels. Frequently had demountable bodywork. Corner poles were mainly used in place of end-ladders. A longer wheelbased type, with broad wheel-treads, was known as the Sussex Broad Wheeled Wagon. Most were drawn by a horse in shafts, although assisted by a chain horse in tandem.

Sweeper. Horse-drawn street sweeping cart or implement, its underside fitted with revolving brushes. Widely used in city streets of Europe and America from the 1880's to the 1930's. Eventually replaced by a motorised or self-propelled type. A few were four-wheeled although the majority appear to have run on two wheels. Driven to a single horse in shafts or pair of horses in pole gear, controlled from an elevated seat at the fore-end.

Swiss mountain carriage. Single-horse phaeton of the 1820's and 30's, hung on cee springs. Seated two on the box-seat and two on a rearward cross-seat, facing forward. Usually constructed with a strong underperch. The front and sides had a strongly ribbed or panelled effect. Lower limbs of the passengers were protected by waterproof aprons carried in rolls. It appeared either with or without a falling hood.

Swiss runabout. Four-wheeled carriage or phaeton for two, with ample rearward luggage space. The bodywork was in the form of a shallow tray with a mid-way cross-seat and low dashboard. Hung on crosswise elliptical springs, like the American Buggy. Popular from the mid-19th century until the 1920's. Drawn by a single horse or large pony in shafts.

Sydney sulky. Also known as the Sydney Brass Sulky. Australian two-wheeled sulky, mounted with highly polished brass fittings. Used for showing purposes and pleasure driving. Hung on sideways elliptical springs. Low-slung, round-backed and well upholstered, including the arm rests. An up-market version of the Stocks Sulky. A slightly less elaborate version, without brasswork, was used as a Town Runabout.

T

Tableau wagon. Circus parade or show wagon/float. Usually drawn by a large team of heavy horses, controlled from an elevated box-seat. The actual tableau or display might consist of gilded human figures in statuesque poses, carved figures or trained animals. These represented scenes from history, popular literature or legend.

Tailor's cart/van. Either a two or four-wheeled delivery van of the enclosed or brougham-type. Used by tailor's, hatters and haberdashers during the second half of the 19th century. Hung on sideways full or half elliptical springs. Drawn by a single horse or large pony in shafts.

Talika. Closed four-wheeled cab of the growler-type. Used in many towns and cities of Turkey and the Balkans, during the second half of the 19th century. Square and boxlike with angular lines. Mounted on sideways semi-elliptical springs.

Tally-ho break. Light sporting break on high wheels. Used by the fox-hunting and horse racing fraternities of the late 19th century. Hung on elliptical and/or semi-elliptical springs. Drawn by a single horse in shafts or a pair of horses in pole gear.

Tandem cart. Two-wheeled dogcart, kept mainly for show purposes. Driven to a tandem pair. The rear seat, occupied by a groom, was on a slightly lower level than the driving seat. Slats at the sides were frequently dummies as dogs were not carried.

Tappell. French – seat tapper. Name widely used in country districts of France and Belgium for a roughly made or badly sprung vehicle.

Tarantass. Punt-shaped Russian passenger vehicle. Suspended on a series of flexible poles between fore and hind carriages. The rearward part, with a cross-bench for three or more passengers, was protected by hood and apron. Driven to a troika or team of three horses abreast.

Tar wagon. Also known as a tar boiler. Four-wheeled vehicle used by corporations and private contractors, in road making/repairing operations. Introduced during the early 1900's. Basically a portable boiler above a small furnace, in horizontal form. The wheels were fairly small and of cast iron. Drawn by a single heavy horse in tubular iron shafts.

Tax cart. English driving or passenger cart taxed very low and – from 1843 – exempt from taxation and duty. Conditions were that the vehicle must cost no more than £12 to make, and have the owner's name and address painted on the side panels.

'T'-cart. A 'T'-Cart Phaeton. *See* Phaeton, 'T'-cart.

Team. American term for a pair or larger number of draught horses and the vehicle they drew.

Telega. Russian passenger or stage coach. Crudely made and frequently unsprung or dead axle. A larger version of the Tarantass. *See* Tarantass.

Telegraph. English two-wheeled chaise of the late 1790's and early 1800's. A compromise between the dogcart and the whisky.

Tennis cart. Light-weight sporting cart hung on a three spring form of suspension. A rein rail of continuous iron rods replaced the normal dashboard. Sides of the bodywork curved slightly above the wheel tops, as with the Ralli Car. Popular during the second half of the 19th century.

Ten-seater break. Passenger break seating four per side on longitudinal benches facing inwards. Two or more could also share the driving seat. Hung on sideways elliptical or semi-elliptical springs.

Thensa. Processional vehicle of Ancient Rome, running on four equirotal wheels. Each wheel had four carved spokes. The forepart was elevated and bow-fronted in the style of a racing chariot. Drawn by pairs of horses or larger teams.

Thespis. Car or chariot claimed to have been used, in the classical world, by the muse of acting and drama. Later a two- or four-wheeled vehicle that could be converted to support the stage used by travelling players.

Three-horse omnibus. Although most three-horse buses, after the original Shillibeer type was banned from the streets of London, were drawn by two horses, in pole gear, there were later exceptions, especially in the provinces. This was apart from the use of extra or 'cock' horses on steep gradients. Several local authorities, including Glasgow Corporation, adopted a three-horse version of the Garden Seat Omnibus during the early 1890's. Horses would be harnessed three abreast rather than unicorn or pickaxe.

Three seat canopy top Surrey. Headed or canopy-top Surrey, with three rows of forward facing seats.

Three spring grocery wagon. American high-sided van, of the open type, drawn by a single horse in shafts. The fore-carriage had crosswise elliptical springs while the rear-carriage had sideways elliptical springs.

Three spring morning phaeton. Light phaeton, frequently having a basketwork body. Hung on two sideways elliptical springs and a set of crosswise full elliptical springs, at front and rear respectively. Drawn by a single horse or large pony in shafts.

Tilbury. Gig designed by the Hon. Fitzroy Stanhope, although named after its builder. It was much heavier than the original Stanhope Gig, although appearing at roughly the same period (early 19th century). Hung on seven springs and two braces, which made it cumbersome but comfortable. Large numbers were exported to all parts of Europe where badly made roads and mountain passes made extra springs necessary. The driving seat was spindle-backed. Mounted by means of bucket-shaped shaft steps. Normally without a buck or luggage space.

Tilt cart. 1. Name used in Scotland for a tip or dump cart, able to discharge its load in a rearward direction.

2. Cart with a canvas hood supported by hoops or tilts.

Timber bog. Same as a Neb, Nib or Pair of Wheels, etc.

Timber carriage or tug. Combined items of limbered or articulated gear, with end-bolsters, joined by a reach pole. Used to transport logs or lengths of felled timber. Usually dead axle or unsprung. Hauled by large teams of heavy horses.

Tip cart/tipping cart. Name used in most parts of Britain for a dump or dung cart. Able to discharge its load in a rearward direction. Usually drawn by a single horse in shafts.

To-cart. French name for a two-wheeled English Dogcart.

Tombrerel. French name for the two-wheeled cart, drawn by a single horse, later corrupted to Tumbrel or Tumbril. Used for both agricultural and commercial purposes. During the French Revolution it was also a prison and execution cart. Usually unsprung or dead axle. *See* Tumbrel/Tumbril.

Tompkin's gig. Small gig, popular in North America during the 1900's. Noted for its slatted under-compartment, similar to the

English Dogcart. Minus rearward seating and with the back fully enclosed. Hung on sideways semi-elliptical springs.

Tonga. Two-wheeled native cart of India, drawn by a pair of large ponies harnessed to a centre pole in a form of curricle gear. Passengers rode dos-à-dos on a broad centre-seat, under a fringed top or canopy. The driver, next to the forward facing passenger, sounded a bugle or trumpet as a warning signal. Widely used by British officers and civil servants stationed in India, also for general military purposes. Native drivers always appeared to be well-acquainted with this type of vehicle and harness. The pole and body of the vehicle – when in draught – tilted in a rearward direction, feet of the rear passengers supported on a tailboard with letting-down chains.

Tortoise. Slang name for a clumsy, cumbersome private coach of the 17th century. So-named as such vehicles were often of a rounded or oval shape, not unlike the shell of a giant tortoise.

Totter's cart or dray. Small dray or trolley, usually flat or low-sided, drawn by a cob or large pony in shafts. Usually had full underlock and hung on sideways semi-elliptical springs, front and rear. Some had an elevated driver's seat on vertical irons, while the shafts curved towards the fore-ends. Brakes were of the screw-down type, applied only when the horse was standing, to prevent it wandering away. Some are still used in the suburbs of large towns for the collection of scrap materials (totting). Modern types frequently have equirotal wheels with pneumatic tyres.

Touring coach. Version of the Stage Coach, drawn by a four-in-hand team, used at British coastal and inland resorts for scenic drives and holiday excursions. Especially popular during the late 19th and early 20th centuries. Many had forward facing roof seats or gammon boards, although the interior compartments – too low or restricted for comfort – were never used and known as 'dummies'. Solid, compact and well-sprung these vehicles were eventually purpose-built but lacked the elegance of earlier coaches. Wheels, although turning in full lock, were frequently heavy and cartlike. Some of the finest touring services in Britain were day-long trips through Snowdonia, starting from hotels in Llandudno and Colwyn Bay. Some Llandudno coaches were twenty-two seaters, not including provision for coachman and guard.

Tower wagon. Near equirotal wagon drawn by a pair of horses in pole gear. This was a platform or base for elevating ladders, raised and lowered at required levels, for the repair of overhead wires, lamps and the gear supporting them. Such vehicles were usually owned by municiple authorities and street tramway companies.

Town chariot. Less formal version of the State Chariot. Seated two passengers facing forward, behind a glass panel or windscreen. Driven from the box-seat to a pair of matching horses in pole gear. Frequently minus the rearward dummy board.

Town coach. Less formal version of the state coach for city or family use.

Tradesman's light spring delivery van. Plain, open van used by retail traders for street deliveries. Drawn by a single horse or large pony in shafts. Up to 15 cwts. capacity. Ideal for steady draught, with high wheels and light but sturdy side-planks/ironwork. Usually constructed with a short wheelbase. Frequently minus a full dashboard. Popular throughout the second half of the 19th century. Hung on both cross and sideways elliptical/semi-elliptical springs.

Trailer dustcart. Four-wheeled dustcart or van. Made of welded steel construction, usually headed or fully enclosed. Drawn by a single heavy horse, its shafts cranked to a low under-carriage. Used by the municipal authorities of many towns and cities in the United Kingdom, until the 1950's. Led on foot rather than driven. Some could be used, with a drawbar in place of shafts, for haulage by tractor units or towed behind motor lorries.

Tram. Alternative name for a Street Car. Usually drawn by a pair of horses, but less frequently by a single horse or pair of mules. Either single or double-decker, according to route. Still used in Douglas, Isle-of-Man, for trips along the Promenade.

Transfer dray. American name for a heavy, four-wheeled dray, used for city haulage. Hung on sideways semi-elliptical springs, front and rear. Drawn by pairs, or larger teams, of heavy horses in pole gear.

Trap. 1. Slang name for any type of light, low-slung vehicle, usually a tub cart.

2. American four-wheeled driving vehicle, informal but of greater elegance than Trap 1. Noted for its high seats but short wheelbase. Grained and varnished with a natural wood finish in the style of a country cart. Drawn by a single large pony or cob in shafts.

Travelling carriage. A large private coach or carriage adapted for the purpose of long distance travel, often using hired horses changed at inns and post houses along the route.

Travelling cart. Type of two-wheeled caravan, fitted with an interior bunk or hammock. Mainly used in colonial territories during the late 19th century. Similar to a Cape Cart or Encamping Cart. Drawn by a pair of horses in pole gear. Dead axle or hung on sideways semi-elliptical springs, although a few may have had thoroughbraces.

Travelling chariot.   A version of the Family Chariot, adapted for long distance travel.

Travelling forge.   Mobile military forge, mounted on four equirotal wheels. Usually attached to a cavalry of artillery unit. Unsprung or dead axle. Carried not only a portable furnace but anvil, bellows and a whole range of tools needed for shoeing and repair work in the field. Featured an arched centre or cut-under for improved underlock. Drawn by a pair of horses in pole gear.

Travelling cooker.   Limbered military vehicle, drawn by a pair of horses in pole gear, controlled by a mounted driver. Continental versions, however, were frequently driven from a cross-seat on the fore-limber. The front or fore-part carried fuel and food, while the rear limber was an oven on two wheels. Supported by props at each corner, when at rest. The tall stovepipe chimney of some types was made to lie flat (with hinges) when not in use. Still in service with some units during the early 1940's.

Travelling wagon.   Similar to the Encamping Cart or Travelling Cart, but larger and running on four wheels. Fitted-out with four bunks or hammock-type beds. Could be adapted for horse, mule or bullock draught, usually in large teams. Used mainly in colonial countries, especially South or East Africa, for long distance travel. Introduced during the second half of the 19th century.

Travelling van.   Open-sided passenger vehicle, hung fairly high on sideways elliptical springs, front and rear. There were two crosswise seats facing forward, protected by a canopy top. Some types had a rearward well or platform for a groom. Drawn by two horses in pole gear. Popular in India during the late 19th century.

Tray sulky.   Australian gig-like vehicle of the late 19th century. Made with an adjustable cross-seat, suitable for a single person only, although some later types were large enough for a driver and passenger, side-by-side.

Tree-planting wagon.   Low-slung wagon in which growing trees or large shrubs could be carried for transplanting purposes. Usually designed with a well-like centre in which roots were protected with soil and straw. Drawn by pairs or larger teams of heavy horses in pole gear.

Trestle wagon.   Military wagon in which trestles were carried, necessary for the construction of pontoon bridges and similar structures. Four-wheeled and dead axle. Usually drawn by a pair of medium-heavy horses in the care of mounted drivers.

Tribus. Three-passenger cab, running on two wheels. Invented by a London carriage-builder named Harvey, in 1844. Drawn by a single horse in shafts. Entered and driven from the rear. Hung on sideways semi-elliptical springs. A later but less popular version was drawn by a pair of horses in curricle gear, known as the Curricle Tribus.

Troika curricle. Large curricle of a type popular in Britain during the second half of the 19th century. Drawn by three horses abreast in the Russian style. The centre horse would be in shafts, curricle gear for both outer horses extended from shafts to pad saddles.

Triolet. French two-wheeled cab of 1826. The bodywork was suspended from cross members of the roof, that also rested on sides of the underframe.

Troll. Cart or truck used by street vendors, especially in the London area and Home Counties. Usually unsprung or dead axle. Drawn by a single pony.

Trolley. Light truck or dray, usually four-wheeled. Low-slung and drawn by a single horse or pony in shafts. Sometimes used at large railways stations to convey mail or luggage from one platform to another, being a version of the porter's trolley mounted with shafts.

Trottle cart. A fore-runner of the Irish Jaunting Car. Mounted on two wheels and having a double row of lengthwise seating. Made from roughly carved timbers, being much smaller than its successors. Usually unsprung or dead axle. Drawn by a single horse in shafts.

Troy coach. American stage or public coach, mainly operating in New York State (U.S.A.), during the early part of the 19th century. Originally constructed in the town of Troy. It has been claimed that the Concord Coach was merely a better finished and more sophisticated version of the Troy Coach. The bodywork of both vehicles would have been mounted on thoroughbraces rather than side springs.

Truck. The name of this vehicle derives from the Latin – trochus for hoop. During the 18th century this was a heavy freight vehicle with two or four wheels, headed by a length of canvas stretched over hoops.

Truck, hook and ladder. Four-wheeled truck or light wagon used in fire-fighting to convey extra ladders and gear. Long and low-slung, mounted on sideways elliptical springs. Drawn by a pair of horses in pole gear, driven from an elevated box-seat.

Truck, hose.   Either a two or four-wheeled vehicle used in fire-fighting to convey a reel of fire hose. Drawn by a single horse.

Truckle car/cart.   Low-slung agricultural cart, used in Ireland and parts of Wales, from the Middle Ages to the late 19th century. A few may have survived much longer, in remote areas. Unsprung or dead axle, mounted on disc wheels. Drawn by a single horse or cob between rude shafts. Difficult to overturn in hillside pastures.

Trull.   Alternative name for Troll. *See* Troll.

Tub cart.   Larger and heavier version of the Governess Car, with which it had many features in common.

Tub cart phaeton.   Small phaeton with a tublike body and curved bottom line. Drawn by a single horse or large pony. Also known as a Tub Phaeton.

Tumbler.   Alternative name for a tip or dump cart.

Tumbler slush cart.   Cylindrical tank cart. Low-slung but with large carrying wheels. Used throughout the second half of the 19th century, especially in country districts, for clearing cess pits of cottages without piped sewerage. It could be tipped by means of a windlass fixed to the rearward end of the shafts. A similar vehicle was also used to carry liquid lime and mortar on construction sites. Dead axle or usprung. Drawn by a single horse in shafts.

Tumbrel/tumbril.   1. Traditional farm cart of a type found in most parts of Western Europe for over three centuries.

2. Type of low-slung ammunition cart, used by many Continental armies throughout the 18th century. Drawn by a single horse in shafts.

Turnout.   Slang name for any type of horse or vehicle, ready for work or show.

Turpentine cart.   Carrying frame on four wheels with end-bolsters. Used in the southern states of North America for carrying barrel-loads of turpentine. Painted with specially strong, repellent-coatings to resist stains from spillage. Dead axle or usprung. Drawn by a single horse in shafts.

Twelve quarter coach.   Coach with twelve panels or quarters, making up the bodywork, some of which could be removed for driving in warm weather.

Two horse cart.   Larger than average cart, up to 45 cwts. capacity. Frequently a tip cart. Used with chain horses in tandem rather than double shafts. Could be fitted with out-raves or

shelving to protect an overhanging load. Usually unsprung or dead axle.
Two-wheeler. 1. Any type of two-wheeled horse-drawn vehicle.
2. Slang name for a Hansom Cab.

U

Underdrawn wagon. Type of freight wagon with its pole or shafts connected under rather than above, the axletrees.
Undertaker's wagon. Any type of four-wheeled vehicle used by undertakers, including the hearse, casket wagon and sometimes mourning coaches. In the United States of America there was also a special tray-like truck or cart of this name used to carry wreaths and floral tributes, when these were too numerous to carry on the hearse.
Universal float. Type of large float on cranked axles and sideways semi-elliptical springs, used for general delivery purposes. Entered from the rear. Drawn by a cob or small horse in shafts.
Utility cart. Two-wheeled skeleton cart, used for breaking young horses. Usually low-slung, its seat near road level and thus difficult to overturn.
Utrecht wagon. Dutch passenger carriage, with panel sides and a canopy top, the latter said to resemble a tent with the flaps down. There was a crosswise seating plan, vis-à-vis, for at least four passengers, while others shared the semi-open driving seat. Later versions may have had doors and windows (lights), although – with the prototypes – there were no doors and passengers had to help each other scramble over the wheels. Usually hung on thorough-braces rather than springs.

V

Vale of Pickering wagon. Neat, light wagon from the Vale of Pickering in North Yorkshire. Used with either shafts or pole gear. Remarkable for its fine proportions. Plank-sided to a height of three planks only. Usually unsprung or dead axle. Out raves were well clear at top and sides.
Van. High-sided vehicle, usually but not always headed or covered. Either two or four wheeled. Used for goods and luggage deliveries, collections, etc. Drawn by a single horse in shafts or, less frequently, by a pair in pole gear.

Vardo 168

Vardo. A Gypsy living van or wagon. Also known as a caravan or house-on-wheels.

Veterinary ambulance. Either a two or four-wheeled horse ambulance.

Veterinary cart. A two-wheeled horse ambulance. Usually driven from a seat over the nearside wheel.

Vettura. Italian cab or hired carriage. Usually four-wheeled and headed. Drawn by a single horse in shafts.

Viceroy. American version of the Skeleton Show Wagon, usually mounted with silver fittings.

Victoria. 1. Victorian pleasure carriage, frequently used for semi-formal or park driving. Popular throughout the second half of the 19th century. Descended from a much earlier type known as a Milord. This latter was greatly admired by the Prince of Wales, on a visit to Paris, one of which he ordered for his mother (Queen Victoria), after whom the English version was named, in 1869.

A semi-open carriage, fairly low and easy to enter. The rearward part was protected by a falling or half-hood. Two passengers sat side-by-side, facing forward. Hung on four elliptical side springs but often having double suspension with rearward cee springs. The Grand Victoria had a rearward or rumble seat for footmen. Although usually driven from a box-seat to a single horse in shafts, larger types may have had a pair of horses in pole gear. One of the most graceful and popular of all 19th century carriages. Could be purchased from £120 upwards.

2. Small, low-slung pony phaeton named after Queen Victoria.

Victoria cab. Same as a Victoria Hansom. *See* Victoria Hansom.

Victoria Hansom. Later type of semi-open, two-wheeled cab, entered through a side door. Further noted for its falling or half-hood. Frequently used in warm weather and at seaside resorts.

Village cart. Light, four-wheeled road cart, driven from the interior. Large enough for two occupants or a driver and passenger, with ample luggage space. Hung on sideways elliptical springs. Driven to a single horse or large pony in shafts.

Village phaeton. *See* Phaeton, Village.

Village wagon. Alternative name for a spring wagon.

Vis-à-vis. 1. French, face-to-face. French name for a passenger vehicle in which the occupants sat facing each other on opposite seats.

2. A narrow passenger or pleasure carriage of the late 18th century, large enough for two persons facing each other. A type of vehicle eventually replaced by the Town or State Chariot.

Voiture. French name for any type of coach or carriage.

Volante. Two-wheeled, hooded vehicle of Cuba. Fairly low-slung with a chaise-like body and long, flexible shafts, which aided the suspension and eliminated sway. Three or more ponies were harnessed abreast, two on each side of a carriage pole. One of the nearside ponies was further attached by extension gear and ridden by a postillion. Hung on rearward cee springs. Large numbers of this type of vehicle were constructed in either Great Britain or the United States of America, exported to Cuba throughout the greater part of the 19th century.

W

Wagga-Wagga gig. Australian gig, strongly made for rough roads or tracks of the outback. It had a well-body with deeply upholstered seats for two. The dashboard was fairly low with a straight rein rail. Shafts were also straight. Hung on sideways semi-elliptical springs, sometimes with a rearward cross spring.

Wagon. 1. Derives from the German or Dutch Wagen, meaning a wheeled vehicle. The original English spelling was waggon, but the extra 'g' appears to have been dropped during the late 19th century, although retained by some, with relation to certain farm or harvest wagons.

In general terms a four-wheeled, medium-heavy vehicle, more substantial and perhaps dignified than a two-wheeled cart. Originally difficult to turn in a confined space – a structure of double 'A' frames on disc-wheels. The problem of turning was later solved – at least partly – by a pivotting of the fore-carriage. Fore and hind-carriage were eventually connected by a reach pole or underperch. Some early wagons were also waisted with a wheel-recess or notch on either side, to assist in locking. During later stages of development there were devices for springing, braking and the use of full underlock. Most early wagons, especially on farms, were without brakes, suspension or any type of driving seat. Horses would be connected to the vehicle in single shafts, double shafts, or pole gear and swingletrees, according to local use and custom.

The main regional types in Britain were either high-sided Box-Wagons of the Eastern counties, East Midlands and Yorkshire, or low-sided Bow-Wagons (having protective side rails or raves bowed above the rear wheels) of the South and West Midlands. There were few wagons of any type in Scotland and the interior of

Wales (apart from a few in the border counties), before the 1890's.

Factory-made wagons eventually ousted vehicles made by village craftsmen, towards the end of the 19th century. The latter types were often crudely made with numerous bolts, nails and metal parts, also having metal rather than wooden naves.

With the exception of certain Dutch and German types, most Continental wagons appear to have been rudimentary, with semi-open or ladder sides. Distinctive wagons of North America were often covered types such as the Conestoga, made for and used by the early pioneers. Later types with tray or box-shaped bodies, were produced by a form of mass production, many having hand brakes and sprung driving seats.

2. Certain types of passenger vehicle – usually four-wheeled – were also known as wagons, especially in North America, from the early 19th century. The name is further given to lightly built, four-wheeled show vehicles.

Wagon, barge. *See* Barge Wagon.

Wagon, boat. *See* Boat Wagon.

Wagon, bow. *See* Bow Wagon.

Wagon, box. *See* Box Wagon.

Wagonette. Four-wheeled passenger vehicle, drawn by a single horse in shafts or pair in pole gear. First constructed in England during the early 1840's. Usually open types, entered through the rear via a small door and step iron. The interior had longitudinal, inward facing seats for three per side, with a fairly low driving seat. A popular family carriage of various sizes, widely used in Britain and North America throughout the second half of the 19th century. Hung on sideways elliptical springs at the front and sideways semi-elliptical springs at the rear. A lever brake usually acted on both rear wheels.

Wagonette brake/break. Large type of wagonette, frequently protected by a canopy top on fixed standards. Able to seat eight passengers. Drawn by a pair of horses in pole gear.

Wagonette omnibus. Wagonette with a raised coach or carrige-type driving seat, much higher than passenger level. A large vehicle frequently drawn by a four-in-hand team.

Wagonette Phaeton. Small, light wagonette with a double driving seat.

Wagonette trap. Four-wheeled American trap or phaeton, with a shifting rear seat. Drawn by a single cob-type horse, in shafts.

Wagon, self-loading. An alternative name for the Excavator. *See* Excavator.

Wain. 1. Early English name for a wagon, especially those used in farm work.

2. Type of two-wheeled farm dray or float used in harvesting. Drawn by a single horse in shafts. Frequently spindle-sided.

War cart. A two-wheeled military cart drawn by a single horse or mule. Similar to the Maltese Cart. A name frequently used in India. *See* Maltese Cart.

Warwickshire wagon. Panel-sided farm or harvest wagon. Noted for its long wheelbase. Sides were much higher at the front than the rear. Able to turn in quarter lock.

Water barrel cart. A large wooden barrel slung horizontally between two wheels and fitted with shafts for single draught. Supported, while at rest, by propsticks. Used for military purposes, also in country districts – without piped water – especially in time of drought. Unsprung or dead axle.

Water cart/wagon. Two or four-wheeled vehicle used to supply water in country districts, also – in military life – to accompany troops in camp or on the line of march. Those owned by local authorities were fitted with sprayboards and used in street cleaning or to clear mud and lay dust, according to season. Sometimes led, but usually driven from a skeleton seat above the tank. Drawn either by a single horse in shafts or pair in pole gear, according to size and capacity. Cost about £40.

Water tank cart. A sophisticated version of the Water Barrel Cart. Either a round or square tank, with top-filler, drawn by a single horse in shafts or pair in pole gear. Made of cemented metal plates supported by a wooden framework. A military version was introduced during the 1890's to replace the less sanitary barrel-type. A Mark II version had filter apparatus and brake-gear. Usually in the care of a mounted driver.

Well bottom gig. Also known as the Well or Welled Gig. English Gig with a dropped front and well floor. It had a much lower centre of gravity than the average vehicle of this type, being more stable and easier to both mount and control. The cross-seat was only a few inches above the axle. Frequently had cane or basketwork sides. Hung on two sideways semi-elliptical and one crosswise semi-elliptical springs. Shafts were slightly curved at the fore-ends.

Welsh long cart. A type of primitive harvest cart used on mountain farms, especially where narrow lanes discouraged the use of larger vehicles. The body was both longer and narrower than the average cart, while the sides were shallow but frequently

depending on side rails – rather than out-raves – to contain an overhanging load. A similar type of vehicle was also used in the Lowlands of Scotland, especially during the first half of the 19th century. Shafts were an extension of the framework or underframe, from which body and platform could be detached. Unsprung or dead axle. Drawn by a small horse of the cob type.
Welsh Ralli car. A slat-sided Ralli Car, known in country districts of Central Wales as a Cart. Shafts were fitted inside the bodywork.
Welsh truckle car. Welsh version of a two-wheeled dray also appearing in Ireland. *See* Truckle Car.
Wensleydale shandry. Strongly built market cart of the Yorkshire Dales. Back and sides of the driving seat were enclosed by a top rail supported on ornamentally turned spindles. The rearward tailboard was strongly made and resembled that of a farm cart or wagon. Some forms of seating were made to adjust on slides to balance a heavy load. Wheels had van-type naves with tapered linchpins. Shafts were of square section. Usually drawn by a medium-heavy horse in van harness.
Westbury luggage cart. Combined luggage and market cart with prominent splashers or mudguards and straight shafts. Made in both pony and cob sizes. There was easy access through both front and rear. Hung on a set of crosswise rearward springs plus two sideways semi-elliptical springs. The crosswise driving seat was movable to balance the load. Frequently appeared with a high dashboard. Popular from the mid-19th century to the period of the First World War.
West End mineral water trolley. Plank-sided, four wheeled delivery trolley, similar to the provincial trolley but having a shorter wheelbase. The elevated driving seat had an under-locker or bookbox for paper work. Usually drawn by a single horse in shafts but, less frequently, by a pair in pole gear. Hung on sideways semi-elliptical springs. Cost between £42 and £46.
Western passenger wagon. Square-shaped, semi-open American passenger wagon, mainly used in states bordering the Pacific seaboard. Seated four or more passengers under a canopy top, with two more on the box-seat. Drawn by a four-in-hand team.
West of England brewer's dray. Four-wheeled brewer's dray used in the Bristol area and the south west of England. Usually made with an open or slatted loading platform. There were four sizes, the largest up to loads of 12 barrels. Supplied with loading skids hung on a framework beneath the rear-carriage, also having a

prominent nameboard at the front-end. Drawn by a single heavy horse in shafts. Hung on sideways semi-elliptical springs, front and rear.

West Gloucestershire wagon.   Similar to the Wiltshire Wagon, having downward sloping hoop raves, continued above the rear wheels to platform level. Sides were fairly shallow and outward inclined, while wheels were much sturdier and further apart than those of the Wiltshire Wagon. *See* Wiltshire Wagon.

West Midlands barge wagon.   Low-sided barge wagon of the West Midlands, an area ranging from South Staffordshire to the Cotswolds. Noted for its long wheelbase, low sides and limited underlock. Mounted with heavy ironwork. Either craftsman or factory-made. Usually fitted with iron naves. Introduced during the second half of the 19th century.

Wheel boat.   Any vehicle that could be converted to a boat or raft for crossing rivers, especially when the wheels were removed. There were several military wagons and carts of this type.

Wheel cart.   Type of primitive slide or sleigh mounted on two wheels, as used for harvesting in the West of Ireland. Similar to the even more primitive Truckle Car, from which it may have developed. Unsprung or dead axle. Drawn by a single horse or cob in shafts.

Whirlicote.   An alternative name for a passenger vehicle also known as the Medieval Long Wagon. *See* Long Wagon.

Whisky or whiskey.   Light one-horse chaise of the late 18th and early 19th centuries. Known by this name as it could whisk over the ground at great speed. Hung on shallow-sideways platform springs. Seldom headed and frequently minus a dashboard. Some had their bodywork covered in canework and were known as Caned Whiskies. The alternative was a panel-sided or half panel type. Seated either one or two people, according to size and requirements.

Whisky-curricle.   Large type of Whisky driven to a pair of horses in curricle gear.

Whitechapel buggy.   Australian four-wheeled buggy, first built about 1900. Hung on crosswise elliptical springs but with a perch-type underbody. Able to turn in quarter lock only. Further noted for its falling or folding hood and near equirotal wheels.

Whitechapel cart.   Type of English or two-wheeled dogcart with a bracket-front and angular bodywork. Sides were open or semi-open but railed-in. Originally used by dealers and businessmen, it became popular as a driving cart for gentlemen, from the mid-19th century. Drawn by a large pony or cob in shafts.

Wholesale grocery wagon.   American, oblong-shaped grocery van or wagon, drawn by a single horse in shafts. Hung on sideways elliptical (platform) springs. The semi-open driving seat was covered by a canopy extension top, supported on pillars, with roll-down blinds for cold or wet weather.

Windsor wagon.   American (box-type) Buggy of the late 19th century. Suspended on side bars and cross springs.

Wiltshire dung cart.   Low-sided, rearward tipping dung cart, as used on farms bordering Salisbury Plain. There was a low tailboard with upward flared sideboards or raves, extending above the wheels. Usually painted dark blue with red or orange wheels.

Wiltshire float.   Large type of farmer's float with cranked axle and mail coach hubs. Hung on sideways semi-elliptical springs. The lower half of the body was panelled while the upper half was spindled to the top line. There was also a curved mid-line or rave. Top or head rails were arched and fully chamfered. Some types had a reverse or damper spring under the rear part. A lever brake acted on the rearward parts of both wheels. Entered through the front, by means of shaft steps. Curved splashers or mudguards protected the wheel tops.

Wiltshire traveller's cart.   strongly built market cart, hung on sideways semi-elliptical springs. The bodywork had a pronounced inward slope or sheer. Upper sideboards or raves were removable.

Wiltshire wagon.   Similar to the South Wiltshire Wagon, with a bowed rear-end and hoop raves above the rear wheels. Unlike the Oxfordshire Wagon, raves were turned downwards rather than upwards, terminating on a level with the loading platform.

Wine cart.   Frequently known as the London Wine Cart. Light-weight and low-sided, but fairly high above road level. Hung on two sideways semi-elliptical springs and one rearward-crosswise elliptical spring. When at rest the straight shafts would be supported by propsticks. There was a slight projection for top loading above the hindquarters of the single horse in draught. Up to a capacity of 25 cwts. Used throughout the second half of the 19th century.

Wine merchant's spring float.   Crank-axle delivery float, similar to those used by dairymen and for farm work, although perhaps more elegant. Made with or without projecting side rails/raves and a square top or head. Notable features were the curved nameboards at front and sides. Hung on sideways semi-elliptical springs. Made in both cob and full-horse sizes. Popular throughout the second half of the 19th century.

Wine merchant's van. Also known as a General Trade Van, although frequently used by wine merchants. Fairly light and open with projecting side raves for extra top-loading. Panel rather than plank-sided. There were check springs over the rear axle, while a screw-down brake acted on both rear wheels, a column of the latter having bevelled gears, operating from the off-side of a single driving seat. Usually sold with shafts for a single horse or pole gear for a pair of horses. The use of either one or two horses depended on the payload and local gradients encountered.

Wire wagon. Articulated or limbered military wagon, drawn by teams of four or six horses, with mounted drivers. Used for laying telegraph wires in the field. Wire was fed-out from spools on each wagon or limber, signalmen riding on the rear body assisting with the paying-out process. This was further checked by an outrider with ringed staff. Unsprung or dead axle.

Wolds wagon. Farm or harvest wagon of the Yorkshire Wolds. A type of Box Wagon, usually drawn by a pair of heavy horses in pole gear.

Wood covered spring lurry. Any type of small delivery wagon with a fixed wooden head or roof and partly enclosed driving position. Hung on semi-elliptical side springs, also having mail hubs and axles. Introduced during the 1890's for house-to-house deliveries. Some later versions with pneumatic tyres, were still in use, as travelling shops, until the mid-1950's.

Woodstock wagon. Alternative name for the Oxfordshire version of the Bow Wagon.

Woosteree. New England name for a type of chaise, having a body similar to the Tilbury Gig.

Worcester cart. Low-slung, two-wheeled dogcart of a type originally made in the City of Worcester. Hung on sideways semi-elliptical springs.

Worcestershire wagon. Type of Bow Wagon noted for its spindle-sides, with highly scalloped/spokeshaved bodywork and outraves. Able to turn in quarter lock.

Worthing cart. Low-sided dogcart of a type formerly made in the West Sussex town of Worthing. Hung on sideways semi-elliptical springs.

Wurst wagon. German hunting wagon of the mid-18th century, also used for military purposes, conveying infantry troops to the front line. Long and narrow, like a German sausage or wurst. Ridden astride, the huntsmen or soldiers having their feet supported by common footboards. Drawn by four or more horses, controlled by postillions.

Y

Yandell buggy. Type of American Buggy, with a curved or Yandell Top, also known as the Doctor's or Physician's Buggy. Hung on crosswise elliptical springs, front and rear. Frequently used by medical practitioners, in country districts, during the second half of the 19th century.

Yellow bounder. British slang name for a Post Chaise, frequently painted yellow or yellow and black.

Yellowstone wagon. Large American passenger wagon, originally used for sight-seeing tours of Yellowstone National Park (U.S.A.), designated a refuge for wild life. There were three or four crosswise rows of seats under a canopy top or head, designed to carry eight passengers. Mounted on thoroughbraces with an elevated driver's seat above the fore-axle. A powerful lever brake acted on both rear wheels. Similar in many respects to the Concord Stage Coach. Usually drawn by a matching, four-in-hand team.

York cart. Light, panel-sided cart, usually drawn by a single horse or mule in shafts. Up to a capacity of 15 cwts. Unsprung or dead axle. Provided, in its later versions, with iron rather than wooden naves. Popular throughout the greater part of the 19th century.

Yorkshire spring cart. Sturdy market cart, hung on one crosswise semi-elliptical and two sideways elliptical springs. The cross seat had a high backrest. Fitted with straight shafts. Up to 20 cwts. capacity.

Yorkshire trolley. Open dray or low-sided trolley, mainly used on farms of West Yorkshire or the West Riding, during the 1900's. A similar type was also used in the West Midlands. Hung on sideways semi-elliptical springs. Able to turn in full lock. Factory rather than craftsman made. Drawn by a single horse in shafts.

Yorkshire wagon. Alternative name for the Bow or Barrel-Topped Gypsy caravan, of a type formerly made in and associated with South-East Yorkshire (now Humberside).

Z

Zomerbrik. Dutch – Summer Break. Small wagonette of Holland, drawn by a single horse in shafts. Hung on sideways elliptical springs, front and rear. Headed by a waterproof or canvas cover on tilts, let down in wet weather. Frequently used for pleasure driving and holiday excursions.

SLEIGHS

Albany cutter. A type of small, open sleigh for two or more persons. Its prototype was designed by a James Goold of Albany, New York State (U.S.A.). This appeared during the 1800's but developed into its final or swell-sided version in 1836. The side panels were frequently decorated with arabesques and floral designs. Also known as the Swell-body Cutter and, at a later period, the Goold Cutter. Some versions had a movable seat at the fore-end. Its style was widely copied or adapted by other builders. Usually drawn by a single horse.

Albany sleigh. A larger version of the Albany Cutter, carrying six persons. Drawn by a pair of horses.

Boat sleigh. A large pair-horse sleigh of New England, said to resemble a boat. Also known as a Large Excursion Sleigh.

Booby hutch. A closed sleigh hired out, during the winter months, in New England, on a weekly basis. Suspended on leather braces and loops. Also known as a Booby Hack.

Bobs or bob-runners. Short sleds or runners used under an ordinary vehicle body, converting it from coach, cart, wagon, etc., to a type of sleigh.

Bob-sled. 1. A short sled used under an ordinary or converted vehicle body.

2. A longer version of Bob-Sled 1, or two smaller versions connected by means of a coupling pole. Mainly used to support open wagons and timber hauling gear. Also known as a Double Ripper.

Bob-sled, lumberman's. Roughy made logging sled or sleigh, as used during the first half of the 19th century, both in New England and the Maritime Provinces of Canada. The hard wood runners were fixed in place by trenails and wooden wedges.

Bob-sleigh. A pleasure version of the Bob-Sled. The sled rather than the sleigh was usually a commercial vehicle.

Coach sleigh. Passenger sleigh, usually drawn by two horses, with the bodywork of a coach.

Cutter. North American name for a light sleigh with one or two seatboards, drawn by a single horse. Some larger types had an additional or sliding seat, which could be folded-down. The latter was known as a 'C'-seated or Jump Seat Cutter.

Dexter cutter. A light-weight version of the Portland Cutter, designed by the carriage-builder R. M. Stivers, of New York City. Named after a famous trotting and show horse.

Dogcart sleigh. A sleigh with the body and upper works of a dogcart.

Double ripper. Alternative name for the Bob-Sled. *See* Bob-Sled.

Farm sled. Simple wooden sled with a forward driving seat and rearward loading platform or compartment.

Land raft. English name for a large sleigh.

Log or logging sled. Strongly built but roughly made sled for hauling felled timber. Its members were frequently lashed together with strips of rawhide.

Pony sleigh. A small or pony hauled sleigh, but with more elaborate fittings than a cutter.

Portland sleigh. Popular American sleigh of the mid-19th century. Usually a double-seater drawn by two horses. First appeared in the streets of Portland, Maine, U.S.A. Sometimes known as a Kimball Cutter, after its designer.

Queen's body cutter. Cutter for two passengers, with a high backrest or rail. There was frequently a small folding seat for a child, facing to the rear. The dashboard would be ornamented with nodding plumes.

Red ribbon cutter. Cutter for two or more persons, its body shaped in the form of a reindeer. Patented by F. B. Miller of Enon, Ohio, U.S.A., in 1881. Drawn by a single horse or large pony.

Shifter. A popular one-horse sleigh in which the shafts may be shifted off-centre enabling the horse to follow tracks of a pair-horse sleigh.

Sled, sleigh or sleigh. Names thought to be of Low German or Dutch origins, for vehicles with ice-runners rather than wheels, slipping over frozen surfaces. As previously noted the 'sled' was a commercial rather than a pleasure vehicle.

Sleigh. Hub-runner. What was normally a wheeled vehicle adapted to take runners in winter. Slides or runners would be attached to the wheel-hubs.

Sleigh, swell body. Large sleigh in which the upper body had the appearance of swelling outwards.

Vasok. A large carriage body of Russian origin mounted on runners.

Victoria sleigh. Sleigh with the upper bodywork of a Victoria or semi-open carriage. Drawn by a pair of horses.

Vis-à-vis sleigh. Horse-drawn sleigh in which the passengers sit face-to-face on opposite seats. Such a name might also apply to the Victoria Sleigh.

Troika sleigh. Russian sleigh of any shape or size, drawn by three horses abreast, as with the Troika Carriage.

DRAGS AND LITTERS

Basterna. A large covered litter carried between two horses or mules. Mainly used by noble families at the time of the Roman Empire.

Cacolet. Type of horse litter used for the transport of sick and wounded men in time of war. Either a form of chair carried between two pack horses/mules, or attached to the near side flank of a single beast of burden. Introduced in the British Army during the Crimean War. Frequently used in both World Wars, especially in the Far East. A type of double chair, made with a single folding hood, was manufactured for the American Army by Lawrence, Bradley and Paree, of New Haven, Connecticut – during the 1860's – but little used.

Dandi. Litter of India and the Middle East suspended from a single pole. Carried either between two men or pack animals.

Forked slipe. An Irish slide car of primitive design and construction. Made from the forked branches of a tree or large bush, boarded across the centre. Attached to the harness of a draught animal by chains or leather traces, etc. *See* Slipe.

Litter. A wheel-less carriage of conveyance supported either between horses or mules in tandem or on the backs of human bearers. In later years it was usually a boxlike structure, semi-open or headed with a canopy top. The passenger rode in either a semi-reclining or sitting position. Thought to be of Asiatic origins (known as a Palanquin), although commonplace in the Roman Empire. Revived in Medieval Europe as transport for the sick and elderly also for some fashionable ladies. Little used in Britain before the early 13th century.

Slide car. A shafted but wheel-less vehicle related to the even earlier Travois of pre-history. More sophisticated versions were used in Ireland and other parts of Celtic Britain throughout the 18th and 19th centuries. Used mainly on farms and small holdings in remote areas. The carrying compartment was a large box or wicker basket at the rear-end, near to ground level. Its prototype, eventually fitted with rollers or disc-wheels was the ancestor of all carts, wagons and carriages.

Slipe. A version of the Irish Slide Car, without shafts, but attached to a beast of burden by crude harness and merely dragged along the ground. *See* Forked Slipe.

Travois or travoise. A wheel-less drag consisting of two or more poles, hauled by a single human being or beast of burden, its apex resting on the back or hind quarters. Space near the base of the 'A' frame would be bridged by thongs, woven twigs or small planks. Widely used by the North American Indians both for conveying the sick and elderly of the tribe or personal belongings.

Travoy. 1. Modern spelling of Travois.

2. Military stretcher used in front line conditions, especially in the Balkans and Near East, during the First World War. The fore-end was harnessed to a pack mule, horse or pony, while the rear-end was supported and steered by a medical orderly on foot.

GLOSSARY OF PARTS AND GEARS

Anchorhead bolt. Bolt-head with a slit or aperture for receiving a spring.

Angle iron. Roller bar of 'L' section used in connection side plates or panels.

Archibald wheel. Patent wheel with an iron nave, invented by E. A. Archibald, in 1871 (American).

Arm rail. Length of wood or metal forming the underline or shaping of a carriage.

Artillery wheel. Military wheel of a type used by the British Army for gun-carriages and supply wagons. Noted for its iron naves and reinforced spokes. Also used on certain heavy-duty civilian vehicles, especially those owned by railway cartage services.

Axle. Bar of metal or wood forming a spindle or axis on which wheels rotate. There are various types supported, as a continuous axle, by a tree or case, or as separate spindles/arms projecting on either side of the vehicle, held by a beam or case but not joined in the centre. Several patent axles have been devised to retain lubrication over an extended period of time.

Axle arm. Spindle-end of an axle, penetrating the wheel hub or nave.

Axle case. Wooden beam or member supporting an axle.

Axletree. Sturdy wooden cross-member supporting an axle. Much stronger than the axle case.

Belt rail. An arm rest on an open passenger vehicle.

Blocks. Wooden blocks used in conjunction with steel springs to raise the body of a vehicle above the axle.

Bodybrace. Iron or steel support for the side of a wagon.

Bolster. 1. Wooden cross-beam of a wagon between axletree and bodywork.

2. Crosswise beam on a timber carriage, to support the load.

Bolster plate. Iron plate on a wagon bolster (Bolster 1) to receive wear and friction, engendered by the constant turning of the fore-carriage.

Bond. Hub-band or loop.

Book box. Box carried at the fore-end of a commercial vehicle, containing order books and paper work.

Book step. Folding step on a coach or carriage.

Boot. Receptical on a coach or carriage to contain luggage.

Bottom bar. Bottom or end bars connecting rockers on the underside of a coach.

Box or box-seat. Elevated driving seat on certain vehicles. Formerly a tool chest.

Brace. Strap or stay used as a means of suspension or structural support.

Brake. Instrument to retard the motion of a vehicle. Usually operated on the wheel with hand-lever, foot-pedal or screw-down mechanism. Connected to the driving position by rods or concealed wires.

Brake block. Wooden, rubber or metal block that brings direct pressure to bear on the wheel to which it is shaped.

Breeching hook. Hook on the shafts or fore-part of a vehicle to which breeching or rearward body harness may be attached.

Bush. Lining of an inner hub or wheel nave.

Butt end. Rearward hub-band next to the actual wheel.

Cant rail. Protective top rail on the roof of a coach or van.

Carriage part. Any part of a horse-drawn vehicle below the bodywork. The Running gear or undercarriage of a vehicle.

Chair. 1. Type of driving seat on certain vehicles, shaped like a chair.
2. Combination of bars and a fifth wheel, on the forecarriage of heavy vehicles.

Channels. Grooves of a wheel into which solid rubber tyres are made to fit.

Closed top. Carriage with a falling hood and permanently or semi-permanently raised sides/quarters.

Collar. Rim or ring on the inner side of an axle arm.

Collet. An axle band on the hub or nave.

Collinge. Axle and hub of English invention, introduced during the 1780's. Also known as the Patent Axle. Contained its own lubricating system. The outer hub secured by bands or collets.

Corner pillar. Corner support or upright in the body of a headed vehicle.

Coupling pole. Under part of a wagon joining fore and rear parts. Also known as a reach pole.

Crane or craneneck. Curved irons on the fore-carriage of a vehicle to clear the wheels for underlock.

Cee or 'C' springs. Curved coach or carriage springs in the shape of a letter 'C'. Widely used from the late 18th century, especially on pleasure or passenger vehicles.

Cut under. Part of the lower bodywork of a vehicle, cut away or raised to improve underlock.

Dash or dashboard. Perpendicular foot or front board, facing the driving seat as a protection from mire and splashes.

'D' links. 'D' shaped loops of iron or steel used in securing cross springs.

Dennett springs. Patent springs first used on a special kind of gig, during the early 19th century. Two sets of lengthways and one crosswise spring under the bodywork.

Dish. The outward cant of wheels providing greater strength and security for the vehicle.

Door stiles. Framing of a coach or carriage door with an aperture for the drop light or window.

Double suspension. The combination of two different forms of springing or suspension in the same vehicle.

Double tree. An evener or connection between two swingletrees or draught bars.

Drabble. The common type of cart or van axle without self-lubrication.

Drag shoe. Skid pan or wedge used as a crude brake, when jammed under a rear wheel. Also known as a Drug bat.

Drayel. Staple or hook on the fore-end of a shaft for the attachment of trace gear or tandem harness.

Drug bat. Country name for a drag shoe.

Dummy board. Rearward platform of a coach or carriage on which grooms or footmen may stand.

'D' wheel. Semi-circular fifth wheel of a wagon forming part of the undergear of its fore-carriage.

Earbreadth. Projection at the side of a wagon or cart to support a metal stay.

Elbow spring. Slightly curved steel spring, once forming the main part of carriage suspension.

Elliptical spring. Curved metal plate or number of plates bolted together, in elliptical or semi-elliptical form. Each plate was a leaf, hinged and hung at their extremities for correct suspension.

ExBed. The axle bed of a heavy wagon.

Falling top. Carriage top that may be raised or lowered according to weather conditions.

Felloe or fellow. Pronounced fellie. Outer rim or segment of a spoked wheel, to the inner extremities of which spokes are attached.

Fifth wheel. Horizontal wheel-like structure forming part of the forecarriage of most vehicles, helping to pivot the carrying wheels.

Front pillar. Upright fore-pillar helping to support the fore-part of a vehicle.

Futchell. Horizontal member in longitudinal form, helping to support the fore-part of a vehicle.

Garnish rail. Wooden framing of a coach window.

Gather. The slight forward set of an axle tree, preventing the wheel from rolling outward, causing it to remain true.

Half patent axle. Version of the Patent Axle, fixed with a single nut at the rear end of the hub or nave.

Hammer cloth. Both a decorative and protective covering over the box-seat of a coach, especially state coaches and vehicles of ceremony.

Hanger. Body. Loop on which springs may be hung or secured.

Head. The roof or top of a vehicle.

Head block. Resting place for the underperch of a vehicle to which it is morticed – forming an important part of the fore-carriage.

Hind carriage. Rear part of the undercarriage of a vehicle.

Hinge pillar. Upright at the side of a coach or carriage door, on which the door is hung and the hinges set.

Hood. A demountable cover or top to protect a semi-open vehicle, especially the passenger seats.

Hoop. Curved member supporting a hood when it is raised.

Hub. Also known as a nave. Centre part of a wheel into which the inner spoke ends are fixed.

Hub cap. Decorative plate fitting over the face of a hub or nave.

Imperial. Roof seat or rack, especially on the roof of a coach or omnibus.

Iron. Protective iron or steel side rail, especially of a driving seat.

Jack. Upright support for purposes of suspension.

Journal. Inner non-rotating part of a hub, through which the axle fits.

Jump seat. Folding passenger seat in a coach or carriage.

King bolt or king pin. Pivot, in perpendicular form, securing either the perch or under-gear of the fore-carriage to the bodywork.

Kneeboot or kneeflap. Flap or flaps in the fore-part of certain open passenger vehicles to protect the lower limbs.

Leader doubletree. Bar or attachment at the head of a coach pole, to which the team leaders are harnessed.

Light. The glass window of a vehicle. Those that may be raised and lowered are known as Drop Lights.

Limber. 1. Separate hind or forepart of certain articulated vehicles.

2. A type of ammunition wagon supporting the trail of a field gun.

Linch pin. Wedge-shaped iron pin securing the wheel to hub and axle.

Lock. The turning circle required by a four-wheeled vehicle.

Locking stop. Projecting to prevent the fifth wheel turning too far beneath the under-carriage.

Mail hub. Patent hub and axle or axletree used on mail coaches and several larger or sturdier vehicles. The wheel is secured to the hub and axle by means of three long screws, unlikely to snap at one and the same time.

Nave. Alternative name for the hub.

Nutcracker springs. A combination of springs in which the sideways half-ellipticals are attached to crosswise dumb springs.

Pad. Central part of a carriage step.

Perch. Pole or beam connecting fore and hind-carriages on certain vehicles, as a means of support.

Perch carriage. Vehicle fitted with an underperch.

Platform springs. A combination of shallow, low-slung, crosswise/ lengthwise under springs.

Pole. Bar or beam to which draught animals are hitched (in pairs) for double harness.

Pole bridge. Bridge or arch securing the rearward end of a coach or wagon pole to prevent it slipping out of place.

Pole cap. Fittings at the fore-end of a pole to which harness chains or straps are connected.

Pole collar. Metal collar securing a pole to the fore-axle or under-carriage of a vehicle.

Pole plates. Plates preventing a pole bearing against the futchells.

Pole socket. Socket on the front gearing or fore-carriage of a vehicle, through or into which the pole passes.

Quarter. Side section of a coach or carriage.

Quarter panel. Thin, upper side panel forming the outer bodywork of a coach.

Rocker. Curved under-support of a heavy coach, found beneath the body-work.

Roller bolt. Upright member attached to the crosswise splinter bar, forming a rearward attachment for traces.

Rumble or rumble seat. Rearward seat on a passenger vehicle. Originally anything fitted between the rear wheels.

Sarven wheel. Patent wheel in which the spokes screw into hub or nave. A type first introduced in North America during the second half of the 19th century.

Scroll springs. 1. Carriage springs in the form of a scroll.
2. Alternative name for cee springs.

Set. The angle at which an axle may be inclined.

Shackle. Staple used to secure leaf springs.

Shackle eye. Link or loop used in securing leaf springs.

Shafts. Also known as thills. Bars or rods by means of which a single draught animal is attached to the front of a vehicle. Double shafts are used on certain types of heavy vehicle, but these are few in number, most pairs (horses, etc.) harnessed to a centre pole.

Sill. Bottom timbers forming the under-bodywork of a vehicle.

Spindle. Side rod or support for a wagon body.

Splinterbar. Crosswise, horizontal bar at the front of a vehicle to which harness chains or traces are attached.

Spoke. Wooden or metal member of a wheel, forming attachment between hub and felloes or rim.

Stagger. Placing alternate wheel spokes at different angles for extra strength and durability. Also known as strut.

Stake. Iron stanchion at the side of a goods vehicle to help retain the load.

Swaybar. Bar connecting the rear part of the futchells on the fore-carriage.

Swingletree. Short, horizontal bar at the rear of a draught animal to which traces are attached.

Tailboard. Rear-end boards of a cart or wagon. Known in America as the tailgate.

Telegraph springs. Platform springs, as used on stage and mail coaches from the early 19th century. A combination of crosswise and lengthwise suspension, secured by 'D' links.

Thoroughbraces. Longitudinal strap suspension of leather or rawhide, for various types of vehicle.

Transom. Crosswise bar of an under-carriage to which the fore-part of the perch is attached.

Turtle boot. Also known as a Turtle Back Boot. Fore-boot beneath the box-seat of certain coaches and carriages, tending to be detached from the main bodywork.

Under-carriage.   Supporting under-gear or works of any vehicle. Also known as the carriage.

Wagon standard.   Upright pole or post, helping to support the fore-end of a wagon.

Warner wheel.   Common type of wheel as used on trade vans and similar vehicles, especially in Britain, during the 19th and early 20th centuries.

Wheel.   Circular disc or connected-circular arrangement of felloes, joined to the hub by spokes. Also the horizontal or fifth wheel under the fore-carriage, used for turning purposes.

Whiffletree.   Alternative name for the swingletree. Also known as the whippletree.

XC plate.   Metal plate treated to prevent rust.

Yandell top.   Patent, downward curved roof or top of certain American Buggies.